To Lorraine and John Orr —
With many thanks for what was
really a fun interview!

Myron Brenton

What's Happened to Teacher?

Books by Myron Brenton

WHAT'S HAPPENED TO TEACHER?

THE AMERICAN MALE

THE PRIVACY INVADERS

MYRON BRENTON

What's Happened to Teacher?

Coward-McCann, Inc.
New York

Copyright © 1970 by Myron Brenton

Library of Congress Catalog Card Number: 79-81012

For my daughter,
Diana

Acknowledgments

THIS book, which seeks to explore the condition of public school teachers in contemporary American society, is based on interviews with more than two hundred and fifty teachers and administrators in various sections of the country; on discussions with officials representing the National Education Association, the American Federation of Teachers, and education agencies on federal, state, and local levels; and on library research that included the reading of more than six hundred separate studies, articles, and books dealing with teachers and education.

But it's not statistics that accounts for the creation of a book of this kind. What makes it possible is the generosity of individuals who submit uncomplainingly to long question-and-answer sessions with no expectation of reward. With few exceptions, the teachers and other educators I interviewed provided me amply with information and insights. Some went far out of their way to perform individual acts of kindness and hospitality. I wish I could thank them all individually on these pages, but it's not possible: They are far too many in number, and it was in response to a promise of anonymity that they provided me with candid answers to my queries. I wish them to know, though, how grateful I am. Needless to say, the "message" of the book is entirely my own responsibility.

There are two individuals I would like to name, however, because their support and encouragement were, without exaggeration, crucial to the completion of this book. They are my wife, Hsi-yen, and my editor, Ellis Amburn.

M. B.

Contents

What's Happened to Teacher?

Part One

PERSONAL AND PROFESSIONAL

[1]

Teachers' Hour

[1]

SOME two hundred years ago schoolteachers were sent to American shores along with pigs and cattle and general cargo; less than a decade ago a former schoolteacher became President of the United States. Thus, swiftly, move the affairs of men; too swiftly, perhaps, for easy transition from one stage to another. The American public school teacher, once a symbol of constancy and stability, has himself become a controversial figure. His life used to be a simple one; in the context of his history he knew who he was—he had a definite place, if basically a lowly one. His validations were the classroom, the books, the blackboard, the dialogue that went on between himself and the learning child. No more, no more. Threats, challenges, demands all fly at him, and he hurls back his own. There are nearly 120,000 public elementary and secondary schools operating in the United States, but wherever the teacher plies his craft, it's the same: No teacher, not even the most insular shut up in the remotest rural classroom, is wholly immune from all that's going on.

It's a well-founded American tradition to go into paroxysms of criticism about the nation's schools and schoolteachers—to go into such criticisms, that is, between long periods of neglect. Since the mid-1950's the criticism has stepped up in pace and tempo, with bitter educational battles about basic *vs.* progressive education, with the phonetic *vs.* look-say reading fight, with the Soviet launching of Sputnik and the shocked American realization that we're not "the best educated people in the world," with the resultant emphasis on science, math, and the gifted child—and now with the stress on the child labeled "disadvantaged" and the issue of community control.

And now, unlike in the past, schoolteachers are speaking up, saying what's on their minds, shouting as loudly as anyone else. Moreover, individually and through their organizations, they've been challenging some basic premises about their rights and responsibilities, about their very place on the educational pyramid. And—a rare phenomenon in the past—they've been walking off the job and brandishing picket signs.

Where are they going? What do they want? Caught between the differing temptations of both professionalism and trade unionism, it seems as if they themselves aren't quite sure. What is sure is that more than most occupational groups they're caught in a network of paradoxes. For instance: Education is said to be at the very heart of the nation's culture, but teachers lack prestige. Schools, it's said, have played a major role in bringing about this nation's affluence, yet many schools and most teachers are largely excluded from that prosperity. Teachers form the largest occupational block in the country, but they have none of the political power of the farm block, which they've supplanted in terms of sheer numbers. Classrooms are places where exciting things supposedly happen in terms of the developing minds of children, but teaching has not attracted, on the whole, the brightest, most creative people.

When teachers are interviewed about themselves and their world, it's these self-contradictions and other conflicts that come through strongly. Some examples follow.

Said a highly rated fifth-grade teacher in Wheatridge, Colorado, "The youngsters don't want to expend the effort. They don't want to learn. After all these years I'm still excited about teaching—why shouldn't the kids be with me?"

Said a golden-haired young schoolmistress from northeast Kansas, "You teach elementary school kids out of 1957 science books; you teach high school kids out of books printed in 1961. All kinds of things have happened since then, so you try to improvise. There's no money for new books, doesn't look like there'll be any coming, so what can you do? You do your best."

Said a Negro woman employed as a resource teacher by the Los Angeles City School System, with great bitterness, "I could fill the schools with qualified black men working in the post office."

Said a high school teacher in Burlington, North Carolina, puzzling over a school bond defeat, "I always thought that in the South support of the schools was as sacred as motherhood and apple pie or something. I thought if you poured out a need to intelligent people, they would react in an affirmative manner. Most haven't reacted at all, haven't voted at all. What few have, voted against the schools."

Said a veteran high school teacher in Chapel Hill, North Carolina, "I think maybe this is one thing you have to worship, so it becomes a religion with you when you're a teacher; it is that you're handling a bit of God in this gray matter, the mind of the child. And that you're doing the most that can be done for him. If you're really sincere about doing that, I think everything else should fall into place. That's what I think. Maybe you could get a bastard for a principal or a superintendent, who would make life miserable for you. If it had happened, I'd probably be an entirely different person."

Said a high school teacher in Newark, New Jersey, "The most exciting thing that could happen, I think, in all of teaching, is that we have honesty. That we say to a person, 'Now look, if you don't like this, if you think you're not cut out for it, we'll find you an equally well-paying job—but for God's sake, get out of teaching.' And then we'd have just those who are excited in seeing a hand go up and a question asked. But sometimes I look

at some of my colleagues, who shouldn't be in teaching. 'Well,'
I say jokingly, 'when are you going to quit?' And the sad part
is that they look at me and say, 'What else could I do?' "

Said a scarred and shaken veteran of the nation's first statewide strike of teachers, in Florida, "The parents never even
saw us. We had to walk out of the classroom—go out on strike—
to get us some attention."

Said a beautiful white girl, a fourth-grade teacher in a
Bronx, New York, ghetto school, when asked about community
control, "I will not—*will not*—have anyone inferior to me telling me how to do my job!"

[2]

Few events in recent American history have created as much
of an impact—and so shaken up teachers—as has the insistence
of the ghetto poor that schools provide their children with
the educational passport to the good life. The poor perhaps
have an exaggerated notion of the extent to which the schools—
under middle-class control—have been their vital link to the
middle-class world. More to the point here, the schools have
become a social and, increasingly, physical battleground. In
the process, a number of assumptions that teachers have long
cherished are being questioned. No longer can they say without
fear of rebuttal that when a child fails to learn, the fault lies
with the learner. Despite much rhetoric to the contrary, schools
have always been highly politicized institutions, but now the
politics has become more intense, pervasive, and open—and
teachers increasingly must choose sides. Though challenged by
some experts, the widely publicized Coleman Report, *Equality
of Educational Opportunity,* has, by concluding that the social
class of a student's peer group is the most important factor in
his school achievement, opened to question the teacher's cen-
trality in the teaching-learning process. The race-class problem as it has now focused on the schools has also given schools,
especially inner-city schools, a new image: that of institutions

where idealistic people can be of service to society. Thus the
Teacher Corps has been created, and Peace Corps returnees are
flocking into the schools, as well as young reformers directly
from the colleges. Whether there are enough of them, whether
they'll stay on and move up into the higher reaches of the
schools' bureaucracies, whether they'll have any real impact—
all that remains to be seen. Many are young men waiting out
the draft; some motivated by altruism, others by opportunism.
At any rate, few are joining the teachers' organizations. What's
sure at this point is that they're coming into collision with the
professionals; value differences are manifest.

The militancy of senior and junior high school students dissatisfied among other things with the curriculum, the quality
of their teachers, the rules and regulations to which they're subjected, is putting teachers into the unaccustomed position of being evaluated by their clients. Passing fad or growing dissent,
whatever the current phenomenon may be, the teacher's traditional authority is being challenged as never before.

A whole confluence of events is having an effect on the classroom teacher, and its long-range effects may well be profound.
The abrupt transfusion of substantial federal funds into the
public schools' arteries; coupled with the creation or growing
strength of educational power blocks like the U.S. Office of Education, the foundations (especially Ford and Carnegie), the
Education Commission of the States, the curriculum reform
groups like the famed Physics Science Study Committee; coupled with the entry into public school business of giant corpora-
tions like IBM, Raytheon, and RCA, all hungrily eyeing the potential educational technology market; coupled with the tremendous amount of in-fighting that goes on at every level of
the educational structure—all such complex events shape or influence major educational policy decisions and ultimately affect
the how's, why's, and what's of the classroom teacher's work.
One evidence of the ferment in education is that the schools
have become innovation-happy. Once accused of never budging,
never changing, many adopt new techniques, new programs,

and new organizational styles one after the other—and often abandon them as quickly, leaving teachers and parents to wonder whether the classroom is fast becoming an educational laboratory with students its guinea pigs. There are some ethical considerations here that have not yet been explored.

The growing pugnacity of the teachers' own organizations— the National Education Association (NEA) and its affiliates, the American Federation of Teachers (AFT) and its locals—is forcing a change both in the teacher's image of himself and in the way the community perceives him. "Front-page pictures of teachers striking and marching, breaking open schools and going off to jail have just about finished off our lingering image of the mythical American educator as a long-suffering pedagogue, sustained more by dedication than hard cash, willing to accept second-class status in his efforts to educate our children," noted Harold Howe in his final report as U.S. Commissioner of Education.[1] Since the 1960-61 school year, 189 teacher strikes involving 263,200 staff members have been called by the rival teachers' groups. They involved an estimated 1,593,638 mandays lost. "Three years ago I made five thousand dollars," said one of the Florida teachers who had struck. "I was offered two outside jobs, one at nine thousand and the other at twelve thousand. But I am committed to staying in the profession, so I'm damn well going to fight for it. We're part of the changing system. We'll make it bend or fall!"

So it seems that the times have caught up with the teachers, or the teachers with the times. But that's only a half-truth because school is one of the most conservative of institutions, and teachers are, by and large, somewhat conservative people. Change doesn't come easily to them, and new roles and new situations not infrequently require them to make painful adjustments. "Far from reducing or simplifying the teacher's task, virtually every recent change in education has enlarged and complicated it," Dr. John H. Fischer, president of Teachers College, Columbia University, has pointed out.[2] To use an overhead projector or tape recorder requires more skill than using a textbook (which may be one reason why so many gather dust on audiovisual closet shelves). New phonics and math systems require greater adeptness than do traditional methods. Better interpersonal abilities are needed to interpret the role of the school to modern parents. Teaching hitherto ignored poverty-group children requires more sensitivity than that needed to teach middle-class youths.

Often, though by no means always, younger teachers are more receptive to change than older teachers. It's not youth that makes the difference as much as exposure to the school's institutional environment. "There can be no question but that the forces which play upon a teacher at his job influence his attitudes and reactions toward pupils, parents and colleagues," states a report on teaching disadvantaged youth.[3] "He becomes captured by a network of activities and influences. In time he becomes a guardian of this network and exhibits the protective behavior expected of one who favors the status quo."

Machines are particularly threatening to many teachers, who much prefer the old combination—themselves and the blackboard. Except perhaps for those who specialize in math and science, few have an "engineering" turn of mind. They aren't very much attracted to the technological adjuncts to teaching.

Much is being written these days about the brave new world of education, with its computer consoles, writing lights, talking typewriters, videorecorders, and other items of educational technology. Already, in scores upon scores of demonstration classrooms all over the country, experimental programs, harbingers of the technological age of education, are being run. In New York City, Philadelphia, and a number of other cities, large and small, children already sit at computer consoles for short periods each day, doing math or spelling drill work. And computerized curriculum prescriptions geared to the individual child and delivered to him daily are being run in experimental public schools in Pittsburgh, Trenton, and elsewhere.

Yet consciously or unconsciously, there is, for the teacher, the specter of a drastic end to the continuing teacher shortage

—of being rendered obsolescent by some new miracle of technology. ("Teacher *vs.* Programmed Texts . . . It's Pointless!" ran the headlined message of an *Encyclopaedia Britannica*-sponsored ad for its programmed text series, intended to reassure teachers.) Computerized instruction may well eventually cause drastic changes in the roles of teachers, in the very nature of the teaching function. But as a Harvard University study points out, not soon, not yet; the costs are tremendous, software (the actual programming) takes years to develop, and schools and teachers characteristically make basic changes very slowly.[4]

"The best teaching machine still wears a tie," insisted a Denver grade school teacher in illustration of that last point. "I firmly believe that the best way kids learn is not through a machine but through the excitement stimulated by an adult. By taking and acquainting him with things, and getting him to respond. To jump into a discussion. The thrill of responding to somebody else's enthusiasm. One of my best tools is my personal enthusiasm, which I've successfully maintained for sixteen years, and I hope I can for sixteen more."

Another male teacher, this one in Cheyenne, talked frankly about the fear many teachers almost instinctively feel when they encounter a radical departure from established routine. He'd been involved in flexible scheduling, an innovative approach to combat the rigidities of the forty-five-minute high school class. The school had been a brand-new one, especially built for flexible scheduling. "We never made it," he admitted. "I don't think we ever reached what we were going after when we first started off. It frightened me, and I was one of the eager beavers when we decided we were going to go this route . . . I felt I might not be as good. In other words, inside I felt I was a good enough teacher in that classroom. And yet we were talking about a team; we were talking about more individualized attention. For example, I wasn't trained to teach ten kids. I was—all of us are—trained to teach thirty, thirty-five, forty. I kept telling myself over and over again, 'If you believe you're a good teacher in this room, you're going to be a good teacher the other way.' But it didn't happen. A teacher who'd been teaching thirty years told me, 'I'm not going to teach that way.' I can appreciate that because I was young and eager and also felt insecure."

It's not only innovative programs but new people that teachers—mostly used to the isolation of the four-walled classroom —must learn to relate to, as school supporting services proliferate. Guidance counselors, who counsel students for college planning and occasionally for emotional problems, provide an example. Though many teachers establish good working relationships with guidance counselors, there has sprung up what may well become a traditional rivalry between the two. "Look here," said a high school teacher in one of New England's most famous school systems, "we have a bright, interesting, capable guidance counselor who would rather sacrifice a class of twenty-nine students to put his one troublesome patient—that's the only word for it, patient—into an environment where he might get a little gain from it. Our goals are antithetical. He's a doctor treating a single patient. I'm trying to educate the nation." A high school teacher in New York City said contemptuously, "Guidance counselors are people who've had one or two more courses in psychology than the classroom teacher. They're the so-called experts." A guidance counselor in San Diego, California, gave another reason for the friction: Counselors tend to identify with the administration. Their position not infrequently is a stepping-stone on the way up.

Paraprofessionals—teacher aides under a new name—also require the classroom teacher to learn new modes of relating. Though teachers continually and justifiably complain about all the paper work and other sundry nonteaching duties that fall their way, when faced with the prospect of another person in their classrooms, they aren't always overeager. An NEA Research Department poll in 1960 asked a nationwide sample of teachers which they would rather have: a class of twenty-five to thirty students with the teacher doing the usual nonteaching duties, or a class of forty to fifty with a full-time nonprofessional taking over those duties. Overwhelmingly, the teachers opted for the smaller class size without the aide.[5] Seven years later an elementary school teacher in Manhattan related how she and thirty other teachers were given a lecture on paraprofessionals at a local university, at the end of which they were asked what their reaction would be if told a paraprofessional would be put in their rooms the following week.

"I was the only one who put up my hand and said I'd be delighted," said the teacher. "The others were scared stiff. They said it would be too much trouble to train somebody. But I think they were afraid somebody would be watching and maybe not approving, somebody might be interfering with their teaching, or taking their stature away."

Often, she said, paraprofessionals tend to do a good job with the difficult children in the class, the ones who are disruptive. If the paraprofessional is reliable, and the teacher doesn't order her about or underutilize her, the relationship eventually works out well. Then the teacher's reaction is, "How could I ever have done without her?"

But if the paraprofessional is too good, she poses another threat. Teachers' organizations have been bearing down hard to control the classroom activities of aides and to keep them from assuming real teaching duties—possibly to prevent the appearance of tangible evidence that some kinds of teaching don't necessarily require a college degree or teaching license.

[3]

A Denver high school teacher, talking about his experiences in an integrated mid-city school:

"I think that for the first time in my life I feel useful. I didn't feel that way at the insurance company when I was pushing buttons and managing people. I managed one hundred fifty girls, but I was just a machine. They were machines; the whole outfit was a machine. But here you're working with exciting people.

I find high school kids are exciting. They're doing things, and they're looking for people to help them do things.

"You're active all the time. I'm active on the outside like crazy. Meetings—two or three meetings every night after school. Integration meetings, association meetings, working for Outward Bound . . . I'm satisfied as a teacher. I inspire kids. I know this from the kind of feedback I get.

"Jerry L——, who I had in one of my classes last year. Very belligerent. Never would speak. Not a word. One time he threatened to wipe out the kid next to him. I said, 'Look, Jerry, let's go out in the hall.' When I got him outside, instead of chewing him out, I said, 'Jerry, go to Mexico with us.' 'What are you talking about?' he grunted, this great big ugly black power guy. Mean-looking. He's on probation. Beat up a grocery store boy. So I started talking to him, tutored him after school a few times . . . Very rarely would he talk. But we took him to Mexico with us. Everybody there was middle-class oriented, even if they were in the minorities. Nobody could understand this cat when we left. When we came back, everybody would mimic his phrases. They all liked him; he was well accepted. He's been writing like crazy, which he never did before. And I've got here three different notebooks which he's given me to read. He may fail. He's still on the verge of dropping out. But he's a lot better than he was at this time last year."

[4]

When asked why they're in that classroom with twenty-five or thirty kids, teachers will typically say they're there to teach them. But "teaching," that good strong definitive word, actually is a vague and imprecise description of what goes on in the classroom. Teachers do not just "teach" the subject matter they've been assigned. Teaching means acting as a test-maker and giver, being office clerk, performing policeman duty, working as materials and equipment handler, and being a janitorial assistant.

But it's not only a question of all the "extraneous stuff" (busy work)—which, one suspects, for some teachers is a way of getting out of teaching. To whatever extent they take it seriously, teachers are expected to perform more than a narrow, purely instructional function. The lengthened school day, the abrogation by the family of certain childrearing responsibilities, mostly the assumptions growing out of the progressive education movement earlier in this century, have prompted schools to take on a host of extra-instructional roles—especially in the area of the children's social and emotional development. "In recent times, the scope of the teacher's role has been vastly expanded beyond its original instructional core to include such functions as parent surrogate, friend and confidante, counsellor, adviser, representative of the adult culture, transmitter of approved cultural values," observes David U. Asubel of New York's City University.[6] That, anyway, seems to be the cultural ideal.

They call it "teaching the whole child" or "teaching not the subject but the child." It's the bane of existence of basic educationists like Admiral H. G. Rickover, who want the schools to bear down hard on basic skill subjects and never mind the "frills." It's also not the most pleasing arrangement for humanistically oriented social critics and educators. These, along with some of the disenchanted high school youths, want to see education embark on a new direction altogether: providing, as a primary thrust, "life skills"—skills of thinking, of reasoning, of relating to self and others.

All this comes under the heading of educational goals and purposes. These are fine for intellectual debate (which may never be resolved) but of little help to most classroom teachers who, typically, are absorbed in meeting day-to-day classroom problems. (Comments S. E. Frost, Jr., of Brooklyn College, "To struggle with basic questions of goals or purposes demands hard thinking, and most people shun thinking . . . Thinking may force the teacher to jettison all he has so carefully prepared and read new books, gather new materials, and recast all his lesson plans. Most people, including teachers, actually fear such up-heavals, and thus avoid thinking as long as they can.") [7] In any event, the teacher's job description is vague (to say the least), his responsibilities diffuse and ill-defined.

In the classroom, then, it's every teacher for himself. The best teachers have always found a way of fitting the subject matter into a larger moral framework, and of being both instructor and something more. What actually happens in that classroom, of course, depends largely on the individual teacher—his temperament, his needs, the aspects of his personality that define the educational tone he sets for his students.

But this is a hit-or-miss proposition that shies away from clearly defined and well-delineated goals whose attainment can be measured in specific increments of time.

[5]

Understand this about teachers: They work in a field that offers extremes to the serious practitioner—moments of joy but also stretches of profound discouragement. When done even reasonably well, the work is far more difficult and complicated than people generally realize. (One close observer of classroom life, for instance, has calculated that the average elementary school teacher engages in more than one thousand interpersonal exchanges daily. Moreover, sometimes these occur nonstop and at breakneck speed.) All this can, and often does, lead to a feeling of real mental and physical fatigue at the end of the teacher's school day. "Good hard teaching is like sex when it's good," cheerfully said a Newark, New Jersey, teacher. "You enjoy it but it leaves you pooped." (Merely being with demanding youngsters all day is fatiguing, something parents who commonly say they're exhausted after a day spent with their own kids sometimes tend to forget.) Though, unfortunately, hard work and dedication don't necessarily add up to effective teaching, even teachers who are ineffective but who try hard come home worn-out (probably more so because of the added tensions). The latter are certainly more to be respected than is the lazy teacher whose time-serving ways make the very act of drawing a paycheck little better than a fraud.

Understand this about teachers, also: Many find it tremendously rewarding to work with children, with their feelings, with their minds. But in some respects the teacher's psychic rewards are tenuous. He can see a child progress, he can see a class "grow," but he can never be sure to what extent he was responsible for it. And in most instances he can't know if he has had any lasting influence on a particular student, or any influence at all, for that matter. The doctor sees his patient get well or worsen; the lawyer wins or loses a case; the teacher has no way of knowing in most situations what the outcome of his labor is.

Then, too, the child moves from grade to grade; the classroom teacher stays behind to teach a new grade the same things he taught the old. To be sure, no two classes are alike; new curriculum materials are added at times; and the teacher may claim that he "learns as much from the students as they do from him." But there are limits to that kind of growth, and teachers concerned about falling into a rut devise little stratagems like tearing up all the previous year's planning notes or teaching a different grade. But there are limits to what they can do in that respect, too. And it's very easy for them to fall into the trap of using with adults the same style, thought, and behavior they use in the classroom with children.

A Boulder, Colorado, teacher of high school science summed it up nicely: "As the years go by, teaching itself becomes easier. But it's more difficult to reach the same degree of satisfaction. It's easy to let oneself become mediocre. Teaching has some built-in tension and frustration."

And understand this about the teaching field: Teachers come and teachers go; the dropout rate is very high. Examining in detail all teacher turnover studies available up to the early 1960's, two Ohio State University researchers came up with this startling picture: For every one hundred college graduates who satisfy state certification requirements, roughly sixty actually take teaching assignments. By the end of the first year, roughly seven more drop out. Five more leave by the end of the second school year. "Two years after the original one hundred prospective teachers graduated," the researchers concluded, "less than half are engaged in teaching and, after ten years, only ten to twelve of the initial one hundred prospective teachers may be teaching in elementary and secondary classrooms." [8]

High turnover is a characteristic of any occupation in which women predominate. Many teachers are "trousseau teachers," young women who'll find husbands and leave to have babies; married women who return when their children are older to supplement the family income, but who leave when their husbands are transferred. As for men, those who can't make it on the salary move into supervisory positions, or new teaching specialties that have been opening up, or into organizational work, or leave education entirely.

Finally, there are the more ambitious people of both sexes for whom, after five or ten years, the challenge of doing strictly classroom teaching palls. Much more than money is involved: They need to prove themselves in other areas. There being little chance for advancement as a teacher, and no formal career ladder within teaching itself, many tend to leave the classroom altogether. It's a melancholy fact that teacher dropouts studies comparing those who leave with those who stay come up with the same findings: Generally, the ones who depart are rated better as teachers than the ones who stay. The ones who depart also have, generally, college achievement records superior to those who remain. The above-average people, then, leave the classroom soonest.

Some who stay defy the statistics, of course—like the former teacher of the year in the Rocky Mountains who turned down four offers to become an administrator. "I would have lost close contact with the boys and girls," he explained. "That's why I'm in education, to work with them. Being an administrator would be like waving to a person—and I want to shake hands with him."

[2]

Profile of the Average Teacher

A FEW decades ago it was no problem at all to profile the average teacher. This teacher was decidedly a "she," for as short a time as thirty years ago only 12 percent of the teaching force was composed of men. She was thirty-one years old, this average teacher, and had been teaching for a decade. She was not married. Her educational background consisted of from two to four years' worth of college. She earned $1,500 a year.[1]

People generally ascribed a fierce sense of dedication to her, believing that this prompted her to go into the profession. A love for children and a pride in teaching may well have nourished her professional ambitions. But to the extent that it idealized her, the community forgot that even love and pride can wear thin when you earn a low keep, are forced into a restricted life, work hard at a draining job, and with every passing year see your chances of getting married and raising a family of your own become that much more remote. The community also forgot—or, more probably, never really considered—that teaching was one of the few professional paths open to a woman who had some education and wanted to use it in a field of endeavor on her own.

Now we have come into the 1970's, and to an extent, the profile of the average public school teacher has undergone a considerable change. It's a multitude of profiles, in a way, that depicts the teacher today. The influx of males into public school education, the discovery of teaching by highly idealistic people as a way of expressing their social concern, the entry of minority group militants into the profession—all such presuppose diversity. Indeed, the teaching profession now encompasses miniskirted swingers, Ivy League intellectuals, former cab drivers, grandmothers, ex-businessmen, Black Panthers, John Birchtypes, Rotary Club rooters, aggressive pacifists—well, the list could go on and on. Increasingly, too, women teachers marry men in other professions, which is another broadening element.

Such diversity of type would presuppose a rich diversity of attitude, the raw stuff of creativity and vitality. It would presuppose an exhilarating atmosphere for the teaching profession and the school children alike. Probably the atmosphere is more like that now than it was even a decade or two ago. Yet if one pieces together the various polls and studies that reflect what teachers do and think outside the classroom—most such taken in the mid-1960's—the composite picture is startling only because it is so unremarkable. If one makes the usual proviso for exceptions, it is fair to say that teachers differ little from the population at large. As will become increasingly apparent, on the whole teachers are very much more a cross section of their society than they are its vanguard. The average American teacher is the average American citizen.

[2]

The contemporary American public school teacher is, on the average, about thirty-six years of age. Chances are he's been teaching for about eight years. Odds are seven to three that he

went to a publicly supported college or university for his training. He has a bachelor's degree and is taking additional college courses. (Nearly one-fourth of all teachers have a master's
degree, most on the secondary level; the number of classroom
teachers holding doctorates is negligible.) College courses and
other career growth activities cost the average teacher from
$100 to $200 a year. He spends some $20 in out-of-pocket ex-
penses for school materials.

Chances are, if the teacher is a man, that he moonlights.
(More than half do.) He's in debt. He and his spouse are buying a home. They own at least one car (over one-third of all
teachers own two cars or more). First choice: Chevrolet.[2]

The average teacher attends church or synagogue. He votes
in both primary and general elections. Politically, he's a conservative; even if he considers himself a liberal, he tends more
toward the conservative side of that spectrum. As Harmon
Zeigler points out in his political study of teachers, *The Political
Life of American Teachers,* teachers are purveyors of middle-
class values and therefore defenders of conventionality.[3]

The average schoolteacher reads one or two newspapers a
day. About half the teachers read a paper published outside the
area in which they live. Almost all teachers read the national
and local news stories; a slightly lower percentage (88.2 percent)
reads the international news stories. Slightly less than one-
fourth of all teachers read the editorials, and 69.2 percent read
letters to the editor. The letters, in fact, are preferred to col-
umnists, with just over half the teachers reading them. Book reviews aren't too popular either; more teachers read the comic
strips, the society page, and the display ads than they do book
reviews. Lovelorn columnist Ann Landers has the edge over
Walter Lippmann, who has been the teachers' favorite political columnist. Quite possibly, teachers do not read book reviews
because they read few nonprofessional books. One recent
survey shows that of the teachers sampled, nearly one-fourth
had not read a single nonprofessional book in the preceding three months. On the other hand, an amazing 10.9 per-

cent had read between six and nine such books. Fiction has the edge.

America's favorite magazine, the *Reader's Digest,* is also the teachers' favorite. *Life* runs a close second. It is a relatively rare teacher who reads *The Atlantic, Harper's,* or even the *Saturday Review.* Hardly any teachers go in for heavy-think or current affairs publications like *New Republic, American Scholar,* or *Daedelus.*[4]

Like his counterpart in the larger society, the public school teacher complains of having little time for recreational activities. Eight out of ten teachers say that preparing lessons and grading papers are a major limitation on recreation; nearly seven out of ten also point to family and home responsibilities. The teacher's principal leisure-time activities are, again like his nonteaching counterpart's, apt to be sedentary. Favorite pastimes are watching television, visiting people, reading, writing correspondence, attending religious services, dining out, going to parties, listening to records (semiclassical, musical comedy, and folk), and going to the movies (historical films are best liked, but only about one-fourth of the teachers attend a movie theatre as often as once or twice a month).[5]

Few teachers like to do more active things, like going out for team sports, acting in dramatic groups, playing musical instruments, tinkering with their cars, sketching, or painting. Favorite sports: football, basketball, and baseball, in that order —but only as spectators. Of teachers who like to be physically active, the plurality (about four in ten) prefer walking or hiking. About one-third like to go swimming. Fewer than three out of ten like to bowl, fish, or camp.[6]

Analyzing teachers' playtime habits, Perry London of the University of California and Donald E. Larsen of Yale University make three points with respect to leisure: (1) Teachers choose activities requiring minimal use of physical energy; (2) teachers choose activities that make few mental demands; (3) teachers aim for escape from workaday life, a life so much more demanding and complicated.

"The net result for teachers," say London and Larsen, "is a somewhat listless, colorless and subdued existence." [7]

[3]

Said a junior high school English teacher in Raleigh, North Carolina, "We've had some top-notch people coming now. They're well-equipped; they certainly have an enthusiasm and interest in students that you just are delighted to find. I think the quality has improved tremendously over the past four, five years."

Said a professor of education at City University in New York, "Some brilliant kids from Harvard, MIT, and other places are coming into the schools. They're looking at the schools as ways of going into social service and government service. This is new. They're motivated by Kennedy, the Peace Corps, the idea of giving. Will they change things? I don't know. They're loners. They don't join teachers' groups or move up in the bureaucracy itself. They see education as a profession with dignity, but after a couple of years some of them also see that teaching children isn't for them. So they move on. You also find some middle-aged people, very successful career people, motivated by the idea of serving. A successful attorney who gives up his practice and teaches high school. A physics professor who goes back into the public schools to teach. But they're a small minority."

Said a professor of psychology at Brooklyn College, "The education majors aren't very bright, but they're nice, decent, polite kids. I like them very much."

[4]

At two-year intervals from 1928 to 1932 two educational researchers conducted an exhaustive study of over 45,000 high school and college students in Pennsylvania. Their findings were startling. They learned that, among college students, education majors ranked at the bottom scholastically in comparison with students in other categories. The median IQ score for 26,000 high school seniors, selected at random, was higher than the median for education students and those ready to receive their degrees at several teachers' colleges. Moreover, in comparing college seniors in education with unselected high school seniors, the two researchers found that many of the high school seniors had actually made better grades in the very subjects the education majors were getting ready to teach.[8]

In the early 1950's, Dael L. Wolfle scrutinized the Army General Classification Scores to determine how intelligence was distributed among professionals and those preparing to enter professional life. College graduates in education scored fourth from the bottom, followed by social science, home economics, and physical education majors.[9] In a subsequent study, researchers determined that Australian teachers' college students with two years' training did as well on the National Teachers Examination as a group of American students trained for four years at twenty-one colleges in the United States. Comparing four-year Australian and four-year American students, they found that the Australians were superior.[10]

In 1965, a USOE study of graduate students' undergraduate achievement showed that only business and commerce majors did worse, that is, got a lower percentage of A's and A—'s, and a higher percentage of C's and C—'s, than education majors.[11] In 1952 education majors ranked lowest of sixteen professional categories on the Graduate Record Examinations. In 1963-64 they ranked lowest again. In 1968 they ranked lowest once more.[12]

Intellectuals will despair; so do some educators, while others place less importance on these findings. Teachers are part of the college-educated group which has an average IQ at least 15 to 20 points higher than the average IQ of the population as a whole. Surprisingly, many research studies fail to show a direct relationship between teacher intelligence and pupil achievement—at least when intelligence is considered as a *single variable* and certain sophisticated math and science

courses are excepted. Some educational experts say research instruments aren't sophisticated enough to measure such aspects
of teacher effectiveness; others suggest that most teachers are
clustered around the 112-115 IQ range, too short a spread from
which to draw any conclusions. But the fact that education
majors as a group have consistently lower grade-point averages
in college may well suggest that their motivation to achieve is
relatively low, something that could affect their teaching efforts.
And it explains the reputation education has for attracting college students who want an easy path to a degree or a career. "If
the most capable people are rejecting classroom teaching as a
career, either at the outset or after trying it for a while, American education is crippled," wrote a Newton, Massachusetts,
English teacher in the *NEA Journal,* which doesn't have a reputation for talking tough to teachers.

[5]

"Q: Why did you choose teaching?
"Mrs. Y: Well, everyone says he likes kids, and I used to. Seriously, though, since I am married, it is a good insurance policy
for me, but more than that, I want to help other children to
learn.
"Miss X: It's what I've always wanted to do. There have been
a few times when I've been frustrated, but I like teaching.
"Mr. W: I went into teaching because in going through high
school I had some classes that were so dull and boring that I
kept telling myself that it doesn't have to be like this, that I
could do better. And I'm trying."
—from "Troubled Young Voices: Interviews with Four
Young Teachers," *Ohio Schools* (January, 1966).

[6]

Teachers are caught in a trap of sorts. Despite the fact that
they're stereotyped unflatteringly in some respects, deep down

the public seems to believe they are (or should be) prompted to their calling by two lofty motives—love for children and love of teaching. Regardless of the extent to which it's grounded in reality insofar as real teachers are concerned, the image is really untenable. Whenever teachers behave in ways inconsistent with it—and it's inevitable that at times they do—the public tends to feel let down, betrayed.

Yet teachers themselves strongly adhere to that same image, the most flattering view possible. That is to say, whenever they're asked why they went into teaching, they usually give reasons that have them putting the best, noblest slant on their motives. Prospective teachers, too, give replies to questions about motivation that have a decidedly inspirational cast. Typical is a detailed study that was conducted with elementary and secondary school teachers-to-be at Northern Illinois University. Nearly all of the prospective grade school and well over three-fourths of the prospective high school teachers ranked "desire to work with children and adolescents" as the primary influence on their decision to become teachers.[13]

Other ranking followed in kind. Nearly three-fourths of both elementary and high school teachers-to-be gave "desire to impart knowledge" second place as a significant influence. Seventy-two percent of the prospective elementary school teachers and 61 percent of the prospective high school teachers ranked "opportunity to continue one's own education" third. "Desire to be of service to society" was the fourth-ranking factor for about two-thirds of the elementary and half the secondary people. As for the fifth-ranking factor, "Liking for a particular subject," only 20 percent of the prospective elementary school teachers but 85 percent of those going into secondary education chose it as a significant influence. And, "Experience in working with youngsters" was a significant factor for 73 percent of the prospective elementary and 43 percent of the prospective high school teachers.

There's no reason to doubt that concern for the welfare of children (most often expressed by elementary school teachers) and strong interest in teaching a particular subject (the big factor with high school teachers) genuinely prompt people to go into the teaching profession. (Quite a few teachers mention other factors, too: such as parents or other relatives who are teachers; the impact of memorable teachers; experience gained teaching in the Army, in summer camps, in the Peace Corps, or elsewhere.) Those, however, are the conscious reasons, the ones readily put down on a questionnaire or given in answer to an interviewer's query.

As will be discussed shortly, there are deeper reasons as well. What motivates people to choose one career over another involves complex psychological forces, many completely hidden even from self, and this applies to the most altruistic of occupations as well as to the more materialistic. It is as unreasonable to expect teachers to be moved solely by "pure" motives (wanting to help children, desiring to further society) as it is to expect doctors and lawyers to be what they are solely out of a profound respect for human life or justice. But teachers, being as human as the others, automatically put their best social foot forward. When nearly two hundred female elementary and secondary school teachers employed by the New York City school system were asked to rate the major factors that influenced them to teach, not even the promise of anonymity deterred them from selecting socially acceptable reasons for making their career choices.[14] Being defenders of middle-class morality, they either wouldn't or couldn't admit to motives at variance with that morality. So concluded the researcher who, writing in the *Journal of Experimental Education,* added, "Apparently teachers are either reluctant and/or unable to admit the powerful sway of motives which are socially less desirable. In private communications, teachers will agree that teaching is a convenient job for a woman. Yet only ten percent regarded this reason as most influential in their choice of teaching."

[7]

In 1950 Yale University published a doctoral dissertation whose contents, at least in part, will bring joy to few teachers. Ponderously titled "The Behavior System and Occupational Type Associated with Teaching," it attempts in a few of its pages that most hazardous of exercises: generalizing on the personality characteristics of an occupational group, that group of course being teachers. In effect, it's a word portrait of the average American schoolteacher, complete with strengths and weaknesses.

Teachers (the dissertation says) are not strongly motivated to enter the occupation or to advance in it. They are at least vaguely dissatisfied with their work, inclined toward the status quo, disinclined toward change. They tend to be cooperative and helpful, and adept at school work. They are more followers than leaders, more disposed to political conservatism than liberalism, more apt to grow authoritarian with time than vice versa. Teachers think of teachers as being different—which renders them quite vulnerable to stereotyping. They lack aggression but have a strong sense of service. Women teachers are rather optimistic, disposed to make the best of a situation. Male teachers are inclined to pessimism.[15]

To be fair, it may be pointed out that the world of the 1950's and the world of the 1960's are quite different and that the portrait might be quite different if drawn in recent years. Fortunately, for the sake of comparison, in 1964 researcher John Gillis undertook to analyze the personality needs of men and women about to enter teaching. Published in *Educational and Psychological Measurement,* the study doesn't paint too dissimilar a portrait. In comparison with people going into other professions, teachers show more cognitive organization. They tend to depreciate and devalue themselves more. They have more of a need for close, friendly relationships. They show more deference to persons they consider superiors. They're more emotional, more needful of giving and receiving love, protection, assistance. They have more of a concern for detail and neatness. They're more erotic in their interests and expressions. On the other hand, they have less need to analyze and reflect, less interest in solving problems, less willingness to gamble or take risks. They're less objective but also less spontaneous. They exhibit less assertive behavior with others.[16]

When men and women teachers are compared with one another rather than with persons going into other professions, the men teachers show more of a need to achieve. They show more need to overcome humiliation and failure, more need for personal power, more aggression and hostility, and more of an urge to manipulate others. Women teachers are more self-abasing, more willing to be submissive, more narcissistic and erotic. They have more of a need to be friendly, to love and be loved. These comparisons would seem to reflect the differences generally found between men and women in American culture. They also reflect the direction teachers' organizations have been taking since a substantial number of men have entered the teaching field.

It's a mistake, though, to view teachers as a professionally homogeneous group. They are one when it comes to teacher welfare and to improving educational conditions, perhaps, but there are many divergencies: among elementary and secondary school teachers; even among teachers teaching different grade levels within a given school; increasingly among white and black teachers; among young teachers and those who have been in their school systems for decades; among teachers who specialize in different areas. Tests with high school teachers confirm the obvious: Music and art teachers are, as a group, much more inclined to esthetics than any other teachers. Math and science teachers score highest on "external validity" tests. English teachers have little stomach for computational work. Mathematics teachers show a strong preference for scientific subjects. In sum, teachers don't all speak the same language.

Many aspects of teacher personality—most, in fact—are far

less evident and far more subtle. Numerous aspects of personality prompting men and women to become teachers find their roots in yearnings and frustrations that go back to childhood experiences, back to all the myriad impacts upon the psyche that shape a human being's inner self. An educator once isolated some twelve possible needs and pressures that motivate teachers. People teach because their own school experiences were exciting and they want to stimulate intellectual inquiry in others. Or because they'd rather repeat childhood successes than function in a wholly adult world that seems too challenging and competitive. Or because they did badly in school and want to return to scenes of failure in order to prove themselves. Or because they lacked affection as children and thus have the need to give to, and become the recipients of, many children's love. Or because their need is to get beyond self, to champion a morally worthy enterprise, and school is it. Or because they need to display strength to others who are not as strong.[17]

Of course such a list, highly clinical in its implications, is a bit mechanical. People's motives generally are diffuse, they overlap, they change with the passing of time and the maturing of self. A middle-aged Negro high school teacher in Los Angeles said that when she first got out of college, teaching was the last thing in the world she wanted to do. She went into it, she felt, because "it was the easiest, most expedient way of building a career—especially because of my race." But after her first child was born, she continued, "teaching became something else again. I realized that it's the most important job in the world."

[8]

What makes for an effective teacher? If one reads all the literature and takes it seriously, one comes up with something like this: The successful teacher is buoyant, considerate, cooperative, emotionally stable, ethical, expressive, forceful, intelligent, objective, resourceful, reliable, mature, vital, punctual, magnetic, enthusiastic, energetic, uses judgment, possesses a sense of humor, and has scholastic proficiency. As J. M. Stephens points out in *Theory into Practice*, he is "held to embody most human virtues along with a great many qualities more frequently attributed to divinity." [18]

What, then, makes for the effective teacher? "The teacher functions as both artist and scientist," notes Lindley J. Stiles of Northwestern University, a highly respected schoolman. "He creates relationships and experiences with students that have the form and flexibility of an artistic production. Much of his professional skill grows from the kind of sensitive observations that support the choice of the right word or suggestion, the most promising procedure, the questions that prod and provoke, and the assessment that motivates." [19] Hyperbole aside (lucky is the child who encounters a couple of such teachers in his school career), it's possible for a person to do a perfectly respectable teaching job without being divinity, artist, or scientist. As for specific personality characteristics, the fact is that six decades' worth of research on the subject of teacher personality hasn't turned up anything of profound value. The most monumental study was undertaken by D. G. Ryans and involved more than 100 separate research projects, 1,700 schools, and about 6,000 teachers. One result of all this labor: Warm, understanding, friendly teachers are more effective than aloof, egocentric, and restricted teachers. Responsible, businesslike and systematic teachers are more effective than evading, unplanned, and slipshod teachers. Stimulating, imaginative, and enthusiastic teachers are more effective than dull and routine teachers. [20]

In other words, the best teachers—and, as confirmed by subsequent research, the ones who produce the most achievement in students—are lively, imaginative teachers caught up in their subject matter and able to present it in a stimulating way. But any halfway perceptive schoolchild knows that. Beyond such characteristics, and maybe hardest to come by, is what David Asubel calls "perhaps the most important personality character-

istic of teachers" insofar as their effectiveness is concerned—
"the extent of the teacher's personal commitment to the intellectual development of students . . . It determines in large
measure whether he will expend the necessary effort to teach
for real gains in the intellectual growth of pupils, or will merely
go through the formal motions of teaching." [21] It's no surprise, either, but it's something to keep in mind—the best
teachers wear a large invisible button that reads, "I give a
damn."

Now for a misconception: It's often said that the best teachers are the stablest ones, the least neurotic people; that neu-
rotics have no place in the classroom. Let us cheerfully agree
that everyone has some neurotic tendencies and that what
counts is not the "whether" but the "how." If enjoying hearing
oneself talk and rehashing ideas are neurotic traits, they are—
to a reasonable degree, anyway—essential for teachers. Of
course, it's not that simple. Some people are so unstable they
don't belong in the classroom working with children. But they
are in the classroom working with children because there's
little or no mental health screening by teacher training institutes, because periodic "mental health" checkups for teachers
are available in very few cities, because there's a dearth of re-
habilitative centers, because teachers' mental health is one of
the several crucial facets of the teaching life that teachers as a
group have been reluctant to face up to. Whenever the unmen-
tionable subject comes up, the first thing any educator does for
publication is to reassure the public that teaching doesn't draw
more emotionally unfit men and women than do other professions. This may be true, but teachers are in a more sensitive occupation than many others. Expert guesses, on the part of educators and mental health experts who have looked into the
problem, is that from 8 to 10 percent of the teachers now at
work are mentally unbalanced and should not be in the classrooms. That would put the number of such teachers at about
200,000.

In 1959 Dr. Louis Kaplan of the University of Southern California scrutinized eleven of the most valid studies of teacher maladjustment. Applying the most conservative estimates to the national teaching force—applying, that is, the minimum percentages of highly neurotic or psychotic teachers—he found that they numbered nearly 120,000 and affected more than 3,000,000 children.[22]

[9]

It is often said that education is a passport to a better life, a proposition almost impossible to refute these days, at least in terms of dollars-and-cents results. No less authentic, however, is the proposition that the field of public school education itself increasingly continues to provide people with the opportunity for a better lot in life. In other words, for many people, a public school career is a definite step up the ladder of success. This fact prompts a variety of consequences, intensifying, as will be seen, teachers' urge for security, their growing aggressiveness, and the tensions between teachers and economically deprived youngsters.

Among educational sociologists there has been much niggling as to just where teachers stand on the status ladder—whether they are on the lower, center, or upper steps of middle-class professions. There's little question, however, either among educators or the public at large, that as a profession teaching is solidly middle-class. That is to say, respectable and, despite some obvious manifestations of disesteem, even imbued with a degree of status and prestige. (Teachers rate their prestige as "medium.") Not every teacher subscribes to that constellation of attitudes and behavior patterns one calls a middle-class style of life; a relatively small number live far above or below this norm. But for the vast majority the patterns generally hold.

That teaching is a middle-class occupation makes it an ideal way-stop on the upward mobility run. To be sure, the profession has, historically, attracted a heavy proportion of women from the middle and upper-middle strata of society. Women, that is, who came from business or professional families. In a sense, though, even these women were socially mobile in that teaching provided a viable alternative to stagnating at home. Many farm girls, too, have been recruited into teaching, and theirs has been a double reward: Teaching got them both off the farm and into a profession.

Now that business and the professions are not as stringently sexualized as once they were, increasing numbers of intelligent and intrepid middle-class women are making breakthroughs in such fields as law, medicine, architecture, higher education, and the executive levels of commerce. As a consequence, some of the brightest, best-educated girls, who formerly would have chosen a career in the public schools, are now turning to other, more rewarding fields. A study of Wisconsin high school seniors illustrates this trend. It shows that nearly half the college-going daughters of unskilled workers but less than one-third of the daughters of professionals or executives plan to become teachers.[23] Of course, many middle-class girls still flock to the schools.

At the very same time that women have managed to push ajar doors leading to a variety of interesting nonteaching occupations, men have found teaching much more congenial than in the past. With men, though, the social-class story has taken a different turn. Very few upper-income males have become teachers. ("When I told my old man I wanted to become a teacher," said a young man from upper-strata Scarsdale, New York, now teaching in the New York City system, "he hit the roof.") Compared with women, the number of middle-class males going into teaching also has been relatively low. The reasons are obvious. Given the comparatively low pay of teachers and the "medium" prestige they hold in comparison with members of other professions, teaching represents a step downward in terms of social mobility patterns for men of upper- and upper-middle-class backgrounds. They can do much better in law, medicine, engineering, and a host of other professional categories. If the pay gap narrows more, this may change. Such middle- and upper-middle-class men as do go into teaching now do so because they prefer less competition than is found elsewhere, because they see teaching as a "helping profession" (especially in ghetto schools) in which they can be actively involved in a concern for people, or both.

For young men from lower-middle-class and blue-collar backgrounds, teaching typically represents a very definite step up on the social mobility ladder. Therefore, the heaviest concentration of males drawn into teaching comes from such backgrounds. "The son of an unskilled worker who's going to college is more than three times as likely to choose teaching as the son of a professional or executive," was the conclusion of the study on the Wisconsin high schoolers.[24]

Wisconsin isn't the whole of the United States, of course, but a USOE study of beginning teachers also bears out this trend. When these beginning teachers were questioned about their fathers' occupations, some interesting differences developed with respect to the two sexes. A total of 51 percent of the female beginning teachers reported having fathers in the white-collar category, the other 49 percent being either blue-collar workers or farmers. On the other hand, only 38 percent of the men claimed white-collar fathers, while 62 percent had fathers who were in the blue-collar or farmer categories—clear-cut evidence of a social leap. Educationally, too, the new teachers made big jumps: Taken as a whole, barely more than one-fourth had parents with one or more years' worth of college education.[25]

In a survey of San Francisco Bay Area teachers, researcher Richard O. Carlson of the University of Pittsburgh was able to pinpoint the social beginnings of teachers further. Basing his conclusions on census tract records, he learned that female elementary school teachers are highest in social class origin, with more than three-fourths originating in the middle and upper-middle classes. Male secondary teachers, on the other hand, have the humblest origins: Half come from lower-class homes.[26]

The political study of teachers suggests that male teachers

more than female teachers are dissatisfied with their jobs and imbued with a great need for respect. Many, whether or not they articulate it, probably feel as does a fifth-grade teacher from the Bronx, New York, a middle-aged man who said with feeling, "There seems to be very little recognition that a teacher is a human being, and that a teacher has transitional stages, that a teacher is modern man, and that a teacher is more than just something that goes into a classroom and, like, teaches."

[3]

Problem Areas

[1]

LET us praise good works. Given the least of what society expects of schools and teachers— (1) to "socialize" children so they'll play by the rules later on; (2) to equip them with the skills they'll need in order to play their economic roles; (3) to provide a custodial service that keeps young kids out of the house and older kids off the labor market—the schools have done a creditable job with the middle-class majority. Illiteracy has almost vanished. At the turn of the century, the nation was 88.7 percent literate. By 1960, and despite the fact that the population had considerably more than doubled, 97.6 percent of Americans were literate. Even with a shocking student-dropout rate of about 30 percent, the schools have actually been retaining an increasing number of youngsters. In 1940 the median number of school years completed was 10.4. By 1966 it was 12.[1]

An Education Testing Service study shows that within the space of two decades there has been a modest improvement in schools from the eighth grade down.[2] No similar improvement was registered for high schools, but one took place just the same.

49

Since each decade sees the high schools holding a larger number of youths of average ability, the fact that there has been no marked loss, say experts in educational evaluation, represents a gain. Moreover, College Board examinations have been growing increasingly more difficult, attesting to the fact that for some youths, at least, schools have been doing a better job in terms of subject-matter skills. And some high school senior honors classes, especially those in science, are offering the equivalent of first-year college courses.

As for teachers, as recently as 1931 two-thirds of all public school teachers in the United States didn't have a four-year college education. Now better than 90 percent have at least a bachelor's degree. Though a degree is no guarantee at all of teaching competence, generally teachers are better educated than in the past.

It's often said that schools were superior, or teachers more dedicated some decades back. Naturally, distance lends enchantment. That one fine and dedicated teacher is clearly remembered, and perhaps in time she may come to seem more numerous than she really was. Anyway, a look at educational literature and statistics for the earlier parts of this century hardly supports the conclusion that things were rosy then. Armed forces entrance examination tests during World War II showed up many scholastic inadequacies. Furthermore, dropouts and nonlearners weren't given the attention they are today; they were simply forgotten.

More to the point, each era has to be judged on its own terms. This is a much tougher, more demanding, era. A good case can be made for the proposition that schools were never better than they are today (most Americans, surveys show, believe they are), but that isn't the question. The question is, how well are the schools doing by a contemporary frame of reference. There's the rub. Though curriculum reform and innovation have been the hallmark of American education since Sputnik first sent shivers down the nation's collective spine, though teacher training institutions have been undergoing reform, though teachers are considerably better educated than they were, though much more in-service education is available for teachers—though all these things and more have been happening, educational literature in the 1960's highlights the same educational problems it did in the 1950's, 1940's, and further back. For instance:

In 1964 *Arithmetic Teacher* reported on a study of a group of elementary school teachers in Colorado. Though teaching upper-grade math, their own math scores were quite low, and they were themselves badly in need of basic math training, especially in the area of basic concepts and symbols.[3] Two years later the same journal published a study with Boston suburban school teachers which showed that the more a teacher is used to teaching math the traditional way, the more resistant she becomes to new math programs.[4]

In 1968 the *Journal of Educational Research* reported on a study with elementary-education majors at the University of Missouri. Fifty-eight percent scored below the norm for eighth- and ninth-graders. Less than 5 percent scored above the ninetieth percentile in the methods courses. These prospective teachers were "particularly weak in their knowledge of the real numbers system, mathematical statements, functions and graphs." [5] A study of full-time mathematics teachers taking an in-service course in math at the University of North Carolina showed that not one of fifty-five mathematics teachers belonged to the Mathematical Association of America (dues, $6), only thirteen belonged to the National Council of Mathematics, few subscribed to mathematical journals.[6]

As 1968 drew to a close, the National Academy of Sciences issued a report which stated that the teaching profession needs "people who can teach mathematics in grade school in a way that will not create a permanent psychological block against mathematics" and "people who are able to teach mathematics in high school and cope with the necessarily changing curriculum." [7] Maybe the authors of this study had in mind a massive scrutiny of American high schoolers—Project TALENT—

which showed that less than 50 percent of ninth-grade youngsters were able to handle a test dealing with arithmetical reasoning, even though "the test items in this skill were not intrin-
sically very difficult and required hardly any computation."
Twelfth-grade youngsters did a little better: 61 percent of the
boys and 55 percent of the girls answered the test items cor-
rectly.[8] Or maybe the authors of the National Academy of Sciences study had in mind the results of a five-year international
math study which had thirteen-year-old American kids ranking fifth from the *bottom*, trailing behind children in Japan,
Belgium, the Netherlands, Australia, Scotland, England, and
France. In that competition American high school seniors also
lagged far behind their counterparts in other countries.[9]

So much for mathematics. In 1965 *School Science and Mathematics* came out with a devastating report on science teaching in
the elementary schools. It stated that training is totally inadequate; that comprehensive courses in the subject are lacking; that some schools allow science to be taught by teachers
who have had no science in college; and that many teachers, consequently, are insecure in teaching science.[10]

In 1968 the *Peabody Journal of Education* reported that
elementary science certification requirements are inadequate.
Many teachers took their science courses so long ago as to be of
little value now, and "in many of our schools, second grades are
studying Archimedes' principle of buoyancy from teachers who
do not understand this principle or who have never heard of
Archimedes." [11]

The insecurity of teachers who teach science on an elementary school level is widespread, and teachers talk about it
frankly. Most elementary school teachers are female; females in
American society are not "supposed" to understand science too
well and are not enough exposed to it. But children in elementary school generally are eager to learn all about science—and
the more favorable the teachers' attitude toward the subject,
the more positive the children's learning experiences in it.
There is the crux of the problem. Teachers tend to follow the

highly simplified, step-by-step procedures outlined in their teachers' manuals. The fact that they must teach from nine to eighteen subjects during the course of the school year doesn't help matters. Understandably, they tend to emphasize those subjects they know best. When faced with an upcoming science lesson she doesn't understand too well, many an elementary school teacher asks her husband or boyfriend to explain it to her. Some teachers admit they have trouble answering sharp scientific questions posed by their brightest students.

(Many schools now employ specialists in certain study areas —science being one of them. However, in big-city systems especially, teachers are sometimes assigned as science "cluster" teachers even if they aren't really proficient in the subject. And at times teachers who don't function well in ordinary classrooms are made such cluster teachers because it's easier to do that than to get rid of them.)

Though elementary science study materials have been specifically designed by the Elementary Science Study Committee to give students the feel of scientific discovery, this hasn't worked out too well either. "As satisfying as it is to see our early efforts come to fruition, most of us at EES are still profoundly worried about the state of education and the plight of teachers and children," the Committee noted in its October 1968 newsletter.[12] "We are more and more convinced that such mastery of prescribed skills, concepts and technique is only a shadow of education and does not, by itself, encourage the development of the drive—or whatever else it is—that distinguishes a committed person from an indifferent one, a human from a machine . . . EES has provided some interesting materials— materials that can help teachers who want to be more sensitive, responsive, provocative, attentive. We have not yet found ways, however, to make teachers want to be these things. We wish we knew how. We also wish we knew how to make ourselves understood as well as heard. Too many teachers and administrators still think we are saying that we are providing a technique—easy lessons about the Discovery Method—when we are really trying to express a way of life, not just a way of teaching. What we want to say is that anyone who tries to teach children to explore and speculate and try things—if he does not himself explore and speculate and try things—cannot carry it off." Criticisms of secondary science teaching run along the same lines.

On to history. Reporting in the *National Association of Secondary School Principals Bulletin,* Robert F. Byrnes of Indiana University's International Affairs Center gave a disquieting report on history teaching.[13] He advised readers of the publication that many of the history teachers in Indiana in the early 1960's had "no intellectual interests whatsoever." The majority hadn't read a single book in the previous five years. Furthermore, "most . . . did not read a single newspaper of any kind—the local newspaper, the Louisville *Courier,* any of the Indianapolis papers, the Chicago *Tribune,* or the New York *Times.*" Earlier, Indiana history teachers couldn't qualify for graduate school fellowships because their grade records were too low. That Byrnes was addressing high school principals nationally suggests the problem is not confined to Indiana.

If history is a problem field, can civics be far behind? It cannot. One may be platitudinous about the subject; paraphrase Thomas Jefferson, for instance, and say that no nation can be free unless its citizens know what freedom is all about. After surveying high school seniors' attitudes for well over a decade, Purdue University's Division of Educational Reference found that the schools have failed to convey the meaning of the Bill of Rights.[14] One out of every four seniors believes the government ought to deny some people the right to make speeches. Sixty-three percent would refuse Communists the opportunity to speak on the radio even in peacetime. Forty-two percent think the FBI or local police are at times justified in using the third degree. Though parents and other influences outside of school obviously have an important bearing on students' political attitudes, taken in context with other studies, the Purdue surveys confirm the inadequacy of civics teaching. The restrictions radical students frequently attempt to impose on free speech likewise confirms it.

When Indiana University's High School Curriculum Center in Government completed its own examination of high school civics courses in 1968, it also found that civics teachers have "little influence" upon their students. Courses are taught mechanically. Approaches are narrow and uninspired: They deal with definitions of political bodies, with forms of government, with the workings of the committee system in Congress, and so on. Courses (and teachers) never get down to gut issues, such as the way real political power is wielded, the place of "community elites," or the manipulations of lobby groups. Calling political education in the schools "often emasculated," the authors of the study say that "kids often learn about politics much the same way as they learn about sex, *i.e.,* from peer groups, casual conversations, adults, the media, etc. What they are often deprived of is learning about politics as a topic for serious, intellectual investigation." [15]

Whether new teaching materials developed by the California Bill of Rights Project and published in 1968 will have an appreciable effect in uplifting civics teaching in the United States remains to be seen. Teachers' attitudes about the Bill of Rights, at least one study shows, fairly closely correspond to those of students'.

Despite the crucial importance of world affairs and despite the importance of having voters and citizens understand the ramifications of U.S. involvements in the area of international politics, little is done in this area. And education majors don't seem to be too sophisticated regarding it. In the early 1960's, a professor on the faculty of Chico State College in California studied education majors' knowledge of world affairs.[16] Only two knew that Lester Pearson was the then Canadian Prime Minister. Hardly any knew who Henry Cabot Lodge (then U.S. delegate to the United Nations) was. David Ben-Gurion, then Israeli Prime Minister, was identified as a "French political leader." Carlos Romulo, the Philippine leader, became the "representative from Cuba" and "President of Mexico." Achmed Sukarno of Indonesia was listed by many students as being head of state of Japan, China, or Pakistan. Ralph Bunche turned into a "union official" and Dag Hammarskjöld into a "Korean." Chou En-lai, *enfin*, became "Ambassador to the United Nations from Red China." The education majors were also unfamiliar with the uses of American tax dollars in relation to international affairs, consistently overestimating the amount of funds spent on humanitarian purposes and underestimating the percentage spent for defense and military purposes.

The study concluded that despite the low scores on the test, "the overwhelming majority" of education majors "felt a knowledge of international relations to be essential for teachers at all grade levels." Furthermore, "paper after paper contained a lament" about how badly prepared they were to meet this responsibility.

In 1966 the American Association of Colleges for Teacher Education asked Dr. Harold Taylor, former president of Sarah Lawrence College, to look into the problem of teachers *vs.* world affairs. "To what extent are American teachers being prepared through their curriculum to understand and to teach about the nature of world society? The answer is, almost not at all," he concluded after an exhaustive look.[17] He estimated that only from 3 to 5 percent of all teachers "have studied in a field which could properly be described as world affairs."

Such knowledge can be acquired separately, Dr. Taylor pointed out, through in-service courses, travel-study, summer institutes, and by other means. But "since, according to our findings, students who are preparing to become teachers seldom possess an initial interest in politics, world society, or foreign cultures, they are unlikely to develop such an interest either on their own or through the curriculum of teacher preparation."

Moreover, Taylor noted, the conservatism of teachers in this respect dovetails with the conservatism of school boards, administrators, and teachers' colleges. All are fixed in a narrow traditional curriculum and pass it on to succeeding generations of teacher-students.

English seems to fare little better than politics or world affairs. In 1964 and again in 1968 the National Council of Teachers of English published devastating reports on the state of English teaching in the United States. The findings have particular relevance in that English—that is, the expression of language—is basic to work, play, and good mental health. The 1964 study shows that two-thirds of all secondary school teachers don't consider themselves well prepared to teach composition and oral skills, 90 percent feel the same way about teaching reading, almost 50 percent about literature and language.[18]

Nevertheless, the vast majority of English teachers fail to take course work in English; nearly one-third of all high school English teachers haven't even attended a voluntary workshop in English. And only 44.8 percent read the most important journal in their field, *English Journal*. The report was also severely critical of elementary school teachers for slighting English both in their pre-service and in-service education even though they spend more than half their class time on English and language arts.

The 1968 report was based on detailed observations of 1,600 classrooms with far better than average English programs. Yet it continues in the same vein. Many students need help with their essay writing, but only 17 percent of their papers show evidence that teachers help them organize, analyze and communicate clearly. Reading programs are "inadequate, uncoordinated and almost non-existent." Language is badly taught, with heavy emphasis on rote drill. Only a few teachers show themselves "capable of effectively leading class discussion." Slow-learning students, and those on nonacademic tracks, are everywhere neglected.[19]

[2]

Innovation, innovation, innovation. For all the prodigious amounts of energy and creativity, and huge sums of money expended on innovative efforts over the past couple of decades, the gain—though indeed there has been some—is less than impressive.

"Every comparison of results with which I am acquainted (and, incidentally, very little bona fide experimentation is available for examination) seems to emphasize one point over and over again—that students generally do about as well as a result of these new endeavors as did students in days past," commented Dr. M. Karl Openshaw, at a conference of innovative-minded educators.[20] "They seldom do worse, but generally speaking, seldom better; and we must accept the fact that student learning is the reason for our existence . . . Under no circumstances would I want to leave the impression that new ideas and programs should not be considered and utilized when possible in improving educational practice. But the results of most of our current emphases and activities reveal that differences in student learning are, at best, only slight and usually for only a small percentage of students."

Team teaching is one example. Rather primitive now, since its modern thrust began in the mid-1950's, it has not proved to be the panacea its proponents hoped it would be. Though specific patterns vary, the basic idea involves a cooperative venture in which several teachers jointly or in hierarchical fashion with a team leader plan, teach, and evaluate specific educational programs, working both with small and large groups of students. In theory, team teaching allows students and teachers to break out of the rigidities of the self-contained classroom, provides teachers with an opportunity to observe and measure one another's work, and allows them the flexibility to use innovative programs and techniques. But the real-life world of the school has its fun with theory. In most schools, the hours are not flexible enough to provide for the kind of interchange team teaching demands. Few teachers are willing to put in all the time and effort required on their own. They show a marked tendency to give intimate, small-group instruction short shrift. Some are reluctant to "share" their classes with other teachers. Personality clashes among teachers is far from uncommon when a couple of teachers are in the same classroom, especially when both carry equal weight. Moreover, they have an almost universal aversion to a no-holds-barred analysis of one another's teaching methods. According to J. Lloyd Trump, associate secretary of the National Association of Secondary School Principals and one of team teaching's foremost champions, too often it degenerates into "turn teaching—I'll teach today and it's your turn tomorrow." [21]

Closed-circuit educational television is another innovation glorified when it was first mass-introduced in the early 1960's. ETV was to alleviate the teacher shortage by providing the means for really large-group instruction. It was to be more effective than the average classroom teacher because only the sharpest, most efficient master teachers were to be used to give the lessons. Instead, as a group of legislators attending a Senate-House Joint Economic Committee in 1966 were told, despite its unlimited potential, instructional television is "perhaps the most expensive and disastrous single failure in the history of educational technology." Many teachers reacted to ETV's advent with fear and hostility. They saw it as an intruder invading the sanctity of their classrooms. Those less effective feared the master teacher would show them up, while the more effective resented the idea of having their curriculum autonomy curtailed. Though they had some qualms about ETV replacing them, numerous teachers used it precisely as a substitute: They failed to provide their students with any preparation for the content of the television lecture, and failed to extrapolate upon it afterward. "It doesn't hurt anything, but it hasn't produced many added gains in learning either, and it generally costs more," is the way Fred T. Wilhelms of NEA's Association for Supervision and Curriculum Development summed up the instructional television situation at the start of the 1968-69 school year.[22]

Fancy and expensive "language laboratories" provide another example of a panacea that hasn't worked out. Relying heavily on electronic gadgetry, these labs have, according to Wilhelms, met one of two fates: (1) Too many classes share a single lab, diminishing student-use time to the point where it does little good; (2) foreign language teachers have little faith in the labs or don't know how to use them, and they remain idle. (A tape recorder, some foreign language experts say, is as useful as a costly lab. But it doesn't, of course, give a school as much glamor.) Curriculum reform has been a booming business in the rarefied atmosphere of the most prestigious universities, but thus far the new materials have not lived up to expectations. Developed in 1957, the new physics curriculum of the famous Physical Science Study Committee was to induce more high school students to take physics. But during the ensuing decade the percentage of high schoolers taking physics actually dropped from 25 percent to 17 percent.[23] Comparisons between conventional and innovative curriculum approaches in math, chemistry, and biology show "no significant differences" in the achievement level of most students—except that the new curriculum materials allow for growth in subject areas and topics not covered by the conventional materials.[24]

After being introduced with a considerable amount of fanfare in the late 1950's, "teaching machines"—forerunners of computerized instruction—have had a dismal history in the nation's schools. By 1967 only 16 percent of the comprehensive high schools were using these programmed instruction devices and many districts, including Newton, Massachusetts, were phasing them out. Materials (the software) were poor, students found them boring, teachers were misusing them, and as participants at a National Society for Programmed Instruction were told, school principals were finding that on the whole they produced "no significant difference in achievement." [25]

Nongraded instruction is still another innovation for which much has been promised and little thus far realized in the way of concrete measurable results. The nongraded concept attempts to deal rationally with the problem of individualizing instruction; its rationale is that each child develops at his own pace intellectually, and that assigning him to a specific grade forces him into an artificial, lockstep framework of schooling. Like team teaching, which it complements, the nongraded approach has had its current thrust since about the mid-1950's. And like team teaching, it has, despite the force of logic behind it, not demonstrated its effectiveness as a superior way of engendering pupil achievement in such skill areas as reading, language arts, and math. Nongrading champions say it inspires pupils to be more independent, adopt a more favorable outlook toward school, and develop better peer group relationships. Unfortunately, this positive assessment—although it may be perfectly valid—is based on the impressions of evaluators favorably disposed to nongrading. What few formal tests have been run fail to show any improved student outlook on the part of those youngsters who are in nongraded classes.

According to Dr. John I. Goodlad of UCLA, one of the foremost exponents of nongraded organization, this "much-heralded revolution in American education is being in large part blunted on the classroom door." Most so-called nongraded schools, he says, adopt the label without really putting into practice the philosophy behind it.[26] Other observers say that, in order to be truly effective, nongrading must be integrated with team teaching, flexible space, individualized curricula, electronic instructional systems, and hierarchies of teaching personnel. In short, it needs a total transformation of school and personnel. A basic problem with nongraded approaches, states a cautionary appraisal in the *Elementary School Journal,* is the teacher: Because of the wide range of achievement levels in nongraded classes, teachers have to be superior, "exceptionally well-prepared and sustained at every step . . . To teach a nongraded class, one must be young in spirit, creative in devising new ways to meet new situations, and eager to meet challenges." The author, a grade school administrator in New York City, added rhetorically, "Does this description fit the typical teacher on the average staff?" [27]

The question points to one problem connected with many innovative programs. Typically, they are developed and tested in "clean" laboratory schools, often located on university grounds or close by, where highly competent teachers under expert supervision work with students of above-average ability. By the time an innovation reaches the "dirty" classroom of an ordinary school for general implementation, however, it has passed before a number of people—the subject-matter supervisor, the principal, etc.—who may alter the original conception. The classroom teacher—who may be poorly trained in the new approach, who may resist it as an unwanted intrusion on established procedure, who must fit it into the realities of the classroom routine—will almost certainly alter it.

In other words, the human element always and unexpectedly comes into play. Thus, programs conceived with an ideal teacher and ideal conditions in mind are bound to fail. It's true that school systems are notoriously slow to change, and that it takes many decades for an idea really to permeate the various school districts. In some form or other, both team teaching and nongrading have been around since the late 1800's. Yet by 1967, less than 15 percent of the nation's school systems had adopted team teaching approaches and barely over 12 percent provided nongraded schools. Maybe only those educational artifacts that fit readily into the complex mosaic of events that comprise the typical school day have real survival value. And the ones that do may be only those that apply to the average administrator, average teacher, and average student.

Part Two

INDIGNITIES AND RESPONSES

[4]

A Sorry History

"THE public school teacher, the one you see in the class-room today, like me, is a direct descendant of the first indentured slave who stumbled off a boat from Europe and was made to teach the pauper kids how to read."

The person who said that was an aggressive young high school teacher in the environs of Denver whose heart and soul are less caught up in the daily struggles in the classroom than in the fight for teacher recognition, teacher respect—in effect, teacher power. This fight he diligently pursues through his professional organization, an affiliate of the AFT.

If there was melodrama in what he said, there was also the barb of truth. It's hardly possible to understand the anger, the needs, the drives, the push for recognition on the part of the contemporary American teacher, without looking at his sources.

His is a sorry history in many respects and not simply because of the way in which teachers were treated—the denial of rights which they endured, the servile manner in which they were expected to behave, the ludicrous wages they received, the political repression and other controls that were placed on them. It almost seems as though a deliberate attempt were being made on the part of the larger society to create a second-rate profession. Such a conspiratorial view stretches the point: The treatment accorded teachers simply reflects the fact that public school education did not, to put it mildly, occupy a very exalted place in the esteem of the nation. The frontier was nothing if not anti-intellectual. To be sure, the status of teachers varied from region to region and from period to period, as differing philosophical, religious, political, and economic forces played upon the concept of education. And always some individual teachers gained respect and recognition in their local communities. On the whole though, even when the hard fight to create a fully public school system was won after the Civil War, in many respects the teachers' place in society was little better than wretched.

To begin at the beginning: In the seventeenth century, long before the advent of mass public education in the United States, "learning" was provided for Colonial citizens by a few very well-educated and many badly schooled itinerant teachers. (A law passed in New England in 1647 required towns of fifty families to provide an elementary teacher and towns of a hundred to establish a Latin grammar school for secondary education. People who could afford to pay did so. Religious instruction was the most important basis for early Colonial schooling.) Many teachers were drunkards. Some were sadists or swindlers. Some pilfered school funds; others piled up debts or disappeared.

It's a wonder more didn't succumb to thievery, considering the pitiful wages they received, equivalent to a farmhand's. Runaway servants obtained jobs teaching school; other servants were, as that Denver high school teacher observed, actually indentured into the ranks of the schoolmasters. Some of these also ran away. As late as 1777, a reward was offered for two runaways in Connecticut, one described as "a schoolmaster, of a pale complexion, with short hair. He has the itch very bad, and sore legs." [1]

Generally speaking, school equipment was abysmally poor, the curriculum severely limited, and youngsters' attendance most irregular. School terms were very short; teaching was in many instances actually a part-time occupation. A number of schoolmasters were also clergymen or, at the very least, had to assume a number of semireligious duties. A number? Take poor Johannes von Eckellen, a New York schoolmaster, and the contract he signed with the town of Flatbush, Long Island, in 1682: He had to agree to clean the church, ring the assembly bell, read portions of the Bible, hear the children recite questions and answers out of the catechism, give them religious instruction, provide a basin of water for baptismal purposes, furnish bread and wine for the communion, act as messenger for the consistory, give funeral invitations, ring the funereal bell, and dig graves.[2]

There was yet another personal indignity: Teachers were "boarded round"—meaning they had to live with a different family each week in order to stretch out minuscule school funds. Generally, turnover was extremely high, though some hardy individuals stuck it out for awesome periods. One Ezekiel Cheever taught for seventy years, thirty-eight of them nonstop in Boston alone.[3]

In the eighteenth century more attention was paid to the moral character of teachers, but crudeness prevailed well into the century. So did inefficiency. Religious orthodoxy was the rule: Teachers couldn't deviate, either in belief or teaching, from the convictions of their employers (who might happen to be townspeople, churches, royal companies, etc.). In the South planters' wives sometimes taught classes as a hobby. In the South, too, Negro slaves, as well as white indentured servants, taught the children of the poor. "Dame schools" for the younger children—often small and dirty corners of private homes, where untrained housewives taught beginning reading—flourished everywhere in the seventeenth and early eighteenth centuries.

This period, too, saw institutionalized the first teacher loyalty oaths, oaths some form of which persist to this very day. Of course there was some basis for the original oaths, inasmuch as teachers were on the payroll of religious institutions promulgating specific sectarian doctrines. Thus the Society for the Propagation of the Gospel in Foreign Parts, an employer of New York-based schoolmasters during the early 1700's, required the prospective teacher to certificate the following: "1. his age. 2. his conditions of life, whether single or mary'd. 3. his temper. 4. his prudence. 5. his learning. 6. his sober & pious conversation. 7. his zeal for the Xtian Religion & diligence in his calling. 8. his affection to the present government. 9. his conformity to the doctrine and discipline of the Ch. of England." [4]

However, during the eighteenth century there was a movement toward vocational instruction, that is, more subjects were taught to promote the seeking of jobs and careers. Bookkeeping, writing, arithmetic, and other subject matter helpful in business, trade, or the ministry began to be widely taught in schools where heretofore they had not been. In other words the notion of real public schooling as a preparation for life was making some headway, as, with the passage of state laws governing education, was the concept of state responsibility for the schools.

During the nineteenth century all manner of changes occurred in the nation's evolving educational attitudes and in the slow development of teaching as an occupation. Educational giants like Henry Barnard and Horace Mann were nineteenth-century people. Through the labors of these and other men a system of compulsory education was established in nearly every state by the time the century had run its course, though not, of course, without considerable frantic resistance from forces inimical, for one reason or another, to forced schooling. (Farmers, whose offspring were economic assets when working in the fields, weren't exactly overjoyed to have them planted in classrooms for a few hours a day.)

A major nineteenth-century phenomenon was the attrition of males from teaching posts, as industrialization and urbanization created higher paying and more attractive jobs elsewhere.

The result was that teaching quickly became tagged as a "feminine" occupation. When, during the mid-1800's, a group of male teachers grumbled about the lack of esteem in which they were being held by the community, famed suffragette Susan B. Anthony told them, "It seems to me that you fail to comprehend the cause of the disrespect of which you complain. Do you not see that so long as society says that woman has not brains enough to be a doctor, lawyer or minister, but has plenty to be a teacher, every one of you who condescends to teach tacitly admits before Israel and the sun that he has no more brains than a woman?" [5]

During the nineteenth century enormous strides were made in the area of educational reform. New and better schools were built. There was improvement in curriculum and equipment. State teachers' associations were formed and journals published. Teacher-training institutions—the "normal schools"—were established in a number of states. So were teachers' institutes—miniconventions where teachers could meet to talk over problems of mutual professional interest. Weighty subjects like the philosophy of education and methodology of teaching were sometimes discussed. More often the agenda consisted of day-to-day classroom problems. For instance, at the Mercer and Crawford Institute held at Jamestown, Pennsylvania, on January 14, 1858, teachers gathered to discuss these questions: Is it better for teachers to board around? Should the teachers encourage pupils to chew tobacco? Should teachers open their schools in the morning by reading a portion of the Scripture? Should the door be closed against pupils who are not present at nine o'clock in the morning? Should the rod be used in school? Should the wages of females be equal to those of male teachers? [6]

Wages? Something else again. Despite educational reform, coupled with compulsory schooling, teachers individually and collectively still fared wretchedly. They remained for the most part among the worst trained, lowest paid, and most shabbily treated of professional workers. Examples gleaned from the

journals of the times: In 1857 teachers in Pennsylvania protested having to teach on Saturdays "inasmuch as six days' attendance upon school was injurious to the physical and mental
faculties of both teacher and pupil." Saturday, apparently,
could be a particularly dangerous day for the teacher. In 1872
Ballard County, Kentucky's school commissioner protested the
practice of people going "to the school house to whip or insult a
teacher." His advice: "If anyone desire to whip a teacher, let
him wait until Saturday." Many teachers in many areas had to
suffer through a tortuous annual examination, a public evaluation usually conducted by a dull layman who would ask the
teacher tricky arithmetic questions and make him read tongue-
twisting passages. According to one historical account, "Rarely
did the examiner ask a relevant question and when he did, he
did not know how to evaluate the applicant's answer."

As for pay, even given the sorry wages that were forthcoming
for both sexes, women were treated much more degradingly
than men. In 1847, for instance, male teachers in Massachusetts
(always the most progressive state in educational matters)
earned a monthly stipend of $24.51. Female teachers earned
$8.07. In Connecticut that same year male teachers earned $16
monthly. Female teachers earned $6.50. In New York State
male teachers earned $14.96. Female teachers earned $6.69. By
contrast, shoemakers, harness-makers, carpenters, blacksmiths,
painters, and other skilled workers often made twice the wage
male teachers did. Seamstresses, factory workers, and even
some servant girls earned more than female teachers did. The
Forty-sixth Annual Report, issued by Philadelphia in 1864,
noted that "a large proportion of the (women) teachers receive each less than the janitress who sweeps the School-
House." [7] In 1867 teachers in a Boston suburb received $2.50
a week. Despite racial discrimination, Negro cooks in the same
area received $3—which speaks volumes about the status of
teachers.

Obviously, the pittances that teachers received did not attract well-educated people in large numbers into the profes-

sion. Even as late as 1890 a mere 20 percent of students going
into normal schools had high school diplomas, while 65 percent
of students had only made it through grammar school. "They
[the elementary schools] are mainly in the hands of ignorant,
unskilled teachers," publicly thundered W. E. Phelps, head of
the teachers college at Winona in 1870. "Poor schools and poor
teachers are in a majority throughout the country. Multitudes
of the schools are so poor that it would be as well for the country if they were closed. They add nothing to the intelligence
or moral power of the country. . . ."

Not surprisingly, there was a 40 percent turnover in the
teaching ranks each year. Many teachers were young women
who intended to teach for a few sessions. Each session lasted, at
most, seven months. Many were shorter, and teachers weren't
hired for more than a session at a time. Annual examinations,
public or private, were the rule. Apparently a large number of
handicapped people went into teaching; a writer in the American Institute of Instruction's *Proceedings* for 1867 stated that
"any one can teach, especially if he happens to have been so unfortunate as to lose a limb, become blind in one eye, or in some
way has become unfit for anything except a teacher. I know of
no other business which has seemed to be so dependent on a
bodily infirmity." As to the image people had of teachers, an
embittered teacher described him in the August, 1864, issue
of *Illinois Teacher,* as "somebody who can parse and cypher;
has little brains and less money; is feeble-minded, unable to
grapple with real men and women in the stirring employments
of life, but on that account admirably fitted to associate with
childish intellects. . . ."

As school systems grew, so did the administrative machinery
to supervise them. Often supervisors were no more adequately
prepared to supervise than teachers were to teach. But the most
lackadaisical superintendent couldn't help but throw up his
hands in despair even if he did nothing more than walk through
a typical school with his eyes half-open. Thus Joseph Fell,
county superintendent of schools in Bucks County, Pennsyl-

vania, painted this pretty grim picture of the results of an inspection tour he made in 1856: "In one school, where I had drawn the map of Pennsylvania on the blackboard, the same diagram had remained for a year, the board never having been used in the interim. In another, not a scholar in the school could tell me in what country he lived, and when I held up Holbrook's globe, the oceans on which were painted blue, and asked what it was, a large boy, at least seventeen years of age, replied, "a bird's egg!" [8] At a third school the teacher saw Fell coming and hastily drew a map of the state on the blackboard. Fell told the teacher he was pleased to see this interest in geography, then quizzed the youngsters about the map. Not one of them knew anything about it. This was their first geography drill, and "they interchanged sly looks with each other, as much as to say, 'Our foxish teacher has been holed this time.' "

Casual educational arrangements, however, did not prevent both male and female teachers from being policed socially and morally and having the most onerous restrictions placed on their private and political lives.

Actually, the leash on the male teacher allowed for more freedom. In a large New England school system, for instance, men could take one evening a week for courting; two evenings if they were regular churchgoers. That same system rewarded both sexes munificently for working hard and well: At the end of a five-year period they got a twenty-five-cent raise (subject, of course, to board of education approval). At the same time they were expected to build themselves a little nest egg so as not to become a burden to society in their twilight years.

Obviously, teachers had no voice in such matters as affected them directly or indirectly, though they were expected to vote —in accordance with prevalent community sentiments. Loyalty oaths, political in nature, were widespread during the Civil War and afterward.

In the first three decades of the twentieth century things failed to change very much. Teachers' pay went up along with everybody else's; proportionately, though, it was as low as it had ever been. School boards manipulated salaries up or down at will. Many unmarried teachers were forced to economize by living in "teacherages"—community-owned boarding houses, a few of which are still operating in such places as Charlotte, North Carolina, and elsewhere. Most teacherages were perfectly decent insofar as their living conditions were concerned. A high school teacher who three decades ago lived in one in rural northeastern North Carolina recalls that it was co-ed, the women upstairs, the men down. It was where he met his wife, and as soon as they became friendly, she moved out. (There has always been a trend toward teachers marrying teachers; not only because there is a communality of interests, but also because two people who are earning low wages are economically better off together than alone.) There were about twenty teachers in the teacherage, mostly women. "It was the greatest living I ever had," the North Carolinian recalled. "I didn't think it was an indignity when I lived on fifty dollars a month, including food." The indignity, of course, lies in the fact that he had no choice; given the relative pittance he received, he had to live there in order to eat and have a roof over his head. Interestingly, this man, who is with the Kings Mountain Classroom Teachers Association, is now fighting for better conditions for teachers in his area.

As for restrictions on one's personal life, while American mores on the whole were loosening up, teachers' remained an appalling anachronism. Who ever heard of a teacher being a flapper girl? (Maybe a few were, but only in the cities and in secret.) As late as the 1920's, teachers who smoked had a hard time getting jobs in California, Tennessee, parts of Illinois, Massachusetts, and other places. Many school boards, representing the thinking of their communities, frowned on bobbed hair: They saw it as a sign of sin, potential or otherwise. Numerous board-teacher contracts stipulated a number of no's: no dates, no petting, no short skirts. In Mississippi and Kansas teachers weren't allowed to attend dances—on penalty of instant dismissal. In at least one county in Ohio teachers who were dating other teachers also faced immediate firing.[9] A town in Louisiana required that its teachers stick around over the weekends and be in bed by 10 P.M.—presumably, if unmarried, alone.

Politically, as rigid state laws in New York, Ohio, Michigan, Tennessee, and many other states made pointedly clear, teachers were to tread an undeviatingly narrow patriotic path. A path that left no room to question any aspect of established American life, either politically or socially, or to present several points of view on particular social issues. "Teachers should know that it is part of American educational tradition that a teacher should have little or no freedom," observed an issue of the Columbus *Dispatch* in 1929. "She is born to be suppressed and harassed by a system of supervision designed to keep her docile."

[2]

Lucky teachers in one North Carolina town signed contracts containing the following stipulations, excerpted here verbatim:

"I promise to take a vital interest in all phases of Sunday school work, donating of my time, service and money without stint for the benefit and uplift of the community.

"I promise to abstain from dancing, immodest dressing, and any other conduct unbecoming a teacher and a lady.

"I promise not to go out with any young man except as it may be necessary to stimulate Sunday-school work.

"I promise not to fall in love, to become engaged or secretly married.

"I promise to remain in the dormitory or on the school grounds when not actively engaged in school or church work elsewhere.

"I promise not to encourage or tolerate the least familiarity on the part of any of my boy pupils.

"I promise to sleep eight hours a night, to eat carefully, etc., etc." [10]

This, remember, was in the wild and woolly 1920's.

[3]

It may not be of great moment, in the face of the complex series of problems facing teachers and their profession today, that three or four decades ago a shy, presumably virginal young thing in Ohio or North Carolina or elsewhere had to forgo the company of men if she wanted to take on a low-pay teacher's job. Yet it illustrates in no small measure the ambivalence with which most communities have regarded their teachers. More fundamentally, it symbolizes the way they've regarded public school education, for the teacher is, after all, its instrument.

To put it simply, the nation's orientation in the main has been pragmatic. Thus, education largely has been viewed pragmatically. The Colonies, deeply rooted in the religious experience, wanted to make sure children knew how to read the Bible. They also needed people versed in skills like surveying and shipbuilding. Free compulsory education for the children of the poor, prevalent throughout the Colonies, served yet another pragmatic purpose, namely, "to protect the rest of society from a working class that might otherwise become vagabond and prove dangerous to life and property." [11]

There was a time, during portions of the eighteenth century, when it looked as though public school education might be humanistically shaped, accenting the individual: his personal growth, his readiness to take part in democratic life, his humanness. But this ideal, lending warmth and breadth to education, soon took a much lesser role. It was the rapid advance of science and technology, the growth of the factory system, swelling competition, the mushrooming of the cities—it was these forces and their requirements that shaped the major task of education: essentially, to provide the well-oiled cogs which could be fitted into their proper places for the smooth running of the economic and social machinery.

Back to that hapless Ohio or North Carolina girl, then, and the price she had to pay for the joys of teaching public school.

Joys? In an atmosphere heavy with functionalism, with educational aims related to immediate and narrow goals, it's questionable how much joy there was. To be sure, the kids were nice, and they learned, and so the teacher took delight in aspects of her work. Many, having been raised to be dependent, probably also derived comfort from the structure all those contractual restrictions provided. But the community's essential disrespect was very evident. It engaged her in a kind of like-dislike relationship. Like because she performed a functional service. Dislike because she and the trappings around her cost money.

One can speculate about all those sex-focused prohibitions the teacher was subject to—don't dance, don't date, don't wear lipstick, don't bob your hair, etc. Obviously, since teachers work closely with impressionable young innocents, there has to be some concern with moral conduct. As the above examples have shown, however, in many instances school boards evidenced less concern than obsession with the teacher's morals. In part good old pragmatism was involved: Keep a teacher from dating, and she won't up and marry and leave the system; furthermore, she'll take less money and more guff when she's single and more dependent on a job. In part the focus on narrow morality probably stemmed from much earlier American days when teaching was centered on religion and teachers had to conform to the requirements of the particular church that sponsored them. In part, too, it probably derived from the strange kind of puritanism that has been so much a part of the American character—a puritanism more façade than fact, therefore needing confirmation in outward symbols of purity, of which teachers provided a spectacular example.

However, the exaggerated asceticism demanded of teachers (especially female teachers) symbolizes something else as well. It symbolizes the curious lack of passion that was felt about the whole educational process. Teaching and learning can be, and at its best is, a sensually moving experience. Give an insight, gain an insight, and the heartbeat quickens, the mind leaps.

But most students and teachers hardly stepped into the classroom for anything so sensual. It was a practical dictum that
governed the school atmosphere: Do your work, get the
grades, graduate, matriculate, take your place in the line of
the world's work. Such schooling, even when camouflaged by a
bevy of "life adjustment" courses, is squeezed dry of life's juices
—just as the community implicitly and explicitly expected the
teacher herself to be squeezed dry, at nineteen or twenty, of
those selfsame juices.

And from such distorted true-life positions as these into
which teachers have been forced come the teacher stereotypes
of old. One researcher looked into the characterization of
teachers in forty-six Broadway plays from 1920 to 1950. He
found that in 68 percent of the plays, teachers were portrayed
as maladjusted. In 37 percent they were having financial trou-
bles. In 33 percent they were experiencing sexual tensions. In
19 percent they were poorly dressed. In most instances the
other characters treated them with pity.[12]

Another researcher dug into sixty-two novels published since
1900 to extract the novelist's image of the teacher. The male
teacher, he found, was pictured as solitary, effeminate, and
impractical. The female teacher fared no better: She was either
young, single, and frustrated or a worn, sexless old maid. And
a third investigator, concerning himself with the lives of teachers in movies and books (to 1950), saw teachers mirrored as
leading monotonous, pedestrian lives—lives they accepted
passively, resigned to their lot. The community, as reflected in
these books and movies, regarded teachers with "pity and
sympathy on the one hand, and with condescension and ridi-
cule on the other." [13]

[4]

And now? Recent books and movies—*Up the Down Stair-
case; To Sir, with Love; Death at an Early Age; 36 Children*—
don't depart too much from the early stereotypes. Teachers

are much more human; some come through with pas-
sions (maybe because for the most part these works have been
written by teachers who themselves had something to say). But
essentially the teacher remains the same: No one can elicit
more sympathy than a teacher caught in a ridiculous bureaucratic web when all he wants to do is teach children; no one
can write with more condescension about teachers than another teacher, especially if he's morally outraged by what he
sees.

Now many of the shameful restrictions that caged in teachers
of the 1930's and before have disappeared. Teachers are better
organized. The majority is teaching in heavily populated urban
and suburban areas where greater anonymity is possible. The
moral climate in any event is looser, freer—even for teachers.

Yet not completely, not everywhere. When the NEA quizzed
its members on community restrictions in 1963, 48.5 percent
reported that their communities did place some restrictions
(though not serious ones) on them. Three percent—about
60,000 teachers, given today's teacher population—felt that the
restrictions placed on them *were* serious.

Even today, in the small towns of Mississippi, Alabama, and
other parts of the rural South, teachers aren't allowed to drink
alcoholic beverages in public. They have to belong to the Bap-
tist or Methodist Church—whichever prevails—and show up
for church services on Sunday. They must be careful to date
only the most respectable members of the opposite sex. As for
sex, there can't be the faintest whisper that the teacher is having any of it. Single women teachers are expected to live in
pairs, in boarding houses. On social issues teachers of both
sexes are expected to be very conservative and, says one small-
town Alabama teacher, "adamantly opposed to the federal
government."

In some local areas in Iowa, teachers have to leave the school
system as soon as they're pregnant. In some small towns in
Wyoming, a teacher has to sneak into an adjacent community
to buy a bottle of liquor (while the teacher from that commu-

nity sneaks into his to do the same). He isn't allowed to play
pool, to tell a dirty joke (or listen to one) in public. In some
cases these restrictions apply to the teacher when he first comes
on the scene; after a while, say after a six- to nine-month
wait-and-see attitude on the community's part, he becomes accepted and the restrictions relax.

Most big-city principals and some in medium-sized cities,
too, are tolerant of miniskirts (within reason), but the small-
town teacher better not try wearing one. A California teacher,
the mother of eight, wore one to school and was promptly fired
by the school board. She couldn't get another teaching job in
the general area because, she said, "no principal wants to be the
one who hires the 'miniskirt teacher.' " In another small town
in California a high school teacher dared grow a beard, and
was dismissed when he refused to shave it off. He appealed the
dismissal and won.

In 1967 the southern section of the California Teachers Association queried many of its members to find out how they
fared in terms of personal freedom. A number of respondents,
mainly from low-population areas, had complaints. "In my
opinion," said a Bonsall teacher, "the private life of a teacher
is about as private as a fishbowl if he lives and teaches in a
small district." Since social restrictions and political restrictions
go hand-in-hand, the issue is obviously wider than having the
right to drink liquor in public or not. As a Palm Springs
teacher wrote the CTA, "What I do, what I say, and how I act
are always subject to public scrutiny. Teachers affect too much
in the community for it to be otherwise . . . We can pull the
shades by keeping quiet, by not making waves, by dropping
out, as it were. Our question then seems to be, are we willing
to pay the price of silence to secure our privacy? If we are willing, can we afford the luxury?"

A former schoolteacher became President of the United
States during this decade, but as recently as 1964 an NEA survey showed that only four teachers out of ten were able to say
that—yes—they were as free as other citizens to take sides pub-

licly on political issues. Finally recognizing the realities of educational politics, some of the teachers' organizations have become as highly politicized as the school systems they serve. New York City's United Federation of Teachers, to take a foremost example, is extremely aggressive politically on both state and local levels.

More teachers are themselves going into politics—running for office—than ever before. (Each month the NEA mass journal, *Today's Education,* publishes a squib about some teacher-in-politics as an inspiration to other teachers.) The NEA is also holding political clinics all over the country for small groups of teachers who want to become more sophisticated in the ways of political in-fighting. Role playing at the clinics conditions the teachers to come up instantly with feasible approaches to simulated political situations. The object is to learn how to work for political candidates favorable to education; how to defeat those who have anti-education planks. But all this is very new to teachers, and many, perhaps most, aren't really involved. ("They think politics is dirty stuff and they don't want to get their hands into it," caustically grumbled a teacher-leader, then in Denver. "Where the hell do they think their paychecks come from?" He didn't realize that educators are partly to blame for this. They've always espoused the myth of "keeping politics out of schools" as a way of reducing formal political activity around education, thereby increasing their own power. In fact, politics and education are inextricably linked and always have been. It's only through political exercises that educational policies are shaped. Moreover, any teacher who doesn't think the very act of teaching, of influencing the young, is political—that teacher is very naïve indeed.)

Because the politicization of classroom teachers is still in its early stages, state education journals still carry occasional articles that deliberate on the morality of teachers politicking (the inevitable conclusion always being that teachers *should* be political animals). The NEA boasts of "protective personnel policy provisions" in new contracts that permit teachers to electioneer and run for office (with sabbaticals for winning teachers)—which shows the extent to which teachers are still vulnerable on this issue. For that matter, there's no shortage in the files of the American Civil Liberties Union and the teachers' groups of cases in which individual teachers are harassed and dismissed for engaging in political or social activities not in keeping with the prevailing attitudes of the community. Civil rights activities and antiwar demonstrations are the most prominent cause for punitive action. But anything not in keeping with the most conventional approach to life can do it. In 1967 a teacher in Alaska was refused another contract because he'd helped bring out a psychedelic tract. Jonathan Kozol, author of *Death at an Early Age,* was fired from the Boston school system for reading to his class a poem by Langston Hughes. In 1969 two Wellesley, Massachusetts, teachers who'd invited an acting troupe to perform LeRoi Jones' *The Slave* as part of a seminar on race relations were hauled off to court. The play contained some four-letter words, and the charge, later dismissed, was that the teachers were introducing "obscene materials" into the school.

Such cases ought to be kept in perspective, however. They occur; they occur much more often than they should; they occur less frequently than might be supposed. Teachers aren't all that often singled out for direct attack. Even during the late 1950's, the heyday of right-wing assaults on the schools, it was textbooks more than teachers that came under direct attack. (Currently, the extreme right wing has launched a highly organized attack on sex education in the schools.) Infringement of teachers' academic freedom isn't more widespread, in part because a vicious circle has been created: Community and school board sanctions inhibit teachers from being more controversial; the climate of conservatism around the schools itself tends largely to draw a more conservative, less adventuresome, kind of teacher. Radical teachers, what few there are, always decry the paucity of radicals among school staffs.

The day has yet to come when students at a teachers' college become wild campus demonstrators. All this is how the prevailing power structure (in every country) wants it. School is always supposed to perpetuate the institutions that prevail, not evaluate them, because evaluation means thinking, and thinking may lead people to make changes, rather than to perpetuate uncritically.

The fact is that most teachers, like most textbooks, shy away from anything that smacks of controversy (which, of course, makes things more difficult for the ones who don't). Consider the race question. A nationwide *Life* magazine poll in 1969 showed that more than half the students, but only 36 percent of the teachers, felt race should be discussed in the classroom.[14] A study of three East Coast junior and senior high schools showed that teachers don't tackle the subject of racial or religious prejudice.[15] On the contrary, they display "passivity and unconcern." Possibly they're not concerned about race, or maybe they want to avoid that particularly sensitive issue because they haven't come to terms with their own feelings about it. But consider a study reported by Hillel Black in *The American Schoolbook*.[16] When 1,251 grade school teachers all over the country were asked whether they initiate controversy in the classroom, 92 percent said no. When asked whether they discuss such subjects, 89 percent said no. When asked whether they should be discussing such controversial subjects, 79 percent said no. Yet when these same teachers were asked what subjects they felt that children might be interested in, they picked Vietnam, homosexuality, Cuba, politics, sex, etc.

Most teachers interviewed for this book gave the impression that at best they skirted around the edges of controversial subject matter, and the ones who explored it in depth with their students made it very clear that they always felt someone looking over their shoulders. A high school Latin teacher in the Rocky Mountain area put it most tellingly:

"I do stand for something in the classroom. And the curious thing is how I get away with it. Because I'm convinced that

the many, many discussions I hold with the students on everything under the sun in this broad universe of ours, and the
ways I try to stimulate interest and thought—well, had I been
a social studies teacher, I think I would have lost my job long
ago. But because I'm a Latin teacher, it doesn't really matter.
Even parents who vehemently disagree with me never make a
fuss because evidently Latin teachers, in their minds, don't
make any difference.

"But if a guy teaching their kids history said this, he's a
pinko, a Commie, something of this kind. I never got into this
even though there were children from families that were
Birchite-oriented.

"I tried invariably to make the point that, now, I don't
want you to agree with my point of view because it's my point
of view. If you think it has some merit, examine it, and examine some others with it. And reach some conclusions of your
own. The worst thing you can do, I tell my students, is to come
out somehow agreeing with me. I want you to be you.

"Some of the kids then would try to draw out some of their
other teachers, and some of course they can't draw out at all. I
don't think a teacher should keep his convictions out of the
classroom. Absolutely not. Why do you think students distrust
teachers so much? Because they're saying, 'Look, you're not telling it like it is.' If you're worried about some kind of repercus-
sions because you hold a certain point of view, I don't know
how you can teach effectively."

[5]

Money Matters

"WE'RE expected to give, give, give," said a disgruntled fifth-grade teacher in Detroit, Michigan. "When we do give, everything's fine and dandy, people are pleased with us, they pat us on the head. When things go wrong, when *anything* goes wrong—the kids don't learn well enough, or they rebel, or there's pollution in the air, or venality in business, or muggers on the street—it's schools that get blamed first. And if schools get blamed, so do teachers. It's the teacher who's attacked first of all. They tell us we're mediocre, we don't do the job we're getting paid to do, we're the dumping ground for failures . . . Well, let's turn it around. I ask you, how good a job is the public doing? To what extent is it giving the schools financial support? I'd like to know the answer because what I see is schools strapped for cash, double sessions, deteriorating conditions. I'd like to have the people who are so handy with their accusations ask themselves that question!"

Money, money, money. Whenever the subject of schools and teachers comes up, money is an integral part of the discussion. Increasingly, attitudes are becoming polarized around the principle that schools and teachers are getting too much of it—or too little. Taxpayers' revolts on school-related issues are growing, as each succeeding year sees a fewer number being approved. In 1966 voters approved 74.2 percent of the amount offered. In 1967 they approved 63.4 percent.[1] In 1969 there was a major wave of tax revolts that prompted even some wealthy communities to go on austerity budgets, eliminating school lunches, putting a moratorium on textbook buying, cutting out after-school activities, and the like. Some observers believed that at the start of the 1969-70 school year up to one hundred or so school districts would remain temporarily closed owing to lack of funds. Inasmuch as some educational economists have predicted a 50 percent rise in the cost of schooling over the next decade, the prospects are for more difficult times ahead. As it is, over the preceding decade, school expenditures were increasing at a rate 25 percent higher than the increase registered for the whole economy. In 1957 current expenditures for the public schools amounted to 10.2 billion dollars. In 1967 they amounted to 25.1 billion dollars.[2]

Putting the situation into another perspective, however, in a given year—1966—Americans spent 55.6 billion dollars on cars and car-related services. They spent 28.7 billion dollars on recreation. They spent 22.5 billion dollars on alcohol and tobacco. They spent 26.3 billion dollars on the public schools.[3]

It's not true, as some people believe, that Americans have been spending more on schools than any other nation. During the early 1960's, for which the latest figures have been compiled, the United States, with the highest per capita income in the world, was spending 5.4 percent of its national income on schools. The Soviet Union was spending 6.1 percent, Finland and Sweden, with per capita incomes less than half that of the United States, were spending 8.1 and 5.1 percent respectively.[4] Another set of statistics: In 1929, at the beginning of the Depression, Americans spent approximately 2 percent of personal income on current operating expenses of the schools. In 1966, in the midst of unparalleled prosperity, Americans were spending 4 percent. Considering education from even the narrowest of viewpoints—namely, the more education a person has, the more money he's apt to earn—one sees that the increase isn't so dazzling after all. Some economists believe more than 50 percent of the upward thrust of the Gross National Product is due to education.

What Americans actually do spend on their public schools varies widely from state to state, city to city. In 1968 New York was spending $982 on current expenditures per child. Colorado was spending $575. Mississippi was spending $346. Within New York State alone, one survey shows, some school districts spend as much as $2,000, others less than $300, per school-going child. Central cities generally spend considerably less than the well-to-do suburban communities that surround them. During the 1964-65 school year Los Angeles was spending $424 on current expenditures per pupil, while more affluent suburban areas averaged $654. Cleveland spent $433 per pupil; its suburbs spent $609.[5] Thus, while some schools are consistently starved, others are run more like private schools.

The taxpayer revolts that have become more and more manifest stem from a variety of reasons: because people are fed up with high taxes and big government generally, and school taxes are one of the few things they can do something about personally; because (especially in some working-class communities) education doesn't carry a high premium; because pro-education forces have done a poor propaganda job or antitax groups have done a good one; because nonparent voters predominate; because inflammatory issues like bussing arouse voter antagonism; or because, simply, people feel they have been bled dry.

At present local sources account for about 51 percent of the schools' revenue, while states pay some 41 percent of the total. Only about 8 percent comes from the federal government, which has the most potent tax-raising powers of all. A number of experts feel the federal government's share of the total school bill should be a full third. Though the need for federal aid to

education has been apparent for some time, powerful conservative elements—including the National Association of
Manufacturers and others—fought bitterly against it. The
National School Boards Association didn't want any part of it,
either. (For that matter, a recent NEA poll shows that 2 out
of 10 classroom teachers oppose federal aid to the schools, and
only 36.4 percent are *strongly* in favor of it.) Significant federal contributions weren't really forthcoming until 1965, with
the passage of the Elementary and Secondary Education Act.
By 1968, however, funds under this act were either rolled
back or leveled off. It's a matter of priorities. Budget figures for
1968 show that forty-three cents of every federal dollar went
for national defense, fourteen cents for the Vietnam War,
eleven cents for all social programs and education (including
higher education). As for state contributions to education, they
have actually lessened over the past several years, as governors
play politics with state legislatures, and state legislatures play
it with city officials and suburban interests. The schools, supposedly "above politics," invariably get caught in the worst
kind of crunch.

[2]

At Saratoga Springs in 1875, according to the NEA *Proceedings* for that year, a convention speaker described the quality
teacher as "manly, forceful, dignified, and practical; a philan-
thropist, patriot, prophet, scholar, philosopher, creator, artist,
and a Christian, though not necessarily a preacher." At the time
teachers were earning $10 to $50 a month.

A handbook for budding teachers, published in 1961, suggests that the superior teacher is a "real person," a "genuine
contributor to society" who participates in "community activities, wide reading, travel," and who has a "zest for life"—a person who enjoys helping charity drives, is devoid of prejudice,
likes people, enjoys responsibilities, finishes tasks punctually
and effectively, and ranks high in terms of personal values.[6] At

the time such paragons, as well as less notable teachers, were earning an average salary of $5,700.

The issue of teachers' pay is full of contradictions and confusions, not the least of them being the enormous regional differences in teachers' salaries. During the 1967-68 school year, the average salary of a teacher in North Carolina was $3,000 less than that of a teacher in California. During that same school year 64 percent of the teachers in New York State were paid $7,500 or more. Yet in fourteen states less than 10 percent of the teaching force made over $7,500. Such discrepancies go far beyond cost-of-living differences and reflect a number of other circumstances—community ability to pay, the extent to which education is valued, the strength of the teachers' bargaining agent.

How much is a teacher worth? That question could bring on discussion on the order of a Talmudic disputation. The worth of a teacher whose inspirational quality changes the lives of children is beyond reckoning. The worth of a teacher who merely coasts by, seeing his job as a sinecure, isn't easy to assess either—no prevailing rates have been established for people who act somewhat like mass baby-sitters. Practically speaking, teachers try to get as much as they can, based on local conditions and the prevailing scale in surrounding communities, while communities try to pay as little as they can decently get away with based on the same factors.

The lack of definition teachers as a group have is very much reflected in their pay and in the attitudes of teachers and nonteachers toward their pay. Teachers are college graduates. They work at an "intellectual" task. Their occupation is termed—and they definitely see themselves—as "socially significant."

But there's the other side to the teachers' coin. Teaching has always been mainly a woman's occupation, and nothing offers a better reason for keeping wages down. Teachers are hired by the city, the taxpayer, who would much rather enjoy the financial advantages of education than share them with teachers, especially since no one has yet been able to prove a direct correlation between high teacher pay and high pupil achievement. The transiency characteristic of teaching—because women predominate and because salaries are inadequate—has worked to make beginning salaries actually more favorable than those being paid teachers on the job for a number of years. The fact that salaries aren't differentiated—that regardless of ability or the market value of their specialty all teachers of comparable education and experience get the same pay—also serves to lower the pay rate overall. Finally, there's the fact that teaching is a part-time occupation—with shorter hours, lots of holidays, and, most significantly, two or three months off in the summertime. Of course, for the married woman teacher whose husband earns a good living and whose own income is supplementary, that summer hiatus is a blessing. It's a lean and hungry period, at the other extreme, for the man who has a family to support. He may ponder that having all that time off actually boosts his take-home pay while working. But it's not much solace when there are bills to be paid, and he must scramble in hopes of finding a good-paying temporary job. For this reason there's a small but growing movement in favor of a twelve-month contract.

[3]

Teachers have made remarkable gains in pay during the past decade or so. During the 1957-58 school year, teachers averaged $4,571 annually. A decade later they averaged $7,423. To put it differently, a single ten-year period has seen teachers' salaries go up nearly 65 percent. They go up from 3 to 8 percent a year. Moreover, comparing teacher earnings with the earnings of all full-time employees working for wages and salaries, teachers come out way ahead of the game: During the 1957-58 period, full-time employees in all industries earned an average of $4,276 annually. During the 1966-67 period they averaged $6,050. In other words, teachers earn more than do all employees lumped together, and the spread between them is increasing in the teachers' favor. More aggressiveness on the part of teachers' organizations, the competition business and industry offer for capable people, and the increased qualifications teachers are expected to meet all play their part in bringing on the increases. They're impressive, but they loom larger than they are because teachers started so far behind.

That teachers still have a way to go before they can, as a group, even claim to be alongside blue-collar workers in terms of straight earnings (not taking into account their shorter work-year) may be seen by a few ready statistics for early 1968. At that time the average pay for a grade school teacher was $7,675; for a high school teacher it was $8,160. But construction workers were making $8,505. Mailmen were earning $7,320. Auto workers were earning $8,740. In comparison with professional fields, teachers were much more disadvantaged; a chemist, for example, averaged $12,000. Beginning salaries reflect the same discrepancies. In 1968 the starting pay for a first-year teacher was $5,940. The average starting wages for policemen and firemen, who needed only to finish high school, were $6,555 and $6,200 respectively. (A garbageman earned more than many teachers in New York City and some other areas, prompting a Los Angeles teacher to comment bitterly, if revealingly, "Pay garbagemen's wages, and you'll get garbage.") Against the teacher's starting pay of less than $6,000, a beginning engineer earned $9,310. A beginning chemist earned $8,520. Beginning accountants earned $8,425. And business-administration trainees were making $7,560 to start.[7]

[4]

Call him Steve. He's a Denver teacher working in a mid-city, predominantly Negro, high school. In his mid-twenties, he's married and the father of two young children. He spends many afternoons in school, working with a colleague on the development of programs that will be more stimulating to his students than the standard educational fare. Other teachers acknowledge that his classes are some of the most exciting in the school. He's had five years of college, been a teacher for three. He's active in his local teachers' association, and works in his spare time for Outward Bound, a special program for economically deprived youngsters. Before that he drove a ski bus on weekends to make ends meet. His wife doesn't work because the children are so young. He thought he should be making $7,000 on his teaching job when he was interviewed in 1968. He was actually earning $5,800.

He said, "I'd love to go to school this summer, but I can't, because I'll be earning $1,500, and that will help. With that I'll be able to pay off the debts I've incurred over the year. It's difficult. It's damn hard. Anybody who doesn't think education is in a deplorable condition in this state is crazy. The seat you're sitting in right now is the departmental chairman's, and he sweeps a church to make extra money—he's a janitor. He finishes his master's, and he sweeps the church. Up until the time I got this Outward Bound job I was running out of money on the tenth of every month. We didn't have enough groceries in the house. We had to charge everything, and I had to scrape around. Yes, it's damn hard."

[5]

Many teachers made this complaint: They said that in educating the youngsters in their classes, they're helping to prepare the doctors, lawyers, businessmen of tomorrow. Yet they say, insofar as their own children are concerned, they'll have a rough financial time putting them through even low-cost or tuition-free colleges. They claim another irony, in that few teachers can live in wealthy communities because real estate prices are so high. And why are real estate prices so high? In good part because the school systems are so good. Few teachers, with the exception of women married to professional men, live in the more well-to-do suburbs they teach in. Some state frankly that it rankles to stand up in front of a class of students who may themselves already have more assets or more worldly experience than the teacher himself can ever hope to get.

A high school teacher in Scarsdale, New York, one of the wealthiest communities in the nation, said that when he talked about Italy, "half the kids in the class had been there already." When he talked about Florida, "some of the kids made it evident their fathers could fly them over any afternoon." Another Scarsdale teacher said some families make it a point to invite teachers to their homes for dinner, "but it's a *noblesse oblige* kind of thing—after the kid leaves school, the friendship peters out." This teacher mentioned pointedly that recent salary negotiations with the school board led to an impasse, and an arbitrator had to be brought in.

In the major urban centers, however, is where teachers have the hardest time maintaining a decent standard of living. Between 1947 and 1967 the average salaries of all public school teachers advanced by 98.4 percent, but the average salaries of teachers in the ten largest cities advanced by only 68.5 percent —*less* an amount than the advance enjoyed by railroad workers, telephone company people, and federal classified employees.

Furthermore, whatever gains teachers made did not in any major urban area with the exception of San Francisco-Oakland meet the U.S. Department of Labor's estimate of what a city worker's budget needs to be in order to enjoy even a *moderate* standard of living. A few examples for the 1966-67 period make that very clear.[8] All are based on a budget for a family of four—a typical American family—consisting of a husband aged thirty-five to fifty-four, wife not gainfully employed, and two children aged six and fifteen. In Atlanta in the fall of 1966 such a family needed $8,434 to live moderately well. The average teacher's salary, however, was $6,564. In Boston the budget called for $10,141. Boston teachers, though, earned on the average $8,093. In Chicago the budget required $9,506. Teachers averaged $8,221. In Minneapolis the budget required $9,495. But Minneapolis teachers averaged only $7,732. In New York City the moderate budget demanded $10,195. But the average teacher pay was $8,966. Such discrepancies with respect to even a moderate standard of living are hardly calculated to attract the most competent and creative people into teaching.

As teachers demand more pay and school boards find it increasingly difficult to come up with the money, some questionable personnel practices have come into being. More accurately, probably, they were always around, but the money pressure has made them more prevalent. Though it inhibits the building of a stable, experienced staff, some districts make it a point to hire for the most part teachers who can be expected to leave before they reach too high a level on the salary scale—young, single women being the most obvious example. There are districts that hire beginning teachers on a probationary basis and dismiss them just before they are due to get tenure. There are districts that hire "permanent substitutes"—teachers who receive no holiday or vacation pay and no fringe benefits— discouraging these teachers from applying for permanent status even though they teach the same subjects on the same basis as the regular staff. Where teachers' organizations become stronger, such practices are less easy to carry out. Denver, for instance, was forced to discontinue them.

[6]

Wry comment heard around well-to-do suburban neighborhoods: "You can always tell the difference between the teachers' and the students' parking lots. The students' lot is the one with all the new cars in it."

And bitter comment from the wife of a former high school teacher from Dubuque, Iowa:

"My husband was a terrific teacher. A terrific teacher. The students said so; the administration said so. But with two kids and another on the way he simply couldn't afford to keep his family. Love is a very great thing, and dedication is a very great thing, but it can only go so far. What's he doing now? He's selling graduate rings—and making a mint!"

[7]

Many teachers drop out, of course, when they find themselves increasingly strapped financially on a teacher's salary. The ones who stay try to find extra work, either within their own schools or elsewhere. Many school districts make non-teaching or extra-teaching jobs available to teachers, who then go on a supplementary pay schedule. Lots of those jobs are in sports—coaching, running the gym at night, and so on. Some educators call such jobs "under-the-table inducements" to keep men in the system, though a number of supplementary jobs— directing the school play, heading the debating society—are open to women, too. Rates of pay vary widely, depending on the activity and its value to the school district. Some districts that say they cannot afford to provide psychological or guidance counseling services nevertheless pay hundreds of dollars extra to the coaches in their schools. During the 1967-68 school year, to illustrate rates of pay, the high school basketball coach in Mesa, Arizona, got $500; in Tacoma, Washington, he got $987; in Philadelphia, he got $1,320; in San Rafael, California, he got $350. In Ashland, Kentucky, the junior high school band leader's supplement was $1,000. A contract between the Taylor, Michigan, Board of Education and the Taylor Federation of Teachers (AFL-CIO) lists nine categories of coaches, whose compensation ranges from 7 to 13 percent of the minimum BA-degree pay. Forensic and debating coaches, band and chorus directors, cheerleader and drama coaches also received percentages of their base pay. Teachers could also make $10 for supervising halls, keeping score at athletic events, announcing, taking tickets, being judges at track meets, and chaperoning dances.[9]

Most teachers who look for ways to increase their earnings put their spouses to work or find work outside the school. A U.S. Department of Labor survey shows that male teachers are more apt to have a second job than any other occupational group. One out of five holds down an outside job. Nearly six out of ten work during the summertime. The percentage is higher still for married male teachers; about 75 percent of this category supplements their basic earnings.

The moonlighting teacher does everything from working as a park ranger to painting houses to being an attendant at a filling station. A teacher who until 1965 lived and worked in a small town in Missouri sold books, ran a movie theatre, drove a school bus, and managed a service station to eke out the $3,600 teacher's salary he was getting. In many rural and semirural communities, the school bus job is prized by teachers as a way of earning more money. The job can become highly contested when several teachers are intent upon getting it. "One year I wanted that job very badly," the teacher from Missouri recalled, "because we were having our first baby, and money was especially short. But another teacher won out. He had a master's degree, and he got the job to make up for the extra money he wasn't getting."

Recounting his experiences as a service station attendant, he added, "You know, it's degrading to serve customers who are the parents of the kids you teach."

It need hardly be pointed out that from any professional standpoint, moonlighting as a way of life for teachers serves neither the teacher nor the children nor the district as a whole. The teacher who has to rush from school to work at another job can hardly be expected to give his primary occupation the time, energy, and interest that it requires. Nor can he be expected to keep up with new developments in his particular area of competence. The U.S. Department of Labor's moonlighting statistics brought out a meaningful trend: Only one-third of all the teachers who moonlight bring their professional skills to bear on their second jobs. The others work at completely unrelated jobs. This isn't the case with people in other professional fields. At least half find jobs closely connected with their primary occupations. But the teacher with a second job feels that he has no choice: Financial realities impose their will.

"It really is difficult to maintain a family," said a history teacher in Burlington, North Carolina. He has been there more than a decade. He has his master's and is near the top of the salary scale. "I've struggled by doing odd things. I operate the football stadium. I operate the gymnasium for the basketball games to pick up a few extra dollars. So I'm still connected with my students; it's not a completely different kind of job. I'm not sure I could have done it then except for a wife who's not demanding or pushy. She's completely comfortable with the things we have. And we don't have a great deal. But teaching is something I've wanted to do. It's a first love of mine. . . .

"A man can do it, and there are many discouraging moments, especially in the summer—the summers are long, I tell you, and you pick up things to tide you over. It's difficult to survive on a teacher's salary. I think you have to have a lot of things working for you. Wanting to stick to it. Loving to do it. Having a companion who's willing to make sacrifices and not have a lot of entertaining or going out or a lot of clothes. I don't think ten thousand or eleven thousand dollars for a man with my training would be a lot of money today. Electricians make that much. Engineers certainly do. The starting salary of policemen here is five thousand dollars same as for teachers. And you need only a high school degree or equivalent. I've taught a few boys now on the force; a couple didn't pass my work. It's sort of peculiar that it happens that way."

[8]

The figures on teacher pay are galling to many teachers, not only because of what they mean in terms of actual living, but also for what they symbolize in terms of status: Financially, teachers are on a par with blue-collar workers rather than with full-fledged professionals (and in some cases blue-collar workers bring home the bigger paychecks). In several cities, on the other hand, there were teachers who admitted they were making "excellent" money; for the most part such teachers turned out to be housewives married to business or professional men, or young girls fresh out of college. Teachers who must support dependents obviously hurt the most insofar as pay is concerned. From time to time people in education propose "dependency allowances" for both sexes (but mainly as a way of recruiting more men). A return to differentials for men were also occasionally proposed before federal law required equal pay for equal work regardless of sex. But all such schemes have little appeal for teachers. They consider themselves professionals and don't want to be paid on the basis of need. Commendably, they want to be paid what they're worth.

There it is again, that awkward question: What's a teacher worth? It's a question that won't begin to be resolved until teachers and their organizations come up with some viable way of measuring teacher worth in direct relation to how successful they are in carrying out their assignments—namely, educating children in specific spheres. This presupposes setting goals and measuring how well they are attained. It's an undeniably complicated issue, but also an issue the teaching field has successfully dodged up to now, preferring to put most if not all of talents and energies into improving the conditions of work. One isn't quieted by the growing criticism of teacher competence and quality among educators themselves—as, for instance, the public utterance of a Long Island, New York, supervisor early in 1969 that half the teaching staffs in U.S.

schools should be fired and replaced with "Peace Corps types." Allowing for the usual exaggeration and for the likelihood that a similar broadside could be hurled at administrators, the fact is that teacher competence varies considerably. But good, bad, or indifferent teachers are all paid on the same basis, one that has nothing to do with competence or productivity.

This topic will be explored more fully in a subsequent chapter. Suffice it to say for now that in the ideal world low-paid teachers wouldn't be expected to subsidize the economic well-being of those who benefit from their services, nor would the schools be a magnet for people who want to settle for moderate pay in exchange for lots of security and convenient hours. Ideally schoolteachers would neither engage in philanthropy nor look upon teaching as an "insurance policy" in case other paths, like marriage, don't work out.

Given the variations in pay in various parts of the country, as well as the variations in teacher quality and productivity, it's safe to say that in some areas *most* teachers are underpaid and in all areas *some* teachers are underpaid. There are also a lot of relatively well-paid baby-sitters around. But, of course, pay can't be considered in a vacuum. It's tied up with fringe benefits and working conditions. The trend, clearly, is to more money, greater fringe benefits, fewer nonteaching duties, smaller classes, more preparation periods, and stronger grievance and due process procedures. The latter are such that it's almost impossible to fire a teacher for incompetence. The parallel is with the factory worker rather than with the risk-taking professional. Precise hours of work, exact length of faculty conferences (forty minutes in New York City), the fractional amount a teacher receives if for some reason he can't be given his preparation period on a particular day, sick leave, pay for extra duties—such items in the best labor union tradition are noted on more and more contracts. Direct classroom contact with children is steadily being reduced, as to some degree it probably should be, given the mental and physical demands good teaching makes upon the teacher. But there's

nothing to indicate that, overall, the quality of what time periods teachers and students do have together is measurably improved.

"If they spend more than fifteen minutes actually teaching,
it's really something," muttered a disgruntled vice-principal
of a high-rated Los Angeles high school. "It's grades, grades,
and more grades; they scurry around giving tests and putting
entries into their books." After a moment he added, thought-
fully, "Teaching is one of the few fields where you can fail, if
you don't fail too badly, and you're all right. You're protected."
Yet if one succeeds brilliantly as a classroom teacher, the ex-
trinsic rewards—money, recognition, prestige—are sadly lacking. The attitude and action of the wider community has
brought all this on, having in the past always tried to pur-
chase education at bargain rates, and kept the teacher vulnerable to salary manipulations, mass layoffs, and the like. That
made it virtually inevitable for teachers' thrust to be in the
direction of unionism (even when they called their organizations "professional associations"), protectionism and security.

In other words, the wider community practically invited
the development of an educational system distinguished more
by mediocrity than excellence. While teacher pay still leaves
much to be desired, certain realities nevertheless have to be
recognized. One, teachers have made precipitous gains in pay
and benefits over the past decade. Two, teachers aim both for a
professional salary *and* the kind of security associated with the
civil servant rather than the risk-taking professional. Three,
as the growing incidence of tax revolts indicates, the public is
becoming increasingly resistant to dipping into its pockets
for the schools.

There's no question but that it's the community's responsibility to provide decently for its teachers, so they won't have
to scrabble for the amenities of life blue-collar and professional
people take for granted. Yet teachers have a responsibility, too.
They have the responsibility to go beyond welfare—to promote policies that will both upgrade the teaching field and

consequently allow for differentiation between the average teacher and the one of superior caliber, between the teacher whose job motivation is relatively superficial and the one who exemplifies high standards and strong commitment.

[6]

Why Beginners Tune Out

[1]

A FIRST-YEAR, fourth-grade teacher in New York City, recalling her first day on the job:

"My father had taught at one time. He talked to me the night before, about how tough you had to be with the kids, let them know who's boss. I got to the school, and all these kids were lined up in the gym, and I didn't know what in the hell I was doing because I had never been in the school before, except for sitting in one day and getting the job. I didn't even know where the gym was. And I didn't know how to get to my room. And I didn't know which key opened the door. I felt like a real idiot.

"What you have to do is have a real bravado about you, and really kind of act like nothing fazes you. I figured the minute I let anybody know I was flustered it would be the end, because they weren't kids who were going to pass it over very lightly, and children make fun of everything, anyway.

"I got one kid to act as class leader—-without knowing at the time that he was the worst kid in the class. Got another kid to open the door. Got them to show me where the class was. I told them to take any seat they wanted. Yes, I was scared stiff. I was just shaking. They were actually very obedient the first day of school, 'what's your name,' that kind of thing. They were feeling me out, too.

"I was very, very sure to act as if I knew everything, as if nothing bothered me. They asked me where I taught before. I lied and told them I'd taught in a school in New Jersey. So they wouldn't question me about the number or the area. I could never tell them I was a new teacher. It was just a day of complete confusion. Part of the time was taken up by giving out books, book labels, things like that. We talked about what they'd done all summer. It was a very awkward day, and I thought it would never end. But it did. Then I thought to myself, 'It's going to be tough, but it'll work out all right.' Maybe some of the other new teachers thought that, too, but five of them quit the first two weeks.

"That first day was overwhelming because all the principal did was give me thirty pounds of books and two monitors to carry them up the stairs. There they were, sitting on my desk —the curriculum. Indoctrination? It consisted of a one-hour meeting on the Friday before school. We sat in the library and were told, 'For the new teachers, these are the regulations; boys must wear ties.' Things like that. Rules about chewing gum, and assembly. On assembly days boys must wear white shirts.

"Each grade had one teacher who was experienced and who was supposed to help the new ones. Mine was very nice, but she was busy, couldn't help me that much; she had her own class. I don't think any teacher, regardless of how many ed courses she's taken, or what kind of preparation she's had— really, once that first day of school starts with a new class, everybody's baffled and bewildered, even those who taught before. Only it's less overwhelming for them. When I came in for that hour before school started, I kind of floundered. They set up their bulletin boards. They knew what books they had, what books to use, they were familiar with the curriculum. They could get all the record cards in shape. I knew from nothing."

[2]

When an eager new teacher takes over his first classroom, he is, typically, in for a few rude shocks. The first shock he endures is the realization of how badly prepared he is for his job. The education of American teachers is periodically under attack. Actually, American education is saddled with three perennial problems that are closely interrelated—the certification of teachers, the pre-service education of teachers, and the in-service education of teachers.

The licensing of teachers has always been a chaotic situation. Certification requirements vary considerably from state to state, but all of them require a minimum number of professional education courses—courses many teachers have been complaining about for decades as being boring and ineffectual. Because of this prerequisite to teaching, many bright people who'd otherwise be interested in a teaching career go into other fields. Because of it, people who are highly skilled in a particular area—say, math or chemistry or art—can't get teaching jobs. There are thousands of excellent teachers who have been teaching for years under "substandard" certificates, but who, because they lack full certification requirements, have inferior status and inferior pay. Moreover, because certification is a different species of animal in every state, a teacher can be highly qualified in one region and unacceptable in another. (Recently there's been a push to make certification requirements more uniform, and several states have entered into reciprocal certification agreements.)

Teacher education has been "undergoing reform" for years, especially since Dr. James Conant's devastating conclusions about teacher training early in the 1960's. Severe criticism came again early in 1969 with publication of the first educational manpower assessment report under the Education Professions Development Act, which is funding new programs in teacher training. According to the report, more than 80 percent of all teachers are being trained at "C" and "D" rated institutions on the American Association of University Professors' scale of faculty salaries. Nearly half went to "D" level schools, while less than 4 percent went to schools rated "A." Furthermore, according to the EPDA report, "higher education has not made a substantial investment in teacher training. The cost of preparing dentists or physicians may range from $5,000 to $12,000 per student per year; the cost of training teachers averages less than $1,000 per student per year." [1]

Now as in the past, teacher training is for the most part based on the assumption that if a person sits in a college classroom long enough, amassing the requisite number of credits from professors who haven't set foot in public school classrooms for decades, he'll wind up qualified to teach. Nobody knows the fallacy of this better than the beginning teacher, who takes over his first classroom and embarks on the beginning of wisdom—by realizing he knows next to nothing about teaching. Educators have traditionally wrangled about the relative importance of content and methods courses, with a third choice being to teach content within a framework of method. Presently, another division of opinion has developed between educators who favor strong on-the-job training with a downgrading of theory, and educators who insist that a strong theoretical background is what the teacher has been lacking right along. A task force studying ways of teaching disadvantaged youth has come out with strong recommendations for a comprehensive teacher education program that's heavy on pedagogical theory, on subject-matter preparation, and on the "shaping" of the prospective teacher's feelings and attitudes. [2]

There are also those educators who say flatly that teacher education has, for good reason, been proceeding on little more than hunches. Commented John Macdonald of Montreal's Sir George Williams University at NEA's National Commission on Teacher Education and Professional Standards (TEPS) 1968 convention, "At present almost nothing is known, as scientists understand knowledge, about instruction and the teaching process; both descriptive and prescriptive models are of a most primitive sort. Thus the source of ideas for teacher education programs is not evidence but an untidy mélange of tradition, the untrustworthy anecdotes of experience, and insights which, however brilliant, are unlikely to survive institutionalization." [3]

As for the continuing education of teachers, those already on the job, it's also beset with problems. To qualify for higher pay, teachers must keep taking additional college courses. With good reason, teachers call them "cash register courses." There's no systematic program of professional growth. Sometimes teachers seek out or find courses that help them become more effective instructors; often they don't. Often, tired from the day's grind, they take the easiest courses or the ones that fit most easily into their schedules. This is the easy way of setting up criteria for teachers' salary increases, but it does little or nothing to improve their competence.

[3]

The second shock the new teacher endures is that, in many instances, he gets little or nothing in the way of meaningful indoctrination. Some teacher-school-board contracts now call for a full day or two of indoctrination, so loudly have new teachers complained about their plight. In other districts, so-called buddy systems have been instituted in which older teachers take the new ones under their protective wings. That arrangement, too, has its limitations. Everyone is busy. Everyone is keyed to schedules. Some school districts provide consultant or supervisory help for new teachers when the budget allows for it; most school budgets these days are hurting.

"When I started teaching here, I didn't know the school provided paper. I didn't know the school provided pencils," said a thirty-year-old Los Angeles man who had been teaching for three years. "You can't get any greener than that. I didn't know a thing. I was given a class with thirty-eight children. I was told to meet on the playground. 'This is your room, you have half an hour to get it ready.' A teacher handed us a little black book with the rules and regulations and went over it with us for an hour or so. But I didn't know how to set up my classroom that first day, and nobody told me. It was three weeks, three weeks, before I got any help."

Much, of course, depends on the individual school and to what extent the administration has bothered to organize help for the newcomers. Contrasts: A young grade school teacher in the Bronx got no help at all, and a month went by before she discovered that a box of cards on her desk contained student records—their IQ's, reading test scores, and other data of more than passing interest. A young grade school teacher in Brooklyn, beginning the same year, recalled that the school's assistant principal and guidance counselor gave her all the help she needed.

Participants in a conference on the training of elementary school teachers, held at Harvard University in 1968, were vociferous in their complaints: Their principals, they charged, weren't knowledgeable enough about the problems of teaching to really help them.[4] Most, they claimed, were not even around to try. "The only contact I've had with my principal was during the textbook check," recalled one conference participant. "He said I was doing a fine job which meant that I had gotten all my reports in on time and that all of my textbooks were properly accounted for." And supervisors? Dictatorial or superficial. Resource people? Rarely seen. The most interesting aspect of these criticisms are the teachers who made them. Their training institutions had especially recommended them as outstanding graduates. They had finished four months of full-time teaching. And most held teaching posts in good suburban schools. Administrators sometimes charge that new teachers are reluctant to ask for help because they are afraid it might be interpreted as a sign of weakness or incompetence. These newcomers to teaching apparently did seek support; in any event it would seem to be an administrator's responsibility to see to it that the atmosphere in his school is nonthreatening enough to permit new and anxious teachers to ask for assistance.

The third shock the new teacher faces is that he's almost completely unprepared for the harsh realities of classroom life. The cry is heard over and over again from the harassed beginning teachers. Everything staggers them; everything is so different from the way they had imagined it: the impersonality of the system, the discipline problems, the slowness with which so many kids learn, the rapidity with which they forget, the countless unexpected little situations that must be dealt with daily. . . .

Did these beginners not go to school themselves to learn how to teach? Yes, they did (although some intensive training programs last only six weeks). Did they not go through a program of student teaching? Yes, again. But student teaching, which Dr. William R. Fielder of Claremont Graduate School has called "ceremonial . . . a rite of passage," [5] is customarily done in a protected environment, one that for the most part is irrelevant to the teaching situation the beginner usually finds himself in. Typically, the school he is assigned to for practice teaching is in a good part of town. It has plenty of facilities. It services a middle-class group of children. His cooperating teacher is one of the best in that school. He is given a limited amount of work to do and learns something about planning lessons and relating to children. But he has little or no opportunity to watch good and bad teachers at work and to contrast their methods. He gets little or no chance to handle discipline, cope with individual differences among children, or practice motivating them to learn; all these responsibilities his cooperating teacher retains for himself. To top it off, the neophytes and their cooperating teachers do not really see eye to eye, even though they may believe they do. Studies show how different their perceptions really are. Cooperating teachers believe their conferences with the student teachers assigned to them are practically ideal. Student teachers, however, feel they need much more support: more encouragement, more inspiration, more warmth, more praise. This represents an astonishing failure in perception. It may be that the tyro teacher is overly sensitive and has exaggerated affective needs. But if the highly experienced teacher is unable to see this need, if she so thoroughly misinterprets the tyro's reactions, it may indicate diminished sensitivity on her part.

The fourth shock most beginning teachers face is the nature of their initial assignment. Logic, if not professional responsibility, would dictate that they be given the easier classes first and, as they build up experience, increasingly difficult ones. However, seniority takes precedence over logic. Contractual rights allow teachers to transfer from one school to another after a set number of years, and most do if the initial school is an inferior one. Seniority gives teachers the right to the better classrooms, and they take it.

"They've taken the garbage detail," said a Denver high school teacher who was highly critical of the practice, "and now it's their turn on the gravy train. It means the least experienced teacher, who hasn't had any exposure to the rough schools, winds up there. Or, in a better school, winds up with the worst classes. It's pretty staggering for the green ones. They suffer; I see them dropping out like flies. But the ones who are really affected are the students. They can't get anything out of anybody who doesn't know how to control them, how to get information across to them, or anything else. The kids are always suffering."

Some schools of teacher education—Brooklyn College and Fordham University, for instance—have devised programs specifically geared to inner-city schools. Late in 1969 the City Colleges of New York were to begin a new teacher education program that would get teacher trainees into public school classrooms at the very start of their college careers. Institutions in other parts of the country are slowly beginning to develop similar models. But the old pattern of seniority rule mostly continues.

The fifth shock many new teachers face, especially if they come to the field loaded with idealism, is the jolt their college-bred notions of "professionalism" get. Nothing will be quite as noble, quite as perfect, as it's painted in the college classroom, in NEA materials, or in books for budding teachers. Meanness, pettiness, thoughtlessness—traits such as these are rampant in every profession, but that decidedly unromantic view of life is not the new teacher's. Not yet. His sense of ethics will be outraged as he hears teachers trade gossip about their pupils, about parents, and about one another. "It's fantastic, the amount of gossip and backbiting that goes on," said a first-year teacher working in a grade school in the Bronx. She made no effort to hide her disgust. "It's like a bunch of little old washwomen—and the men are as bad as the women!"

Strongly dedicated to the children, to the conviction that they deserve the utmost in respect and civility, the idealistic new teacher will be offended by the treatment some veteran teachers may show them. He may realize that this is not a conscious effort to be malicious. It simply doesn't occur to some teachers to take the feelings of the youngsters fully into account. "It's insulting and patronizing the way some teachers carry on about the kids, right in front of them," said a junior high school teacher in Los Angeles. He also taught in elementary schools there and observed the same phenomenon. "They'll make remarks about the kids' intelligence, about their home life—I had one so-called colleague of mine talk about a mother's drinking problem with her son right there, playing it dumb but listening to every word. . . ."

Beginning teachers sometimes naïvely think that their newness is an asset, that they'll be able to bring a fresh perspective to a staff hidebound by years of teaching. To be sure, there's a certain amount of arrogance implicit in this attitude, but it's also true that newcomers to a profession can bring some novel approaches to traditional ways of doing things, even if these do not always work out as first conceived.

Some older teachers do react with good humor and receptively to the brazen ideas of the arrogant young. "I help them; they help me," said a matronly teacher in Plainfield, New Jersey. She had graduated from normal school in 1933. She was teaching in a school that had made the by-now familiar transition from catering to a predominantly middle-class Jewish clientele to one mostly composed of low-income Negro children. She continued, referring to new teachers, "They're energetic; they come with ideas about how to appeal to children. Older teachers are more likely to stick to the book."

But other older teachers don't forget that the beginners rank below them on the teacher status scale. Some try to be helpful but convey their dominance in various subtle ways. Others aren't so subtle and tend to ride roughshod over a new teacher. A twenty-four-year-old elementary school teacher in Brooklyn's ghetto district, Bedford-Stuyvesant, told how she had used the wrong traffic pattern in taking her class to the yard during her second week at the school. One of the older experienced teachers had bawled her out for it in front of both their classes. But this newcomer was more assertive than most, and she had no compunctions about establishing what she considered her integrity. She told the imperious teacher, "In the future, if you have something to tell me, say it in private." It took no time at all for the entire school to hear about the incident, and that noon in the teachers' cafeteria, her colleagues stared at her unbelievingly.

The new teacher naïvely assumes that if there is some way he can reach so-called unreachable children, he'll be applauded for his efforts. And of course, some of his experienced colleagues will applaud, even if they have strong feelings of resignation about such children. But others feel quite threatened when a student of theirs is successfully taken in tow by another teacher —especially if the teacher is a newcomer.

A young woman who taught the fifth grade in New York City for one year related an experience of this kind. One of her students was a bright, appealing little boy, and she was very fond of him. While with her, he did extremely well in math. As soon as he got into the sixth grade and had a new teacher, however, he began flunking out. One day he came sheepishly back to his fifth-grade teacher, explained his predicament, and asked her to help him. She volunteered to spend her lunch hours giving him special tutoring in math. He did well, passing all of the tests he hadn't been able to pass with his regular sixth-grade teacher. That teacher began to make snide comments. Poking the younger one in the chest one day, she said, "I hear you're wasting your lunch hours. Well, you'll learn." Soon after that incident she forbade the boy to get this special tutoring help, telling him he was "disrupting the lunch period." She also complained to the principal that "there was nothing good anybody could say about this boy." And the fifth-grade teacher? It had just happened, and she felt terrible about the situation. "But I can't," she said, "for the sake of peace in the faculty family, help him any longer. But you know? He'll probably really flunk out with this teacher with whom he has no rapport at all. . . ."

The discrepancy between their image of professionalism and the actuality of daily classroom life is a factor many new teachers take into account when they decide that teaching is not for them. "Whoever tries to defend the position that teaching is a profession might just as well give it up now," wrote a young junior high school teacher to her professor at Cornell University. She was explaining why she was abruptly quitting teaching. "I've heard everything in teachers' rooms from dirty jokes to 'dirty niggers.' There's no professional pride—it's just a job to them. And gossip about the kids is their second most favorite type of conversation. As a sick footnote, one of the married teachers has asked if he could see me some night when his wife goes out to her bridge game. (But of course any man could do that—it just rankles that he asked me in front of my class.)"

The disillusioned girl's letter found its way into the pages of the professional journal *Clearing House*. Was the journal trying to tell its teacher readers something?

[4]

Much remains to be known about the relationship of teacher preparation to teacher effectiveness. However, it seems reasonable to assume that teachers will not arbitrarily be assigned to teach a subject for which they have had no preparation whatsoever. Yet, either because no specialist in that field is available or because it's inconvenient to hire one, such misassignment is rather commonplace in the public schools. Beginning teachers or those on the staff a year or two often get the brunt of misassignments because they have built up no seniority rights to help them get the assignments they would like, but it happens frequently with experienced teachers, too. The beginner, of course, is more disadvantaged in the situation than a teacher with five or ten years' worth of experience. Unsure of himself to begin with, the inappropriate assignment only makes him more so.

A nationwide misassignment study sponsored by the NEA gives some hint of how prevalent it is.[6] A total of 1,035 survey questionnaires were returned, describing 677 cases of misassignment. The actual incidence is probably much higher, since 40 percent of all the educators to whom the questionnaire was sent failed to return it. Fifty-nine percent of the cases involved lack of subject-matter competence. (Another common type involved the assignment of a teacher to a grade he was not prepared to teach.) Where corrective measures took place, it was usually due to the corrective action taken by a state accrediting agency, not due to pressure of parents or administrators.

The administrators, obviously, make the misassignments in the first place. The NEA survey shows that they don't consider it a potentially serious problem. Their idea apparently is that if a person is a teacher, he can teach anything. It's an expedient

view to hold, but it shows the extent to which the administrator
is removed from the teacher's frame of reference. Theoretically,
there may be something to the viewpoint that a teacher's talent
basically involves the act of teaching, but whether the information to be taught, the subject at hand, is of such slight importance is a very dubious proposition. Anyway, most teachers
seem to think of themselves as specific *kinds* of teachers first—
elementary, English, math, etc. This is the way they were
trained and, possibly, certified. It's an important consideration
with respect to self-confidence: A teacher's image of himself is
by no means unrelated, after all, to his performance in the
classroom. An elementary school teacher in New York City
spoke with real panic about the assignment she had just gotten,
for the following term, to be a science teacher—"and I hated
science in school." A guidance counselor in South Carolina told
of taking a course in sociology after being assigned to teach the
subject in her high school—"but it was very foolish of them."

A junior high school teacher in North Carolina talked at
length about this particular facet of the teacher's life. He was
not a beginner, but he had been given varied assignments from
his beginning term. His teaching stints had included public
speaking, creative writing, mathematics, general science, earth
science, and social science.

"There's a real problem in the junior highs, where we have
so many electives," he explained. "It's good for the child to try
many things—theoretically. But if you don't have many people
who are qualified to teach these different things, it seems to me
you're defeating your purpose. Because, obviously, if the
teacher does not enjoy teaching fine arts or public speaking or
creative writing, this rubs off on the children, and they know
—they know when a teacher likes a subject and when a teacher
does not.

"For a while I wasn't qualified to teach half the subjects I
did. Went straight by the book. One year I had to teach the new
math, and I didn't know any more about it than the students
did, frankly. Fortunately, this was a slow group. If I'd had a

bunch of more intelligent students, they'd have run me out of the classroom. Because I had a hard enough time just keeping ahead of these slow students.

"This is a shame, and this is a side to school the public never sees. They never see what's going on in the classroom, and nobody bothers to point out that teachers are not qualified to do this or not qualified to do that. I accepted these courses because I had a good liberal education. I felt I could handle these things; I didn't necessarily feel qualified. I felt I was competent, but I don't think I did a good job teaching. I mean, I kept the classroom together, we kept busy, the students probably learned a little something. But as far as doing a really good job of teaching—I did not. I'd be the first to admit that.

"Now, in college you get the idea you're going to be a specialist. If you majored in college, for instance, in biology, and you say, 'Oh boy, I can't wait to get to senior high or junior high and have my biology classes!' And then you get out there and find out that you're lucky if you're even teaching biology . . . Or you may be a specialist in European history in college, but then you get out in the schools and you find yourself teaching North Carolina history to seventh-graders. You're not told this in college. You get out of college and you find out that the idea that you were competent and qualified in certain areas, and that you'll be able to stay in those areas—well, this whole thing just collapses. This is depressing to a lot of college graduates. It turns them off."

[7]

The New Militancy

To parents from Pawtucket, Rhode Island, to Portola Valley, California, the most distinguishing feature of today's teacher is his militancy. "Where's the spinster lady devoted to her boys and girls? Where's the Mr. Chips who used to teach when I was a boy?" rhetorically demanded a father from Pittsburgh, Pennsylvania, which was hit by a seven-day strike in February, 1968. "The men talk aggressively; the women wear miniskirts. They parade around in front of the schools they've closed, with picket signs—and have the gall to say they're doing it for the children!"

He was a middle-aged man obviously taking an old-fashioned view of things. But if a Gallup poll published in 1969 is any indication, he has plenty of company, because almost two-thirds of the sample of Americans quizzed were against teachers having the right to strike. This puts them in direct opposition to the teacher, who with increasing fervor strikes and registers his conviction that he has the right to strike. There were five strikes during the 1963-64 school year, twelve the following year, then eighteen, then thirty-four, and the jackpot in terms

117

of teacher walkouts occurred during the 1967-68 school year, when teachers and their organizations had lashed themselves into such a paroxysm of anger that there were one hundred fourteen explosions. Even that figure hardly tells the scope of the action, since it includes three statewide strikes: 67 school districts struck in Florida, 590 in Pennsylvania, 940 in Oklahoma. By the time the school year ended, according to the NEA Research Division, 163,000 teachers had been involved in strikes that cost 1,400,000 man-hours of instruction.[1]

Whenever the NEA takes a poll on the subject, and it's doing so with growing frequency, a higher percentage of teachers indicates that they're ready to walk out as a last resort when contract conditions aren't met. In 1968, nearly 60 percent of the teachers polled said they were ready to strike under "extreme conditions" of negotiation breakdown or where negotiation was refused, while a hard core of almost 9 percent was ready to lift picket signs even before the state of last resort "the same as employees of other occupations." Moreover, more teachers are now saying they're ready to walk out on issues other than those directly related to salaries, fringe benefits, and the like. Nearly three-fourths of the teachers favoring strikes in the 1968 poll indicated they would strike for smaller class size or to improve the instructional program. Almost 90 percent of these teachers said they'd strike to remedy unsafe conditions for children.[2]

They strike, but how do they feel about striking? There's no simple answer. Each man worships God in private ways, and holding a picket sign aloft is also a matter for the inner self. Moral outrage in one teacher can be a feeling of anguish, of pressure almost beyond enduring, in another. "I don't approve of the strike; I think it's ghastly," said one such anguished lady who was among the 50,000 teachers participating in the three strikes that shut down New York City schools for three weeks in 1968. "I can't cross the picket line, I just can't. Those are my friends; those are the people I work with." And a married woman who participated in one of the numerous strikes that plagued Michigan in 1968 said, "What can I do? I don't need more money—but the men do. Is it fair to them if I don't join the strike?" On the other hand, there are many women teachers who feel it's high time for drastic action and some men who are revolted by the idea of striking. It was a man, a high school teacher involved in the Florida strike of 1968, who gave the most poignant description of one striker's feelings: "This was the most traumatic thing I ever had to face. It hurt real bad, worse than when my mother died. I cried like a baby for three days. But deep down in my heart I knew I was doing the right thing."

The strikes, and the ringingly affirmative votes in polls on strikes, shouldn't obscure the fact that the overwhelming majority of teachers haven't struck and many—especially among older teachers—are offended by the very idea of teachers shutting down a school. As one travels throughout the country, talking to teachers, one senses a real generation gap here. There are numerous exceptions, of course. At NEA headquarters they're fond of referring to the "little old ladies" who write in, approving of NEA's new militancy. But the older the teacher, the more apt he is to be resentful of this new world of picketing educators. He remembers when he worked long hard hours for $50 a month, sees contemporary teachers taking their workaday cares much more lightly, getting fat salaries (in comparison with the old days), and walking off the job besides.

Yet the generation gap seems to go deeper and broader than merely the attitudes involving money and other facets of teacher welfare. It illustrates, in a sense, the predicament the contemporary teacher finds himself in. The teacher in the little red schoolhouse or in the small city of forty or fifty years ago may have been shabbily treated by the community, but his was a much less equivocal role than that of today's teacher. Whatever the lacks in his education, he was usually better educated than most of his pupils' parents. Moreover, many of his charges were children of immigrants, coming from families with a strongly ingrained respect for education. Thus, the teacher enjoyed an

authority not present these days, an authority over parents and
students that gave him a feeling of professionalism, despite the
fact that he wasn't among the community's elite. Paradoxically,
even the social restrictions and other community mores that set
him apart helped confirm his sense of identity. And there was
no question of a mass media, of a child's peer group, of a host
of other forces acting as "teachers of children." They may have
been there, but it wasn't said then, as it is now, that a child
learns at least half of what he knows outside of school. Learning took place *in* school. And the teacher, who saw his charges
grow up, who taught the sons and daughters, and sometimes the
grandsons and granddaughters of his original students, had
some visible connection with the product of his labors. It meant
something. It meant a great deal. Furthermore, in terms of his
professional life, though he was supervised and though the curriculum was handed down from above, the experienced
teacher had a good deal of autonomy in the classroom. And
the principal was not only boss but, in part, co-worker. Thus,
in some important respects, the teacher's life had continuity
and definition.

There were always voices raised in protest against the
teacher's lot, of course. But the classroom teacher's discontent
didn't become widespread until social conditions within and
without teaching changed, lessening the earlier satisfactions
and creating new tensions. This thrust began in the prewar
years, with the growing shift from rural to urban patterns, the
growth of the city schools, and their consequent bureaucratiza-
tion. The number of principals, supervisors, and special teachers grew rapidly, which had the effect of putting the classroom
teacher still lower on the status scale, not only in the community but in his profession, too. Conversely, administrative status
—and salaries—swiftly increased. Thus, already in 1920, according to a history of the NEA, "a superintendent bewailed
the rift between administrators and teachers; a high school
teacher referred to the stultifying effects of being told what to

do; a normal school teacher deplored the practice of appointing committees of teachers and then ignoring their recommendations . . ." [3] Already, teachers were protesting paternalism and domination.

That earlier discontent, though, was like a few lost voices in the wilderness compared to the cacophony of angry sounds that would come in the postwar years. Three main factors that have brought this about were the baby boom, the higher educational qualifications demanded of teachers, and the entry of men in large numbers into the teaching field.

The baby boom brought an army of schoolchildren hurtling into the public schools which were unprepared to handle the sudden new load; it created overcrowded conditions, a teacher shortage that became chronic, a perpetual problem in terms of school financing, and a tremendously bourgeoning school bureaucracy. In California, for instance, there was one administrator to every twenty-four teachers in 1923; one to every seven in the 1950's. In New York the ratio of nonteaching to teaching personnel was 5.5 per 1,000 pupils in 1958, 8.2 per 1,000 in 1968. More and more, then, teachers have become mass production workers on an educational assembly line, removed from the sources of power and alienated from the institution that employs them, somewhat the way a factory worker is alienated from the plant that pays his wages but with which he feels little sense of identification.

Then there's the upgrading of teachers' education and preparation. As recently as four decades ago few states made a college degree a condition of teacher certification, and most that did required it in connection with secondary teaching. Four decades ago some 70 percent of the teachers then working had no degree. Presently, every state but California and New York requires a bachelor's degree for full certification even on the elementary school level, and the latter two states require a fifth year of college. There's nothing in the research literature to show that, say, a third-grade teacher who has had four or five years of college is any more competent and effective than one who has gone for three. ("No wise man will seek entrance to heaven on the argument that it has been absolutely necessary in the past for a man or woman to graduate from a four-year college in order to teach the third grade," stated Francis Keppel, former U.S. Commissioner of Education, in *The Necessary Revolution in American Education*, "though the education profession has sometimes made it sound that way. With the new curricula that seem to be ahead of us, college becomes more necessary.") [4] The point here, however, is that the more college a person has, the more value he seems to have both to himself and society, the greater his expectancy of rewards from that society.

Finally, there's the unprecedented entry of men into teaching during the postwar years. In 1940 about 20 percent of all teachers were men. By 1968 nearly 32 percent were men, an increase that commands more respect when one considers that the total number of teachers has undergone a whopping increase, so that in terms of sheer numbers there has been a drastic change. In point of fact, the decade between 1958 and 1968 saw a 73.4 percent increase in the number of men teaching, as contrasted with a 39 percent increase for women teachers. Some 15 percent of all elementary and 53 percent of all secondary school teachers are men (these ratios having remained fairly constant for a decade).[5] There is, of course, more than coincidence to the fact that the drastic rise in teacher militancy has occurred contemporaneously with the equally drastic increase in the number of males teaching. A cadre of bright, aggressive, organization-minded young men has been developing. As the teacher-leader of a local West Coast NEA affiliate put it, "There seems to be a very determined effort on the part of younger men who are intent on making teaching their livelihood for the rest of their lives, and who will depend on a teaching salary for their entire earnings, to gain control of the power structure in the various organizations. And they will fight."

[2]

The year 1956 saw the publication of a book, *Education as a Profession*, that did its share to crystallize the dissatisfactions and militancy of teachers.[6] Written by Myron Lieberman, an expert in professional negotiations for teachers, it made a number of harsh points contrasting teaching with medicine, law, architecture, accounting, and many other professions. Unlike such others, teachers' pay is wholly inadequate to a professional remuneration. Unlike the other practitioners, teachers don't control the state boards that license them; many states, in fact, don't even allow educators on their teacher licensing boards. Teachers don't control textbook selection in numerous states. They don't control—and often have little say about—the curriculum. They have very little voice insofar as their teacher training institutions are concerned. Lieberman also called teaching a "feminized" field, the preponderance of women who drift in and out of the field seen by some as depressing salaries and retarding the raising of educational standards.

Teachers didn't need Lieberman to tell them—this they were acutely aware of as a result of everyday experience—that they don't control hiring, firing, staff deployment, and many other matters of direct concern to them in their schools. In individual schools teachers are increasingly being invited to help formulate policy decisions, but such participation is sporadic and informal except in those instances where they've made it a contractual right. Teachers are also being invited to participate in curriculum decisions, textbook selection, and the like; but in actual practice, many complain, they're merely asked along for show, and their decisions are disregarded. Alternatively, they say, only those teachers sympathetic to the administrators' point of view are invited to participate. In any event, the prerogatives rest with laymen, with principals, with college professors, with supervisors, and with the superintend-

ents of schools. As education becomes more and more complex, lay boards of education too lose some of their authority,
and increasingly, the superintendent emerges as the most powerful figure on the local educational pyramid.

At the same time, however, schools and teachers have been
saddled with a host of social problems and tasks, problems and
tasks ranging from sex education to providing effective education for low-income youths to getting suburban students into
the best colleges. Such responsibilities have made teachers'
work more complex and difficult—all the more so since they
aren't adequately trained to handle them, lack the authority to
initiate programs they feel are required, and frequently find
educational facilities wholly inadequate to the need.

By this confluence of forces the contemporary teacher has
arrived at the stage of militancy. His loyalty to the school has
lessened as the school has grown increasingly bureaucratized.
Finding himself at the bottom of a professional hierarchy, lacking a sense of identification or continuity with the community,
better educated and expecting the status of the educated person, leavened by the greater aggressiveness and pragmatism
of the young men who have come into the teaching ranks, feeling insecure about or cornered by his many duties—the teacher
still sees himself as a second-class citizen, underpaid, without
the esteem or autonomy that confirms the fully functioning
professional. What he sees makes him angry. The superficial
support many communities give their schools makes him an-
grier still. He recalls what the history of teachers has been like.
He's affected by the climate of protest and action that charac-
terizes other groups' efforts to shake off second-class citizenship.
(Some of the militant teachers interviewed bitterly referred to
the treatment of teachers in the past, and also acknowledged
the civil rights movement as an influence on their activities.
They talked with relish of "teacher power.")

Militancy or teacher power doesn't in the first instance
mean strikes. It means making demands that previously were
unheard of or could be shrugged off; it means, specifically, en-

croachment on the powers and prerogatives others have been accustomed to. "Basically . . . teachers desire a better definition of their role in the hierarchy of the American school system," notes a policy statement of the New York State Teachers Association. "They want acceptance as working equals, equality of status, and recognition of their competencies in their own area of responsibility . . . Putting it bluntly, they do not want to be talked down to but they do want to be talked to at eye-level . . . In the dignity of their professional competence they do not appreciate being directed in every detail of their daily function." [7] Which is what some of them had said in 1920.

But this is not 1920 and in their push for power, teachers have legitimatized collective bargaining with school boards in about a dozen states, and more states will pass such laws. The NEA has introduced into Congress a professional negotiations bill that would permit teacher-board negotiations in every state, provide for arbitration machinery, and allow strikes as a last resort.

Though teachers have a long way to go in terms of power (having started from almost nowhere), their contracts now include dozens of items that go far beyond salaries and fringe benefits. In recent years teachers' groups to varying degrees have encroached more and more on the traditional powers of school boards—negotiating on such items as class size, curriculum development, and building schedules. These are powers which, as a Seattle Teachers Association official put it, were "formerly held sacred as managerial prerogatives." New York City's United Federation of Teachers (UFT) has made its widely publicized More Effective Schools program, a strong educational program geared to ghetto schools (and, not incidentally, toward making the lot of teachers in those schools easier) a contractual matter the past few years. Moreover, on the state level, the NEA is endeavoring to establish professional practices commissions and professional standards boards that would have all segments of education participating formally in the areas of teacher ethics, standards, and competence. Not

surprisingly, school boards and school superintendents are be-
wailing the reduction of their former authority, while teachers'
organizations are alternately boasting about how far they've
come or bemoaning the distance they still have to go. Boards
are further charging that intense rivalry between the NEA and
AFT is goading each to a dangerous escalation of demands as
they compete for members and for power. Such competition
was especially evident in a series of teacher strikes that crippled
numerous Michigan communities in 1968.

When strikes occur, they obviously do so because there's
a breakdown of negotiations, an impasse between school boards
and teachers' groups. The fact that negotiating is a new art
for both sides doesn't help matters. Many a bargaining collapse has been precipitated by ineptness, intransigence, or in-
sensitivity on the teachers' or the school boards' side. (Contract
talks proceed most smoothly when both sides hire attorneys
experienced in this field to do the negotiating for them.)

Beyond the immediate cause of a strike, however, seems to
be the whole confluence of forces that have so radically changed
the lives of teachers and weakened their identification with
schools and communities. The accelerating sweep of teacher
power and teacher strikes suggests that teachers as a group are
at a particularly difficult point of evolution—a point where they
neither have the securities of the past nor the advantages of a
well-defined profession. They're no longer satisfied with what
they regard as crumbs, either for themselves or for education,
yet they're not getting what they want either, certainly in no
way as quickly as they would like. Their position parallels that
most difficult of human stages, adolescence. Their anger, their
frustrations, their need to dispel the image and reality of second-class citizenship makes even otherwise conformistic and
status quo-oriented teachers susceptible to the angry strike
calls of their leaders. In the case of some strikes it has almost
seemed as though ephemeral forces beyond the power to control have swept the teachers into mass walkouts. The Florida
strike, triggered off by an extremely complicated set of polit-

ical and educational circumstances, seemed to have had some such element to it.

Striking is for the teacher no less than for the factory worker a way of saying, "Here I am, I exist, I'm important." It was a Florida teacher who said, "I thought people liked me and respected me. I couldn't walk into the supermarket weekends without a lot of people stopping me and talking to me about their kids. Well, now I know better. They pay lip service to good education, but the majority want baby-sitters, that's all. We'd been telling them for six months that if we can't get support for the kids, we're going to resign. And they'd say, 'Yes,' but they weren't really listening. When we called meetings to explain things, our grievances, just a handful of people showed up. Now it's different, now that we actually went and did it." What some other striking teachers in other parts of the country had to say was quite similar. The anguish many teachers feel about striking is real, but so is the satisfaction, conscious or unconscious, that comes with thrusting oneself into the sun's light and forcing the world to acknowledge one's existence.

[3]

An AFT teacher-organizer in the Rocky Mountains, addressing a group of disgruntled NEA-affiliate members who are thinking of switching allegiance:

". . . But there's tremendous value, I think, in teachers being organized. We go down and lobby at the state legislature occasionally, where the money comes from, and one of the first questions they ask is, 'How many people do you represent?' If you represent forty-five, fifty, a hundred, the first thing they do is start looking over your shoulder to find someone else to talk to. They aren't interested in talking to that small a group of people or to representatives of that group. So there's great value in being organized, and there's nothing dirty about being organized.

"And the second point I'd like to make is that it's best to be organized in the American Federation of Teachers. Maybe we can go back just a little bit. As you all know, I assume, being members of the NEA, this organization of yours is over one hundred years old. The NEA was formed shortly after the Civil War. It had about ten thousand administrators at the time and stayed that way for a great number of years until coincidentally in 1917 the AFT was organized. John Dewey held Card No. 1 and said, 'I think there ought to be an organization for teachers only.' And he had a hand in organizing this group of teachers. Well, overnight the NEA jumped from a group which had lain dormant with ten thousand members. The handwriting was on the wall. Either you expand the nature of your organization, to take in a larger group of people, or eventually you're going to be outnumbered. Because obviously there are more classroom teachers than there are administrators. . . .

"I think for a long time there has been an erosion of teacher dignity. This is really the thing that moves me. I have no ambitions, believe me, to hold any paid office in the Federation of Teachers. All I want is to be a classroom teacher. My neighbors are still saying to me, 'Are you still a classroom teacher?' As if —well, they don't ask the doctor who lives next door to them, 'Are you still a doctor?' Certainly he's a doctor. 'Haven't you been promoted?' There's no promotion as far as I'm concerned. I want to be a classroom teacher. And when the NEA local people spend half their time talking about how you get promoted, to me this is the kind of philosophy we don't need in a teacher organization. How you get to be a better teacher ought to be the issue. How you turn out a better product. This is what we ought to be talking about. . . ."

[4]

NEA headquarters is located in an $11,000,000, Washington-modern edifice all its own, a brisk five-minute walk from the White House. It houses 34 departments (like audiovisual instruction, elementary school principals, etc.), 18 headquarters divisions (educational technology, research, radio and television, etc.), 25 commissions (budget, credentials, educational television, etc.), and an elaborate internal decision-making structure to encompass the needs and wishes of its 59 state and more than 8,000 local affiliated associations. Theoretically, policy is set by the 7,000 delegates to the Representative Assembly, which meets annually. Practically, the executive committee, receiving direction from the powerful state associations, has much to do with the shaping of policy. The ordinary classroom teacher, remote from the sources of power, tends to find himself in as much of a bureaucracy in the NEA as in his school district.

NEA's membership in 1968 was past the million mark, including teachers and administrators. In terms of its potential power, it peaked several years earlier, however, at a little over 50 percent of the nation's teachers. This has become a troublesome fact of life for the organization, which keeps pushing hard for new members. In conjunction with its affiliates, though, the NEA affects the welfare of more than 1,750,000 teachers. Its 1968 budget was over $15,000,000.

The NEA has had a considerable share in raising the standards of the teaching field and upgrading education in the United States. (In recent years its National Commission on Teacher Education and Professional Standards [NCTEPS] has been especially active in this area.) The NEA has helped bring to fruition several major federal aid to education bills, particularly when it reversed its traditional stand against federal support for private and parochial schools. Along with the AFT, it called for federal aid long before it became popular to do so; then, as now, extreme right-wing groups accused it of being Communist.

But for the most part during its history the NEA has shied away from controversy and was often more facile with slogans about quality education than with action to bring this about. Until the past few years the NEA was dominated by administrators, even though the majority of its members are classroom teachers. The image it gained was of a stodgy, status quo-oriented establishment institution, one it's trying to live down. In its earlier years, in fact, as a recent historical account has it, the NEA was more of an instrument for controlling teachers than for helping them.[8] Furthermore, one of its major thrusts has been expansionist; it has been a major player of the membership numbers game. Though the practice has been waning the past few years, administrators in school districts all over the country coerced teachers into joining the NEA. Applicants for teaching positions were handed NEA membership blanks along with employment application forms, or were otherwise pressured into signing up. In the eyes of the administrators, membership in the NEA and its affiliates was equated with "professionalism"—while the teacher who didn't want to join or, worse, joined the teachers' union, was looked upon askance.

All in all, the NEA's impact overall, legislatively and otherwise, is far from commensurate with its prodigious expenditures of time, energy, and money. This is so despite the fact that during the Eisenhower regime the NEA had the reputation of practically running USOE. (The then-Secretary of Health, Education and Welfare, Arthur S. Flemming, had the habit of phoning NEA headquarters from his limousine to report on important legislative matters.) In recent years the NEA has lost considerable power and influence to a coalition of tough-minded, change-oriented men from the foundations, from the upper echelons of a newly powerful USOE, and from elsewhere.[9]

Though it has always operated under the credo of "one big happy educational family," the past decade has seen members of that family increasingly at one another's throats. Much of the dissent has come from angry, impatient, urban-centered young teacher-leaders of their local NEA affiliates. They no more liked the idea of being paternalized and dominated within the NEA than within the schools. Nor did they like the spectacle of a brash, aggressive AFT grabbing off such plums as New York City (whose ninety-odd NEA affiliates it whipped into a union in 1960), Chicago, Boston, Washington, D.C. (in the NEA's own backyard), and other major cities. And those angry young men had considerable distaste for the conservatism of NEA's administrator-leaders, who had come from small towns or rural areas and had little feeling or concern for city problems. Many of its powerful state affiliates still are conservative and administrator-dominated. Thus, NEA's civil rights record was, until recently, poor: It avoided taking a stand on school desegregation until the Supreme Court decision of 1954. It had no cabinet-level Negroes in its hierarchy nor did it elect a Negro president until 1968, and the last of its white and black separate Southern affiliates were to be merged (with considerable pressure from the NEA) in 1969. It wasn't until 1968, in fact, that the NEA organized a task force to deal with urban school problems and a human relations center to deal with the human rights of students and teachers; previously it attacked such problems in piecemeal fashion. But the NEA has fought hard for the rights of Negro teachers dismissed from Southern school districts in the wake of desegregation, and has contributed substantial sums to help them.

The past decade, then, has seen an intensive amount of infighting within the NEA, and the balance of power has been shifting from administrators to teachers. Squeezed by AFT victories on the one hand, and the demands of its own aggressive teachers on the other, in 1967 the NEA reversed an historic stand against strikes and passed a resolution okaying work stoppages as a last resort. (Prior to that time its ultimate weapon was "sanctions"—blackballing a district by warning teachers not to take jobs there.) By 1969 the school superintendents had become so affronted by teacher power that the relationship between their group, the American Association of School Administrators, and the NEA, was organizationally very tenuous. And power fights were being played out among other conservative, moderate, and militant factions in the NEA family.

The AFT, too—160,000 strong and, despite its puny size, in control of some of the biggest cities—is far from running a harmonious shop these days. Traditionally allied with American labor's liberal wing, it has concentrated on teacher welfare and also been strong on academic freedom and civil rights. Its civil rights record has, until recently, been a much better one than the NEA's. It backed school desegregation years before the 1954 Supreme Court decision, ran freedom schools for Southern Negro students, and desegregated or suspended its own few Southern locals. But as salaries and working conditions have improved, its members have become more protectionist-minded. A number of locals, for instance, have veto power over transfer of teachers to ghetto schools, preventing the integration of faculties and overloading those schools with inexperienced teachers.

Despite the fact that his union was strongly identified as alienated from the low-income communities, Albert Shanker, president of the UFT, became the top vote-getter of the twenty persons elected to vice-presidencies at the AFT's 1968 convention. Disenchanted with the outcome of this convention, which also saw Shanker successfully weaken a strong community control resolution, dissidents promptly formed a new caucus.

The UFT is the foremost example of a formerly progressive teachers' union grown increasingly powerful, political, and protectionist. In the early 1960's it backed a school boycott, the pairing of schools and the reorganization of the middle grades —all to promote integration. It gave substantial sums to support civil rights demonstrations in Selma, Alabama, and urged its members to vote for a civilian review board to hear cases of police brutality. But from the mid-1960's on, things changed. Ghetto militants became more vocal in denouncing the failure of the schools to educate their children, and some accused teachers of incompetence. They were outraged by the union's consistent refusal to bend on the transfer issue. Many teachers themselves reflect the general bias against nonwhites, as recent studies indicate. The union refused to back a second boycott of the schools. With the establishment of community control demonstration centers at IS 201 in Harlem (followed by two more, in Brooklyn's Ocean Hill-Brownsville slum and in lower Manhattan) repeated clashes between the union and the black community occurred in 1966 and 1967. Clashes would probably have come anyway, but they were more frequent and intense because the Board of Education's professionals—hostile to the idea of community control—hadn't given the demonstration districts clear guidelines as to their powers.

At any rate, black teachers began to break away from the UFT. Many of the whites were unable to empathize with the black community's efforts to better its schools; all they could see were threats: growing black militancy, more violence in the schools, intrusion into professional matters (there were demands that district superintendents be locally elected and teachers evaluated by the community), the irrational fear that people were literally going to invade their classrooms and tell them how to teach.

Late 1966 to early 1968 saw a continual series of confrontations between the UFT and IS 201, the latter also having plenty of problems getting Board of Education cooperation for even the most trifling matters. In the fall of 1967 the UFT struck the city for three weeks over issues that left many teachers frankly confused. One action that preceded the strike—an inflammatory "disruptive child" clause the union wanted inserted in the new contract, giving teachers the right to summarily remove any child from class—bitterly offended the black communities. Their schools remained open during the strike, which was ostensibly called to force the Board of Education to expand the UFT's More Effective Schools program. A lot of rank-and-file teachers, however, thought they were staying out to get a better pay package, as well. When the strike ended with no wage gains other than those already won, many teachers were furious. (Some observers saw the strike calculated to serve a few more subtle purposes: to defeat a new negotiations procedure the city was attempting to set up, and to show the troublesome demonstration districts a little teacher muscle.) Then Shanker was jailed for having violated the state's anti-strike law and the anger of rank-and-filers understandably melted. As one union official unofficially put it, "Even teachers who felt he'd let them down now backed him. He became a martyr."

Throughout the whole of 1968 there were ugly clashes between white teachers and people in the ghetto areas, the main focal point now being the Ocean Hill-Brownsville community control district. (Of earlier incidents, commented sociologist David Rogers in a study of New York City's school bureaucracy, "It is unfortunate that teachers and parents, who are both victims of the school system, should become so involved in power seeking that they take it out on one another." [10]) At one point the UFT struck the district to protect teachers the district didn't find acceptable. It lobbied heavily and expensively in Albany, the state capital, whose lawmakers were considering bills to decentralize all of New York City's cumbersome school system, being rewarded with the passage of a very weak decentralization bill.

By fall of 1968 the confrontation had focused dangerously on nineteen teachers the district claimed were sabotaging community control efforts. Ocean Hill-Brownsville's governing board dismissed them from the district and ordered them to report to central headquarters for reassignment. Charging that the teachers had been "fired," claiming due process violations with respect to involuntary transfers, and brandishing "mob rule" signs (which the black community saw as racist code words), the UFT struck. It didn't strike alone. It formed a solid alliance with the Council of Supervisory Associations, a highly conservative body of school administrators that had fought almost every desegregation measure the union in calmer days had supported. The UFT-CSA alliance notably shifted educational politics in New York City. The alliance came about because the CSA was even more fearful of community control than the UFT was: The ghetto communities, tired of being educational colonies, were demanding the right to bypass the city's so-called merit list of (white) principals and to choose their own black and Puerto Rican administrators.

Fifty thousand teachers (out of about 55,000) stayed out of school, along with the administrators and—a couple of weeks later—the custodians, who shut off boilers and changed door locks in an effort to keep nonstriking teachers, parents and students from entering locked schools. A few schools were forced open and kept open, though most white parents supported the UFT. Thus, more than 1,000,000 schoolchildren were deprived of a month of school. The disturbances gave the UFT ammunition with which to demonstrate to Albany lawmakers that community control (or meaningful decentralization) wasn't viable in New York City. The union had a number of concerns. It couldn't afford to lose its hard-fought right to bargain on a city-wide basis. It wanted no part of any decentralization scheme that would allow thirty-odd local boards to hire, fire, and transfer teachers. It was also worried about its dwindling membership in the demonstration districts: Few of the teachers who volunteered to teach there—though largely white and Jewish, just like the bulk of loyal UFT teachers—signed up. (Before the end of the strike the union sought to gain an "agency shop," which would have had nonunion teachers paying dues, as a price for settlement.) For their part, the community control districts had some compelling interests of their own—most importantly, to consolidate and build on their very tenuous power base.

Aroused by the union leadership, rank-and-file teachers were genuinely frightened by the prospect of community control, or even decentralization. The actions of a few black extremists and rising anti-Semitism in the black areas of the city didn't help matters. During the strike some anti-Semitic leaflets were stuffed in teachers' mailboxes in a few ghetto schools; the union reproduced these by the thousands and the city was flooded with them, making the threat of anti-Semitism loom much larger than it was. By this time the city was polarized, mostly along racial lines. It became increasingly clear that the UFT was out to kill decentralization. The complexities and virulence surrounding the strike were exacerbated by the failure of the Board of Education, Mayor John V. Lindsay, and the Ford Foundation, which financed the demonstration districts, to provide effective leadership.

The strike ended on November 17 with a complicated agreement that put observers into the Ocean Hill-Brownsville schools, established a state trusteeship over the district, and gave the union right to full grievance procedures in the case of involuntary transfers. The agreement also added forty-five minutes to the school day, eliminated holidays, and shortened vacations —ostensibly to help students make up instructional time, but in fact as a thinly veiled mechanism for allowing teachers to make up pay lost during the strike. The makeup time brought more tensions: It prompted high school students to demonstrate and was a factor in fresh disturbances surrounding UFT teachers, this time back at the IS 201 district. These occurred precisely when lawmakers in Albany were getting ready to vote on new school decentralization measures, and Shanker warned of the possibility of new city-wide strikes.

The UFT lobbied heavily in Albany, as before, and also spent much time, money, and energy attempting to defeat local politicians, up for reelections, who had been strong for community control. It found itself in the ironic position of backing lawmakers hostile to community control but who had voted for strong anti-strike laws directed at public employees. In Albany a very weak decentralization bill was passed—one that also gave the union what it had wanted right along, the elimination of the three decentralized districts. During the strike the UFT had dismissed a vice-president from its hierarchy, one who was publicly protesting its policies. Now many remaining dissident UFT members quietly dropped out, and organizational changes made it very difficult—or next to impossible—for those who remained to protest union policy with any kind of effectiveness. The new decentralization bill considerably strengthening its members' rights, internal opponents melting away, the UFT emerged more powerful than ever.

[5]

Presently, the NEA and AFT are locked in bitter jurisdictional battles that cost them heavily in money and talent, both of which could obviously be put to more constructive use on behalf of education. (In Michigan alone, according to one informant, both sides spent around $200,000.) There's good reason to believe a merger between the two organizations will at some time, possibly by 1975, take place. Merger talk has been in the air for years, both overtly (the AFT periodically makes a grandstanding offer, via the press, for an NEA-AFT merger) and covertly (secret talks between members of both groups are held from time to time). Major obstacles to merger are said to be NEA's administrators and the AFT's union affiliation. As the distinctions between the two organizations keep blurring, these obstacles may well disappear. How power would be divided may prove a bigger problem in the long run. At any rate, there are signs that mergers between locals in various states will precede a national merger.

Such a merger would create one powerful educational monolith—a teacher's organization with the ability to shut down most or all of the nation's schools at once. It's not the most comfortable prospect to contemplate. "It may be necessary to have a nationwide stoppage," David Selden, AFT president, has said, "to bring about a reallocation of resources for the schools."

Whether or not that possibility is a remote one, some implications of growing teacher power bear considering. The fact of the matter is, most teachers aren't committed to their careers or their professional organizations. Housewives and housewives-to-be, or men who run from school to a second job, may work hard and may work well—but they have little interest in what goes on beyond their classrooms. "Teaching is just a job," admitted a teacher, the mother of three, who perhaps typifies the attitude of many women in the field. "I began to teach because I enjoy working with children, because I didn't like to come home in the rush hour . . . It's a job that's very convenient for me as a mother. My hours are excellent. My pay is good. Maybe I'm a little better educated than a lot of women. Maybe I put a little more into my work. But it's still just a job." Such people aren't very active, inquiring members of their profession. *The Political Life of American Teachers* shows that teachers join their organizations because they think they'll be helped professionally and intellectually, because they're asked to or expected to, or because they can "increase their political power" by having the teachers' group "lobby for them and, if necessary, defend them against community attack." Most teachers join for the first or second reasons. Only about 15 percent are active in their organizations in the sense of giving much time and effort to them.[11]

Teachers have turned to the NEA or AFT and their affiliates in large numbers because, lacking the former deep identification with school and community, they can identify with their group, and be helped by it. But that doesn't necessarily mean they're any closer to the sources of power—to the "front office" so to speak—of their organizations than they are to the power sources of the school or community. It doesn't even mean they're interested in being close to it. All this has considerable import as teachers' organizations grow stronger, more militant, more political, and demand an increasing voice in educational decision making.

What's good for teacher may be good for education, and then again, may be in fundamental contradiction with it. It only muddies the waters to say, as teacher-leaders sometimes do, that everything benefiting teacher benefits students— especially when some teacher groups now come to the conference table with a couple of hundred contractual demands, most of which can be narrowly defined as welfare items. As for strikes, they may revolve in straightforward fashion around the surface issues, and then again they may have underlying political significance whose ramifications go far beyond. Issues of which the rank-and-file may be as unaware as the general public. None of this is to suggest that teachers shouldn't ask for more power or be denied the right to strike. But teachers can be cogs in their organizational machine as in any other. In teachers' healthy quest for greater autonomy, for the right to run their own show, this is the danger.

Part Three

RELATIONSHIPS

[8]

Power Plays

Possibly not often enough emphasized is the fact that the
school is a social institution. As such, it imposes a variety of inevitable pressures on those who function in it. Students, teachers, administrators—all are expected to conform to certain
well-established conventions. At times these conventions are
shaken up a bit, as when teachers strike or students demonstrate for greater autonomy, but neither strikes nor demonstrations have caused impressive changes thus far. In fact, teachers
are only second to students in the number and variety of regulations they must obey. Teachers must punch in and out on time
cards. They cannot, any time they please, take a coffee or a
smoke break. They cannot simply leave for a quick trip to the
lavatory when the urge is upon them, although, of course,
many do. Their hours of work are strictly governed—one of a
number of regulations teachers themselves, through their organizations, have had a hand in formulating. In many districts
their style of dress and the length of the men's hair is regulated,
as are the growing of beards and mustaches.

Teachers must, in many schools, prepare lesson plans on a

weekly or monthly basis. They are evaluated with respect to their competence (at least theoretically). They are expected to cover a certain amount of classroom material at given periods of time. They are required to use textbooks and follow curricula imposed on them from state or local boards of education.

Teachers are the handmaidens of the educational bureaucracy. They're hired by public agencies and paid specific monthly sums. They're governed by contracts that in some districts run as long as eighty pages. They're subject to the dictates of outside institutions in the bureaucratic chain: state boards of education, local boards, superintendents, supervisors. They're also subject to the wishes of their own professional organizations which, as they grow stronger and more powerful, are able to exert considerable pressure on their own members as well as on the agencies they negotiate with. Teachers receive a host of bureaucratic benefits; among them, a high degree of job security, insurance, and retirement pay.

Like any social institution, the school expects those who function in it to conform to a formal and fairly rigid hierarchical pattern. Power passes from the principal to the assistant principals. Then to the department heads (in high schools) and grade-level representatives (in elementary schools). Then to guidance counselors and cluster teachers. The rank-and-file classroom teacher is right there at the bottom of the professional pyramid. As in higher education, prestige accrues to a staff member in inverse ratio to the amount of time he actually spends teaching. When schoolchildren become older and more sophisticated, they see with ever-greater clarity that among the professionals, classroom teachers don't occupy a lofty position.

But a pecking order, it seems, is subject to innumerable gradations. Among classroom teachers the more experienced ones are on a higher status than those less experienced. High school teachers have more prestige than junior high school teachers, and junior high school teachers rank above those in the grade schools. A fifth-grade teacher has more status than a first-grade teacher; a ninth-grade teacher has more standing than a seventh-grade teacher; and so forth.

The formal power structure of the school is clearly defined. Everybody knows how the chain of command goes and that the principal is boss. But every social institution has both formal and informal power structures, and the school is no exception. In every school there are informal power groups, as well as individuals who wield considerable influence over its workings. A principal new to a school in a Denver suburb explained what his first move was after arranging his office to suit his taste: He set about discovering where the power lay among the staff. "You get to know individual teachers, how they act, their relationship to each other. Pretty soon you find out the power structure. You know which teachers are held in tremendous awe and respect by the other teachers."

An analysis of faculty structures, "The Social System of a School Staff," shows that even though generally teacher turnover is high, informal power groups tend to remain stable over the years. Informants in various schools point to age, seniority in the profession or building, interests, social involvement, and activity in teachers' organizations as determining factors in the formation of cliques. In New York and other cities where the union is very strong, chapter chairmen carry special weight, not necessarily because the administrators like them but because of the trouble they can cause.

Since the Reverend Martin Luther King, Jr., was assassinated, there has been a marked increase in the formation of separate groups among black and white teachers where staffs are integrated. A white woman teaching in a Harlem high school said that in her school some white and Negro teachers are in the same clique and sit together in the cafeteria. But the more militant black teachers have formed a separate group, and whenever an outsider attempts to sit at their cafeteria table, they say, "Sorry, we're having a meeting."

In New York City as a whole, the teachers' strikes of 1968

have caused a radical realignment of cliques in many schools and the establishment of new power factions.

Not infrequently, when asked whether there are any cliques or influence-seeking groups among their staffs, administrators and teachers respond, "Oh no, we're one big happy family." This implies a democratic environment in which everybody functions as an equal, but it never turns out to be true. Further probing always reveals that certain teachers are closer to the principal than others, and therefore do have more control over internal school affairs than does the majority of the faculty. Why is this fact so often dodged? Possibly this is "inside" information of the kind outsiders should not be privy to. Possibly the teachers interviewed were themselves members of the informal power structure and therefore felt it to be more politic to adhere to the fiction of democracy. Informal influence wielding at all levels of politics is, after all, more influential for being unseen. There is also the possibility that some teachers do not know and do not care to know too much: The classroom is a refuge *from* tensions, as well as a place where a different quality of tension is generated. For a considerable number of American public school teachers, the classroom defines the limits of their workaday world.

Many teachers, then, find it a simpler, safer world when roles are clearly defined and the principal is the leader. Women teachers in elementary schools particularly tend to see the principal as a highly supportive figure, a father figure. For them and for others, it's enough to know that he's there when needed, that he'll back them up in disputes with parents and pupils, that he'll be fair in assigning workloads and extracurricular duties, that he'll be consistent in his policies.

[2]

A teacher in a well-to-do suburban community in the Rocky Mountain area, describing the political situation in his school and district:

"Of a staff of seventy, about fifteen are very opinion-ated, progressive, aggressive, creative, intelligent. They don't knuckle under when somebody tells them to do something. Sometimes they literally have to be forced to acquiesce. It's a very challenging staff to work with, never boring—but they keep the pot stirred up so there's always ferment, something always brewing.

"Sometimes it gets tiresome; you wish they'd just go home for a while so you could do your job. But they're good for you, too, because the main hazard a teacher runs is to get bored and complaisant. He teaches the same things the same way and pretty soon all of the kids begin to look alike, too.

"There's no friction among the activists and nonactivists on the faculty, because the nonactivists usually pick an activist to support. But there's a lot of division among the activists themselves. There's never any common ground, usually three or four camps regardless of the issue. The principal is caught in the middle, with this very aggressive, demanding, difficult faculty to work with. He's a nice, low-pressure man who gets pushed around. Not the right man for here.

"At faculty meetings, some of the teachers make disparaging remarks about the principal—not personal remarks, but in terms of his professional competence. Mistakes he's made. Either he's doing things he shouldn't be doing or not doing things he should be doing. The superintendent is something else. He's aggressive, ambitious, pushy—he's pushed people into innovations they didn't want. One of the big complaints is that teachers have the illusion of involvement, but decisions are made before they are ever involved. One thing the super-intendent wants to do is integrate the elementary, junior high, and high school systems into a giant nongraded system where teachers are switched around to teach everywhere. Some teachers are sympathetic but feel they're being asked to sign a blank check saying they're in favor of it without really know-ing what it is they're in favor of. The principal? He has re-placed a strong, dynamic, forceful principal who was kicked upstairs because of personal problems. This one was hired in reaction to the aggressiveness of the other. But the pendulum has swung too far, and now they're interviewing for another principal."

[3]

The principal is in an unenviable position. As the foregoing tale of educational intrigue suggested, he can be ground to pieces as the middleman between the superintendent and the staff. He also has parents to deal with, of course, individually and in groups, and the nonprofessional school staff—clerks, custodians, paraprofessionals, and the like. All must be kept reasonably happy or, at the least, kept from creating too much turmoil. Turmoil is something superintendents and school boards definitely do not care for.

Ostensibly, the principal of the school is its "educational leader," the "teacher of teachers." This is how the professional literature is wont to describe him. It stresses—and this is true—that a principal with leadership qualities can turn an average teacher into a far better one. It creates the illusion that he is an educational superman through whose intervention the school is a beehive of intellectual activity. An NEA survey of principals conducted in 1968 shows that elementary school principals judge themselves as giving 30 percent of their time to supervisory work.[1] In fact, taking all levels of principalship into account, and with special reference to the bigger schools, principals tend to spend very little of their time in the role of "teacher of teachers." This is exactly the way most teachers like it. They want him on their terms, when they need him, not hovering around at any time of the day. Many districts now provide curriculum coordinators and supervisors to help teachers (although there are plenty of complaints about them, in that they are either inefficient or rarely available). High schools have department chairmen who provide guidance.

How's the principal's time spent? Budgets, building pro-

grams and problems, curriculum development, overall discipline problems, red tape in triplicate from the central office,
parent and community pressures, meetings, meetings, meetings—thus, much of his forty-five-hour average workweek is
eaten up. In large schools, especially on the high school level,
the secondary administrative staff has been expanding enor-
mously. Literally months may go by before the principal even
knows all of his teachers' names. But for even the most auton-
omous-minded teacher, this much impersonality is apt to rub
raw. "Until April he kept calling me by another teacher's
name," chuckled a Manhattan junior high school teacher. "It
infuriated me—wanted to punch him in the nose every time
he did that."

There are monthly faculty meetings, but almost no teacher
depicted them as more than a dreary ritual given over to trivial-
ities or a superficial, hour-long discussion of something basically
as serious as bigotry. When principals and teachers get together
for a mass confab, merry intellectual music does not often result. A Los Angeles elementary school teacher, throwing up
her hands in disgust, gave a typical reaction to questions about
faculty meetings: "You've had a hard day, you sit there, you
look at your watch and hope it'll be over soon." At the last
meeting, she recalled, the discussion centered on the best place
to buy cookies for the forthcoming Easter party.

Thus, many teachers in bigger schools have minimal contact with their principals. A high school teacher in San Diego
described his relationship with a just-departed principal as
"casual—I saw him three times a year, at Open House, where
he greeted parents. One day I committed a heinous crime. I
gave out too many warnings to the kids on the last day when
warnings were due. The principal called me in. 'How come
you gave so many warnings? Must be doing a lousy job.' I told
him I thought warnings were to make the kids do better and
bring their grades up. It was the first time in three years we
had a professional talk."

When principals acknowledge that they don't see enough

of their teachers, they plead red tape. They're overworked, inundated with paper work, and can't spend anywhere near the time they would like to spend with teachers. There is obviously another viewpoint. "A lot of it is 'busy work,'" snorted a guidance counselor in New York who has worked with administrators on both coasts for over two decades. "They don't manage their time properly, and some of what they do could be done by paraprofessionals." She told of a situation that required an important administrative decision. The principal avoided coming to any firm conclusions, claiming he was too busy with other matters. "The very next day I tracked him down in the book room—he was stamping the school name on books." A teacher in El Cajon, California, insisted that a common administrative failing was overconcern with public relations, adding, "I think the best public relations is just to do a damn good job of educating the kids." Public relations is, of course, the easier task.

To be an effective educator of educators presupposes a sharp, broad educational background. Otherwise one could envision situations in which teachers are more expert at their trade than the principal who is supposed to guide them. And in numerous instances this is exactly the situation that prevails. Many principals taught only for a few years before going the administrative route. Many have physical education or shop teaching backgrounds. Since at least some principals eventually become superintendents, the problem of inadequate training proliferates to higher levels of the educational hierarchy. Thus, the mediocre teacher becomes the mediocre principal becomes the mediocre superintendent of schools. This is borne out by a University of Oregon study of school superintendents, which reveals that the superintendents themselves "claim there are too many incompetent administrators operating schools and holding membership in administrators' associations." [2] It indicates that administrative training programs give essential sociology, history, philosophy, political science, and psychology courses short shrift. Many administrators, according to the study, fail to take a stand on issues. They evidence a low *esprit de corps*. They provide inadequate educational leadership in the community. They lack courage and vision. They are poor organizers. Since these reactions were based on the candid responses of administrators themselves, one must conclude that their accuracy is not open to question. In fairness to superintendents it should be emphasized that few administrative jobs today invite as much pressure and produce as many ulcers as theirs. It is in lots of ways a thankless job that many competent men shun.

A number of teachers, reacting to their own administrators, noted that there isn't necessarily a correlation between excellence in teaching and excellence in administration. They see some highly competent teachers leave the classroom for more lucrative and prestigious administrative jobs and flop dismally. Furthermore, a former official of the Denver Classroom Teachers Association pointed out that once he becomes immersed in administrative implementation a principal loses certain teaching knacks. This makes it less easy for him to help or understand the problems of classroom teachers. An official with the Winston-Salem Classroom Teachers Association said that teachers who are "gung-ho about the problems of teachers" when classroom teachers themselves, tend to change once they go up the administrative ladder of success. Then, he explained, their attitude is, "I got where I was by not rocking the boat, by following all the rules and regulations. Why don't you?"

Some teachers—and administrators, too—feel a principal should devote a portion of his time to actually teaching classes. According to Carl O. Olson, assistant superintendent for curriculum, Fredonia (New York) Central School District, this would keep them attuned to the realities of the classroom, make them more understanding of teachers and students, help them identify problems and evaluate programs, and reinforce the idea that the teaching and learning process is a school's most important function.[3] According to the NEA report on elementary school principals, 4 percent of their workweek is given over to regular teaching. Very few principals actually teach classes on a regular basis, however (except for those in small districts who are teaching principals). The problem with having principals teach is not that it isn't logical, but that it is too logical. It presupposes that there is nothing a person who has left the classroom would rather do than to return to it—a rather doubtful proposition.

A principal must, if he's at all effective, be a good politician. That is, he must be able to deal skillfully with the various factions that exert pressure upon the school, both from within and without. Most teachers and administrators would likely echo the sentiments of the Winston-Salem teacher who said, "Just as I set the tone in my classroom, the principal sets the tone in the school." The phrase is often heard in reference to a principal and his school, but what does it mean to "set the tone"? The successful teacher does not force the learning process. The successful teacher creates an atmosphere in which the children are carried along by their own curiosity and enthusiasm. The teacher, in effect, shapes and manipulates the educative environment.

There's a parallel with respect to principals and their constituencies. Principals of the old breed still have the "I'm-boss-and-you'll-do-as-I-say" attitude, but this approach no longer works the way it did. The "new breed" of principals and those long-established ones who are sufficiently flexible also create an atmosphere. The best of them engender a free, stimulating, creative aura that encourages teachers to explore better ways of teaching and leads them to *want* to teach more effectively. Even those who are more restrictive, however, shape their environments just as, in another sense, the environment in which they function as administrators shapes them. They manipulate people. "Manipulation" when used in this way may seem to imply criticism. No value judgment is intended. Whether one uses that word or the more polite "skilled in interpersonal relations" or "versed in individual and group dynamics" or "superb at motivating people," it amounts to the same thing. One aspect of the principal's job is to gauge the power of the formal and informal groupings with which he must deal. If he's sharp, he plays them off to best advantage, neutralizing as best he can the forces he deems troublesome or destructive. He cannot, because of his own vulnerable position in the educational hierarchy, afford to make waves.

The outcome can work to the best interests of the school and the children it services. Where there are conflicts, however—for instance, when a decision might favor the children's welfare but antagonize the teachers or put the administrator's position on the line—it's another story. Only the rare person— be he school administrator or anyone else—will consciously make a decision whose outcome renders him highly vulnerable. And as the University of Oregon's study of administrators shows, courage is not the most readily available commodity among them. The principal with integrity must constantly be wary of his own motivations in relation to his administrative actions. When he plays off one group against another as a way of life, it becomes easy for him to make the maintenance of his position the primary end in itself. Thus, some principals are seen by teachers and parents as petty schemers and liars. It's an occupational hazard.

In the course of studying administrative power and educational decision making, Ralph B. Kimbrough of the University of Florida observed the workings of a junior high school he dubbed West Town.[4] The school provides a vivid illustration of how a clever and strong principal can manipulate his staff. The principal, Mrs. Goff, had served there for twenty-four years. She had "developed one of the strongest PTA organizations in the state" and carefully hired a teaching staff that she had molded "into an overgrown matriarchal family with herself firmly established as the head of the house." Mrs. Goff used "some orders and classes of confidants" through which she made decisions. The final decision was hers, but "made only after she had held an order of formal discussions with the favored members of the 'family circle,' composed of older women on the faculty."

One of the "family circle's" notable functions, a function hardly unique to this particular school, was teacher indoctrination. Peer group pressure is a highly effective weapon in stabilizing a staff and having it conform. A young woman described how it worked at West Town: "When I came here, I was assigned a buddy. I was given advice even to the point of how to teach by the Old Guard. [The Old Guard refers to Mrs. Goff's confidants.] They would meet me in the hall and talk to me or pass around notes. I was advised how to vote in elections for offices in professional organizations. I was told it was best to listen to the old heads who knew best. The Old Guard had a hold over Mrs. Goff. I was advised to visit the [women's] lounge if I wanted to be better liked."

As Dr. Kimbrough has pointed out, nonconformists can be subjected to some intense and continuing pressure. At times, if teachers don't care to conform, it's assumed that they don't care to teach at that school and, when the year is over, are treated accordingly. At times the object of the pressure gets mad and counters by forming a clique of his own—something the principal might not wish to see happening.

In order to have control over his faculty, the principal needs information. "Company spy" is an unlovely expression, yet the teachers closest to the principal do sometimes provide him with the kind of gossip he finds useful in judging how to deal with people and situations. The teacher-informants don't see themselves as spying and would be sincerely shocked if so accused. They're caught up in the system; it has become their whole life, and when they reveal something untoward about a colleague, it is with a sense of righteous duty. Newcomers to a school may not only be subjected to the blandishments of the inner circle, but if they seem resistant, may be warned by teachers outside the circle not to talk about certain things when particular teachers are in the room.

Parents who have become part of the principal's little educational establishment may also play a useful role; they can sometimes warn him of impending actions of more troublesome parents. The principal who cares to use them also has other intelligence sources available to him, notably, the clerks in his office and the school custodians, who tend to identify much more with the administration than the teachers do. "It might be said of a great many schools that the second office of the principal is in the boiler room or the receiving room," write the authors of *Introduction to Education,* with rare candor for an educational text.[5] "It behooves the teacher to listen politely to the complaints of the custodian . . . and to do what one can to make the custodian's job easier, even if the pupils must help tidy up the classroom before dismissal." Apparently more teachers need to read that book for their own protection. A grade school teacher in New York City, for instance, said her custodian had snitched on her when she allowed the children to write on the blackboard, something that is against the rules. A custodian in San Diego tattled on a teacher who allowed her students to put up anything they wanted on the bulletin board. Another San Diego teacher rated the custodian in his high school "one of the three most influential people in the school."

He explained, "If you don't have a good relationship with the custodian, you don't get anything. If you're on good terms with the custodian, you send a kid over for a ream of paper, he sends it back. If you're not on good terms, the custodian sends the kid back with the message, 'I haven't got any' or 'You'll have to send the official form' or 'You'll have to wait till the end of the semester.' The relationship with the custodian is far more ticklish and far more tender than it should be. I've had my run-ins. I've wanted to use my room for kids to make up experiments after school. The custodian wants to clean it up. It's really a power question. Which is the most important job —to have kids making up their experiments or cleaning up the room at exactly three ten? The principal, he keeps nicely out of it."

[4]

A teacher in New York City recalling the way things were in New York schools before the teachers' union became a power:

"Lesson plans—you had to hand in lesson plans. You still have to hand them in, but there's a difference now. There's a difference in spirit now. At the time it was a spirit of 'do it or else, do it or something terrible is going to happen to you.' But you didn't really know what it was that was going to happen to you. So you had people copying from each other lesson plans which they were never going to use. On a Monday morning, if they hadn't done them over the weekend, the panic—'I haven't done my lesson plans!' And copying them down and seeing to it that they'd have them ready in time to hand in to the administrator. It was an awful atmosphere.

"The administrator walking in to observe you. What the union has done hasn't made these things any more meaningful, but you're less afraid. What the fear was then I didn't know. It was sort of a vague fear that everybody had—that you could be given an unsatisfactory rating or sent to some terrible school or be out altogether . . . So teachers watched carefully, but you didn't ever look at the children. You looked at the administrators. You didn't discover the individual characteristics of the children you were teaching. But you did discover the individual characteristics of the administrators. And you followed through on those.

"There was one principal who did not permit teachers to talk to each other. Mrs. S——. They called her, 'Chickenshit S——.' She did not permit teachers to speak to each other in the hallway. You were not allowed to talk to your colleagues, ever. There was no time at all that you were not supposed to be in your classroom, teaching. Teachers didn't talk to the principal about policy. The principal was the person who made all the decisions, and that was all there was to it. You didn't question his authority. And furthermore, the way a principal became a principal was a political thing. There's this whole myth about the Board of Examiners. Well, you had your friends on the Board of Examiners, and you knew who was testing, and so on.

"The assault on the teacher was so great. The feeling of being raped by these politicians was so great. In elementary schools in particular, because elementary school isn't considered as important as high school. So principals came out of high schools—as though there's nothing to be known about how small children function. So you have principals with high school mentalities.

"If your class was disorderly, that was the worst crime, because it was the worst crime in high school apparently. You were terrified of being caught with disorderly children. Therefore, if the children were orderly everything was all right, no matter what you were teaching or what you weren't teaching. It didn't make any difference.

"One day the principal came to my table at lunchtime and asked me if I had a special religion. I didn't know what he was talking about. Turned out he wanted to know why I was so kind to the children. He didn't want me to be different from the other teachers. I was the 'crazy teacher.' The day the union contract was signed I changed in his eyes from the crazy teacher to the dedicated teacher. . . ."

[5]

The traditional relationship between principal and teacher —that is, the historical one—is highly patriarchal. Another way of putting it is that the principal-teacher relationship runs a close parallel to the teacher-student one. A high school teacher in Los Angeles put it bluntly: "The good teacher is like the good student. You keep your nose clean and don't cause any trouble." A patriarch can be benign, going on the assumption that he knows what's best for his underlings, and he can be harshly authoritarian, especially in dealing with people he considers uppity. Both types were and to some extent still are to be found among principals. Even today, the air redolent of teacher militancy, there's no shortage of teachers who are afraid of their principals. This isn't surprising, after all, if one considers the personality characteristics of persons who go into teaching. After completing a national tour of United States schools, Dr. Ruth G. Newman, co-director of the Institute of Education Services, Washington School of Psychiatry, concluded that all too often the school atmosphere was depressing and teachers treated like children by their administrative superiors.[6]

Dr. Newman cited one representative instance in which, at a faculty meeting, the principal strode in twenty minutes late, said, "Good afternoon, teachers," and the teachers in unison chorused, "Good afternoon, Mrs. C——."

In the South it seems to be Negro principals in particular, accustomed to running segregated schools like little fiefdoms because white-run school boards almost wholly neglected such schools, who are most authoritarian to their teachers. In Southern communities many teachers, both black and white, complained while being interviewed for this book about their treatment at the hands of black administrators. "They can't adjust to the fact that teachers have some rights, too," said a black elementary school teacher in Raleigh.

But to an extent this is the cry of teachers of all colors everywhere—those teachers, at any rate, who are the more assertive and independent-minded ones and who set the pace for the rest. As teachers demand increasing say in matters of school policy, curriculum development, items affecting both teacher welfare and classroom instruction, the principals see themselves literally stripped of their former authority, especially with teacher groups and school boards negotiating over their heads on matters that affect them directly. Members of the National Association of Secondary Principals stressed, at their 1968 convention, that they are "being traded out of existence." That same year, at a conference of the National Committee for Support of the Public Schools, a principal with the Philadelphia schools gave voice to the principals' dilemma: Everybody wants power, he said, but the principal's power in the typical school system is far short of what it should be for dealing with his broad range of responsibilities. The principal, he said, typically has no power over instructional resources, supplies, and equipment; over selection and assignment of personnel; over staff size, counseling services, clerical help; nor does he have the prerogative of making teacher ratings "meaningful in terms of their performance." [7]

It's self-evident that as one group makes claim to more power for itself, the one from whom the power is being wrested will insist it's losing too much to function effectively. Even as teachers claim they have no autonomy in the schools, they have been having much of it within limits in the world they jealously guard as their own—the world of the classroom. Not many, perhaps, would agree with the statement of a Los Angeles training teacher that "the teacher is God in her classroom." But even those who deny the validity of that remark can't deny the fact that, with the door to the classroom closed, and within the limitations imposed by the curriculum, most teachers have a great deal of informal autonomy. One teacher admitted that "teachers can stand on their heads inside the classroom if they want to"—and proceeded to describe a colleague who was a Yoga enthusiast and actually did stand on his head and teach at times!

As for the principal, he thinks he's losing power, and to an extent he is. But part of his problem is that he must deal with old relationships in new ways, and he is literally unprepared for the task. It's a learning experience for him, as for anyone caught in a new situation. This is a time when everybody—not only teachers, but students, parents, and, in low-income urban areas, community people—wants to see a shift that will give them more authority than they have. One may imagine that many a principal, taking a moment's respite from the day's round of harassments, reflects nostalgically on earlier days, easier days, days when, as one sympathetic teacher put it, "he could gather his children under his wing, you know, and counsel them and help them."

Nevertheless, he's hardly left powerless. If he is shrewd enough, he realizes that power shifts don't have to mean depletion of authority, only that authority is played out in a different way. A bright, tough administrator with the reputation of being a clever politician explained that, in response to a demand for greater teacher participation in school affairs, he had established a teacher council. Now when some matters come up that affect teachers directly, he encourages teacher participation. "I do it for selfish reasons." He shrugged. "Rather than stick my neck out on issues that are of little concern to me insofar as the outcome goes, I'd rather put it in their hands and let them decide for themselves. This to me is the best way to handle it administratively."

Nor is the principal defenseless in the daily running of the shop. Teachers are not apt to take over the schools—not yet, at any rate, much as some more vociferous ones might give the impression that they will. The principal today, as always, pretty much holds the key to staff morale—something even militant teachers admit. This hardly bespeaks administrative impotence.

As always, the principal is still in most instances the purveyor of patronage and still has, if he wishes to exercise it, the power to harass. Many advantages can accrue to the favored members of the principal's inner circle. A teacher can be given choice duties (or less of the less desirable ones). He can get the best rooms (the newer ones or the ones on the sunny side). He can get preferential treatment with respect to equipment, etc. He can get the least troublesome classes, if the principal wishes him to. Teachers in a Manhattan school described how a few of their colleagues regularly take off when the tough math lessons are supposed to be given. A high school teacher in Winston-Salem, reporting on his school and district, said, "If you want a certain position, you pal around, you become a crony of so-

and-so, and you eventually get the position. One teacher told me, 'Our school administration is government by cronies.' I have to agree with that."

It would be a mistake, however, to consider the interplay between the principal and the members of his informal power structure too simplistically. More goes on than conformity and narrow self-seeking. A strong informal power group can help shore up a weak administrator, thus keeping chaos at bay. The tension that results from the rivalry between the principal's pet group and another teacher clique can, if not so intense as to tear the place apart, spark new approaches and better solutions to old problems.

Moreover, favored teachers are not necessarily only those who curry favor. Some principals make a sharp dichotomy in their minds between run-of-the-mill teachers and those whose teaching is exciting and dynamic. Even if the latter are not well liked, they may be given special leeway to work out their own innovative ideas. A highly experienced woman who teaches the primary grades in Manhattan remarked that she is always coming up with new ideas to put to use in the classroom. Some she can implement on her own in the privacy of her classroom; others require the principal's okay. Unlike more cautious principals, he has never refused to give his permission. But he always says, "Don't tell any of the other teachers. They couldn't handle it."

The teacher does not like his attitude—his putting down the potentialities of the others—but she plays along. She remarked that her relationship with her principal is very strange: They are in collusion for the sake of creativity, and at the same time they are in collusion against it.

[9]

Teacher's Day with the Kids— and Vice Versa

[1]

As the concerned teacher watches his students file into the classroom, he fervently hopes it will be a good day. He hopes Johnny will not throw his books on the floor in a temper tantrum, Alice will not burst into tears because she fails to understand the lesson, Eddie will not race around the room in a fit of youthful exuberance, Kenneth will not hurl a swearword at him, and it will not be necessary for him to reprimand half a dozen other youngsters for half a dozen other assorted transgressions. As the kids file into the room and push themselves into their seats, the teacher hopes they will be interested enough in what he has to offer to make at least half the time he spends with them worthwhile. As the boys and girls settle down to the day's work with varying degrees of enthusiasm, the teacher hopes not too many things will get in the way of the classroom activities. He hopes there will not be too many interruptions from the office, but realizes that that may be too much to ask for.

Said a first-year third-grade teacher in Manhattan, outraged by it all, "There's a school intercom, and the principal is on there buzzing her mouth off like once every half hour. Invariably when you're in the middle of a lesson. Some unimportant little tidbit like, 'It is raining today so you will not go out at lunchtime.' 'John Jones, come to my office.' The principal could just buzz Jones' room and tell him to come, but she doesn't—the whole school has to know. Just that damn intercom buzzing the whole damn day long."

Said a sixth-grade teacher in Los Angeles, with grim precision, "Paper work, paper work. The nurse wants the health cards, so you have to stop and get them. Another teacher wants one of your record cards. The principal wants to know how many social science books you have. Somebody else wants to know if you can come to a meeting on such and such a day. Forms to fill out, those crazy forms: Would you please give a breakdown of boys and girls in the class; would you please say how many children you have in reading grade such and such. Forms, messengers—all day long."

When the concerned teacher begins his day with his students, he knows that some of them will act up in class, will act up because they are in bad moods, because they had fights with their parents, because their home lives are miserable, because they have headaches, because they have a lot of excess energy to release, because—who knows all the reasons why? The teacher may also be in a bad mood, have had a fight at home, be beset with personal problems, be not feeling well, be more inclined to take a swim in the ocean or a drive in the country than be locked up with thirty youngsters—but he must control himself. Being human, teachers do convey mood, of course, and do snap at the children more on one occasion than on another. But unless they are lacking in stability they make sustained efforts to control their emotions. Few are so much in control of themselves—in the early grades, at least—that they keep from yelling. A common spectacle in a great many elementary schools is the one of teachers yelling or screaming at the boys and girls to bring the classroom under control.

In other ways, however, teachers habitually feign mental states. They make an effort to be cheerful, though worry about something assails them. They pretend to be interested in students' questions, identical to questions they have heard hundreds of times before from other students. They pretend to be absorbed in textbooks which, insipid on first reading, now bore them to distraction. They pretend that the new directive from the principal's office makes eminent sense, when in reality they think it's the silliest thing they ever heard of. They may be convinced a particular child is the most offensive brat they ever came across, but they stifle the urge to give him the sound whipping they feel he deserves. There are educational critics who contend that, yelling aside, teachers are much too much in control of their emotions in the classroom, and students never really see them reacting like flesh-and-blood human beings.

Said a junior high school teacher in Brooklyn, "There are days when you feel like chucking the whole thing. You can go along and have a wonderful day; you're teaching and the kids are listening, and you're bringing the subject across. And then five minutes before the end of the period one kid will act up and start a fight with another kid or maybe just become insolent, and the whole day's ruined. So you can go home and feel you've had a terrible day and five minutes is all it takes."

Said a fifth-grade teacher in Newark, New Jersey, "Children can really bring out the worst side of you. At home you can flare up. Even at another kind of job, if somebody annoys you, you can always say, 'You're an s.o.b.,' and get it out of your system one way or another. With a child, you've really got to think three times before you do anything or say anything. And there are times when you feel so completely inadequate, what you want to do is take your hand and just smack them—some of them. You can't do that. At least I can't do it. So it takes such a great amount of inner discipline, rigidity, that you walk out of there physically and psychologically exhausted at the end of the day. Because they drain you and test you constantly."

The concerned teacher knows that at the end of his six-hour day he'll be tired, knows that if it's a particularly difficult day he'll be wrung through the emotional wringer. Teaching is not simply a matter of handling information, even for teachers who teach as if it is. Largely, it is a very complex series of interpersonal relationships—with the class as a whole, with a variety of subgroups, with children individually—all occurring at the same time and in all kinds of unpredictable ways. After minutely studying life in elementary classrooms, Professor Philip W. Jackson of the University of Chicago concluded that the teacher "typically engages in two hundred or three hundred interpersonal interchanges every hour of her working day." [1]

The teacher must react perceptively, intuitively, if chaos is not to ensue. He must instantly decide what to do about the unexpected—and there's always something unexpected happening during the course of the school day. He must react both intellectually and with a marshaling of his emotional forces. He must deal with children having a wide range of backgrounds, abilities, and interests.

It's the diversity of intellectual and emotional responses in the typical classroom that drives many teachers wild. There's a common misconception that such diversity is found only in classrooms where children are placed heterogeneously, without regard for their achievement levels. These may represent an extreme, but the fact is that variation runs deep and wide, even in classrooms in which all the children are supposedly "equally" bright or slow. (Teachers used to teaching only fast classes or only slow classes run the risk of assuming all the students are alike, and overlooking important individual differences.) Though "meeting individual differences" is one of the hallmarks of American education, the extent to which even the best-trained and most-skilled teacher can do so is limited—especially in a classroom of twenty-five or thirty children, all of them supposedly learning the same thing the same way. Often overlooked, too, is that teachers are individually different and may have problems meeting the needs of one type of child or another. (In some experimental schools, teachers and students are matched in terms of temperament.) Individualizing instruction is one of the biggest problems of new teachers; many never get the hang of making even relatively gross adjustments for the children as individuals. They slide naturally into the habit of gearing the instruction to a vague common denominator that serves the indeterminate "average" students far better than it does the brightest and the slowest.

Said a fifth-grade teacher in New York City, "If I discuss something on the level of the brightest kids, the slow ones are completely lost. If I aim the discussion to the level of the slow kids, the bright ones turn off and start getting ready to throw stones out the window or something. Maybe some teachers have the knack of drawing all the kids out, getting the best out of them all. I don't."

Said a resource teacher employed by the Cheyenne school system, "I'd like to have the ability to feel the individual differences in the classroom. To know just what each child needs. To know what to do, have the time to do it, and the means to supply it."

One thing teachers know for sure: Some youngsters will catch on swiftly, almost before the point is made; others will struggle slowly and painfully through the learning process. It might be supposed that teachers would prefer the quicker learner, and most do. But some shun the brightest, cleverest students.

Said a junior high school teacher in New Haven, Connecticut, "Some of the slower children mind you a lot more. You say, 'Open the book'; they'll open it. But some of the brightest children are real discipline problems."

Said an elementary school teacher in San Diego, "I like to work with slow learners rather than with fast ones. I don't enjoy working with very intelligent kids that much; I don't think

I'm that intelligent. I have a feeling that what I can give them isn't nearly as great as what I can give the slow learners."

Said a woman who teaches fifth grade to mostly Spanish-speaking or bilingual children in the Bronx, "The bright kids are the more selfish ones. With the bright kids you work from your head; with the slow kids you work from your guts. There's almost a parent-child relationship or satisfaction that comes with the slow kid. You don't eat yourself out from the inside with the bright kid."

The best teacher is, in his own way, as sophisticated in dealing with groups as the most skillful group therapist. Like the therapist, he must, if he is ethical, watch himself with respect to favoritism. Many teachers wrongly deny even to themselves that they prefer some pupils over others. It's the denial which is ultimately harmful, not the awareness of feelings which can then be handled and governed.

Said a white elementary school teacher in an all-Negro Raleigh school, "I try not to, but when a child does everything on time, does just what you say and all, you have a tendency to show some favor to that child. You get a little impatient with children that you have to remind over and over about everything they do, and they never seem to do it right. But—I can see that child has a special need and a special problem. And that's my job."

Said a shop teacher in an inner-city junior high school in Manhattan, "You can have favorite bad kids as well as good— because the bad kid may be just mischievous, and you would just laugh at him in another situation. The kids who are noticed most are those who are very good or very bad. The kids in the middle, the ones who give no problem and don't shine, are little noticed. Sometimes you don't even know they're there. A kid like that, you don't consider him a favorite, because at the end of the term you say, 'You've been in my class all term long?' The first names you learn, the first day, are the bad kids. The kids who don't give any trouble but aren't outstanding, their names you learn the last day."

(Teachers delude themselves into believing they're entirely fair, at least, in the way they grade. And many try very hard to be objective. Some admit they agonize over grades and hate the whole procedure; they become somewhat emotional about it. But research studies indicate that teachers really aren't fair in the way they grade; on the contrary, unconsciously they tend to favor the children they like best, children with whom they have the most affinity. Dovetailing into this is another conclusion many classroom observation studies come to, namely, the teacher, especially the female teacher in the elementary school, inclines much more to the girls. Women teachers are found to be less supportive with boys, chide them more, are harsher with them when doing so, and send them down to the principal's office in cases where girls, acting up the same way, simply are reprimanded.)

Cutting through all the complexities of the teacher's work is his hope, each day, that it will be more than an ordinary day. He hopes that the classroom chemistry will react in its mysterious ways to produce something special. It's what he really came to school for.

And then there's the student. More than likely he, too, is irritated by the constant interruptions, unless the classroom atmosphere is deadly dull, in which event he welcomes them. The student, too, feigns mental states in his day-to-day classroom encounters with the teacher, since he's sometimes far more angry than even his acting out would indicate, and at such moments only his fear of punishment serves to govern his real impulses. (Some aren't fearful enough, the teachers would say.) The student, too, acts and reacts constantly on both the mental and emotional levels, and tires toward the end of the day. He, too, can work better and learn better with some persons than with others but is forced into at least a measure of cooperation with all. In kind, then, if not in degree or complexity, teacher and student go through somewhat the same emotions in their relationship with each other. Even to the hope that something above the ordinary will happen during the school day.

[2]

"Sometimes there's a white spot amidst the dark, you know?"
said a young woman who teaches school in a semirural area in
northeastern Kansas. "Like when you're teaching the kids
something, and they're all eager to learn." A man close to retirement, who teaches high school Latin in a Denver public
school, smiled reminiscently. "Once in a while you will have a
particularly good part of Cicero, and everybody seems to get it,
and you feel thrilled for that day," he said. "We take so much
garbage, I sometimes think I must be a real masochist to keep
on with it," commented an elementary school teacher in Manhattan. "But then you get one of those glorious days when
everything goes right, the kids catching on to everything, smart
as a whip—and then I wouldn't trade being a teacher for anything in the world!"

They call it, as that young woman did, a "glorious day."
They refer to it as a "magic time." They say it's "like a current
of electricity flowing through the classroom." They're describing that most thrilling moment of all for the teacher, the moment when teaching and learning come harmoniously alive,
and the whole classroom, teacher and pupils, go through a stun-
ning educational experience.

It makes up for the dull days. The draggy days. The days
when the most obvious point does not seem to get through,
and all that is in the air is a kind of sluggishness. Few teachers
can say that it happens with any kind of gratifying frequency.
"I haven't had any of those wildly exciting times lately," said
a high school teacher from New Haven, Connecticut. He was
wryly philosophical. "You keep trying."

For most teachers the short-lived peaks are terribly important. It is what gives them emotional sustenance during the
arid stretches, when teaching and learning are slow and pon-
derous. Not many are so possessed of vitality and enthusiasm
that they bound into the classroom daily with almost innocent

determination to coax and cajole and badger and bait some intellectual excitement out of their students. Not many are like a supercharged high school English teacher in Newton, Massachusetts. He said, "You're in emotional contact with the students. You say they're motivated, they're interested, they want to learn. It's ephemeral. At that moment I may make a point that will change the lives of four kids in that room. You can't do that without quiet, concentration, determination, homework for the teacher and the students—a long, steady progression of work from day to day. You can't do it without the assumption on the part of the student that when he comes to school, he's going to work."

Not many teachers, even among those who initially sustain the enthusiasm, can sustain it steadily. The daily grind *is* grinding. The routine *is* stifling. The act of relating to twenty-five or thirty youngsters *is* draining. But few teachers don't secretly hope to produce some miraculous change in their charges, and few are less than delighted when on rare occasions it happens. It's true even of the incompetents, the pure and simple baby-sitters. It may be only a spark, but it is a factor in the complex of motivations that brought them into teaching. Teachers at almost every level of ability and enthusiasm, underneath it all, want to feel that they have even to a slight degree been responsible for change, for growth, for learning, for insight on the part of the boys and girls in their classrooms. They want to feel the thrill of accomplishment.

One can take a cynical attitude. There are teachers whose stock in trade is the incisive sarcasm, the hurtful remark. "I hated him," said a junior high school girl in Denver, referring to her previous year's Latin teacher. "I'm not always very graceful in my gestures, and he kept calling me, 'Toscanini.' " There are teachers so insecure they become competitors with the children they teach, unconsciously subverting the very learning process they are supposedly encouraging. "They make fun of your questions or the things you want to try," said a Los Angeles teenager, describing such teachers. "One I know makes

fun of test grades even when the kid tries the hardest. Most
kids are afraid of a teacher like that. They won't go to them
for help even when they need it badly." But even those teachers
boast of their successes.

The wish to feel in some measure responsible for something
good happening to their students is a universal one among
teachers, but how it translates itself is an individual matter.
For some, who haven't really thought deeply and perceptively
about their roles, it revolves around the accomplishments the
teacher's higher-ups expect of him: getting through the curriculum, doing the work assigned. There are teachers who
glory in high achievement for their youngsters. For other teachers a spectacular leap on students' achievement test scores is
much less important. It is enough if Johnny overcame his aversion to math while in their classes; if Jean is less reticent, more
interested in school, readier to relate to her classmates by the
end of the term.

There are fine teachers who have very definite personal
teaching philosophies with which they weave their classroom
tapestry, such as the Raleigh junior high school teacher who
said, "I want to give them learning. I want to give them interest in all that lies about them. Respect for others—for people
who differ with them, too. Desire to keep growing. A chance
to express their views and to develop flexibility. I think appreciation is something I strive for—for people and places—and
these qualities I hope would be instilled in them. I think an
awakening of all that lies ahead is more important than what's
in the textbooks—they soon forget that." A Newton high
school teacher said flatly, "I start with the assumption that
they're ignorant, prejudiced, and incompetent—and I want
them to leave me with knowledge, an open mind, and skills
. . . In humanities the question that keeps coming up is, 'What
is it? Who cares?' And I challenge the kids on this. I say, 'So
you can have a happy, interesting, wonderful life—so you can
have the world open up and see double meanings in everything

around you—so you can have closer contact with the world.'
But I say, 'Practical, no, forget it. It's not practical.' And I think
that's the only motivation a person can have or ought to have
in the humanities. It's psychedelic. I seduce them into learning."

For teachers the biggest thrill is to have a former student
walk into the classroom years later and say how much the experience with that teacher meant to him. This is what gives
meaning to his work and confirms him as an educator. But it
happens seldom.

"It was a tremendous experience at the end of the year,
when a young man I once taught came back to visit me," proudly
said a sixth-grade Denver teacher. "He's a West Point cadet
now. I asked him, 'Why in the world would you want to come
back and see me?' You know what he said? 'Well,' he said, 'you
were the only teacher who ever sat and talked with me sometimes. . . .'"

[3]

Unfortunately, most children aren't ecstatic about school.
And they have little lasting regard for their teachers. When
asked, most kids say they like school. But a substantial minority—about six youngsters out of thirty—are very negative in
their feelings about school. And when the positively reacting
students are more searchingly questioned, it usually develops
that there are many aspects to school they don't like at all. This
is what Jackson discovered after a thorough scrutiny of six studies of grade school students' attitudes, studies that spanned a
quarter of a decade.[2]

How, then, does the average run of students feel about
school? A study conducted with elementary school children in
1940 is descriptive of the results of more recent surveys. Conducted with more than 600 sixth- and seventh-grade students
in three New York City schools located in high-, middle-, and

low-income neighborhoods, the study reports that students "do not look at school as a place of joy or pleasure. There is no exuberant enthusiasm displayed. There is no zestful approach to the school situation. The children attend school with consciousness that it will help them out in later life. School is not pleasurable for itself." [3]

There are other indications of the way children feel about school. One such is the high school dropout rate. Another pertinent signpost is the way students feel about teachers, since it seems reasonable to assume that the way a child perceives his teacher is a strong determinant of the way he feels about school generally. According to the findings of a Purdue University poll, *The American Teenager*, 80 percent of the high school students surveyed stated that they liked school.[4] Yet 75 percent also said they didn't want to become high school teachers. Another study of high school students' attitudes, sponsored by the Committee on School and College Relations of the Educational Records Bureau in the early 1960's, pinpoints why.[5] According to the author of the study, David Mallory, for many students a teaching career seemed "unthinkable, even ridiculous or contemptible. These students spoke of the teaching profession as requiring dreary repetition, underpaid drudgery, and intellectual death."

Could the students have been viewing their own school roles as similarly uninspiring? A clue may lie in one's remembrance of teachers who played a meaningful part in one's life. Most people, after a dozen years of schooling, can recall no more than two or three teachers as having made any significant impact on them. In the early 1960's, G. W. Allport of Harvard University asked 100 college undergraduates how many teachers had exerted a powerful influence on their intellectual or personal development. Though in the aggregate these college students had encountered 4,632 teachers, they could recall only 8.5 percent as having made a really strong impact on them. And of all those thousands of teachers, better than three-fourths were wholly unremembered.[6]

[4]

A Hunter College (New York City) student, recalling her high school calculus teacher, the one who endures in her memory:

"She was beautiful—she was enchanted with her subject and capable of conveying it. A very literate woman. She didn't put us through humiliating things, like work that's unstimulating. She flattered us by having us do the work less as punitive assignments and more as new ideas. She treated us as adult human beings."

The girl sighed, mulled over her public school experience as a whole, and said, "Most teachers have no sense of the fragility of young people."

[5]

Children do not, of their own free will, take on the role of students. They may come to love school, they may come to understand that education is related to ultimate material success in life, but in no sense are they a self-selecting clientele. Especially not in the first eight or nine years of schooling, when the option of dropping out is less available to them. Whatever enthusiasm they show in the classroom, the quality of it is contaminated by the fact that they must under law attend. The truth is that we literally grab our children by the scruff of the neck when they are five or six years old (or, given the trend to kindergarten and prekindergarten, much younger), dump them into classrooms, and in effect tell them, "Your days of freedom are over, this is where you'll be from now on." It may be a lovely school—all glass and mosaic tile and gaily colored walls and movable desks and carpeted floors—but it is still a place where a child is imprisoned. He is a captive. He may be lucky enough to have teachers who tickle him into thinking, stimulate him into learning, encourage the flowering of his

personality, give him in school the things that will enrich his
life outside. But he is still a captive. He cannot—even if at the
moment his psyche demands it—goof off, daydream, skip a couple of days, run out of class, let out a yell, fall asleep at his desk.
At least, he cannot do these things without being reprimanded,
sent down to the principal's office, given a bad mark, put
through the humiliation of having his parents contacted, or
otherwise reminded that he has absolutely no choice in the
matter.

"I don't think we're motivated to learn, as a way of life,"
said the high school teacher from Newton. "Most people are
motivated to stretch out like a cat and go to sleep in the sun.
We learn in spurts, things that catch our fancy. Other courses
are approached with the idea of getting by. Especially here in
this country. People are required to go to school, but it's an
anti-intellectual country. So the kid is stuck in class, and there's
the teacher, the source of his anxieties."

The custodial function of the public schools is nothing new,
though it should be kept in mind that when compulsory schooling initially was introduced, most children were still valuable
commodities to their farming parents, who were not exactly
eager to see them march off to school. What *is* new, compared
with even a couple of generations ago, is that the school day is
longer than it ever was, and the "children" are already young
adults by the time they graduate from high school. What is new,
as well, is that all children—even those most antagonistic to
and disorderly in it—must attend school. These factors accentu-
ate the custodial aspects. Thus, as Oswald Hall of the University of Toronto has pointed out, teaching takes its place among
"the other great custodial occupations of society. Here teachers link hands with nurses who take charge of patients confined
to a hospital, and with jailers, the reform school personnel,
the army sergeants, the penitentiary guards, the baby-sitters,
and all those whose occupation is to maintain control of people put in their charge." [7]

These aren't the most pleasant of comparisons. They're

stressed here to point up some of the difficulties and tensions surrounding the teacher-student relationship. Many teachers will protest that they try hard to establish warm, friendly, open relationships with their students. They'll point to their pretty new schools and demand to know whether they bear any resemblance to jail. Yet the fact is that no matter how nice the teacher or how attractive the surroundings, the child has to be there. He must arrive and leave at set times. There are various skills and subjects he's expected to master. Regardless of his feelings, he's expected to take tests or answer questions on demand. He must jump to the order of bells. He must produce passes on demand. In other words, the school institutes a host of rules, and students are expected to obey them.

But school is more than a place where a child is conditioned to submerge his feelings, take his place among the group, and learn to obey higher authority. It's more than a place where skills are mastered, or facts pounded in to be spewed back on demand. It's the teacher's job, presumably, to awaken the child's curiosity, encourage his absorption in learning, lead him to the delights of inquiry. This requires a more open relationship, mutual respect, a downgrading of conformity, and a minimum of anxiety. The two climates are more or less antithetical, one of the complexities of the teacher-student relationship. There are teachers who feel this deeply. "I keep trying for rapport with the students," said a high school teacher in Los Angeles, "but the whole setup—it becomes more like a master-slave relationship. Three-fourths of the time you have to be a policeman." A professor of education at Teachers College, Columbia University, explained, "What's promoted is conflict—divided loyalties. If you're going to stay in the system you have to wall off much of your concern or you're torn apart." He commented on the absence of sensitivity to students' needs and to a lack of respect for students he has observed in many schools.

There are many ways a lack of respect is shown. Gossip about children (though unethical) is endemic among teachers. Rules and regulations are often formulated (by teachers or administrators) from the standpoint of what's most expedient, rather than from the viewpoint of what's best for the students in the long run. There are teachers who assign homework and then throw it away. It's commonplace to lie to the children, and to talk about them in a patronizing way while they are present.

It's easier for teachers and administrators to assign schoolwork as a disciplinary measure, set up detention halls for problem children, and use corporal punishment than to search for the alternatives that would make schools and learning seem less punitive. A survey by *Grade Teacher* shows that 62.7 percent of the nation's elementary schools permit physical punishment, 63.2 percent of the teachers favor a school board rule permitting teachers to hit unruly youngsters anywhere except above the shoulders, and nearly half of the respondents had used corporal punishment during the preceding year.[8] Twenty percent had done so more than five times.

Of the many teacher comments reprinted by the journal, only one was anti-corporal punishment. The dissenter, from New York, said, "I think the teachers should be trained and screened for their self-discipline. After all, isn't striking a child an act of no self-discipline?" Yet it's not always easy for the teacher *not* to be punitive when the situation overwhelms him. A grade school teacher in the Bronx, New York, barely six months on the job, teaching the "slow" class on her grade level, said sadly, "There's a tremendous amount of futility, and that's why I've been so disappointed with just this year of teaching. It's taken a tremendous amount out of me. I'm drained all the time. I try everything I can think of as far as new methods go. I try very hard to keep my temper and not allow the ten or fifteen disturbing influences in the classroom to override me, run me, and it just becomes a battle to see who's the strongest one. Sometimes I feel like a real shrew or a witch. I'm not a rigid person to begin with. I'm not that tough, and I'm not really a disciplinarian at heart, but this is a role that has to be maintained very, very strongly as long as the classes are so big. Psychologists say you can be more flexible, and you can be lax.

You don't have to be that screaming witchy figure up there, they say. But I find it very difficult to be otherwise when I have thirty children to take care of."

The custodial aspects of school manifest themselves strikingly in high school. Student councils, in which students supposedly have a voice in matters of direct concern to them, are usually administrator-controlled and faculty-managed. The right to political expression—by wearing buttons or in other ways—is expressly forbidden to students in many schools, especially if the politics is not popular with the administration. The ACLU fought all the way up to the U.S. Supreme Court the case of three Des Moines, Iowa, high school students who had been suspended for wearing black armbands to protest the Vietnam War after having expressly been forbidden to. (The Court ultimately ruled in their favor.) "Student-run" school newspapers are not student-run at all; they are, in fact, under complete faculty control. When students show initiative, imagination, and independence—supposedly three great American virtues—and establish underground newspapers, they are suspended or expelled. This has happened in Long Beach, New York, San Diego, California, Seattle, Washington, and elsewhere. Repeated incidents of mass suspensions occur with regard to long hair and miniskirts—to the point where it becomes evident that schools are far more preoccupied with controlling students' dress and appearance than they are with matters like bigotry, poverty, riots, and pollution. This preoccupation even takes the form of flouting official rulings: Though in 1966, the then New York State Commissioner of Education, James E. Allen, ruled that girls may wear slacks to school, administrators and teachers all over the state have still been enforcing no-slacks prohibitions. While the current school demonstrations and ever-increasing violence have their roots in a number of causes, one of the more important is surely the overcontrolling atmosphere of the schools. In an NEA poll teachers overwhelmingly favored the schools' right to regulate student dress and appearance.

Because many New York City high schools have been subject to unrest and violence, especially in the aftermath of the 1968 teachers' strike, the New York *Post* sent a reporter posing as a student to Taft, a typical middle-class high school.[9] There had been no violence at Taft, and the object of the reportage was to find out what life was like inside a "decent" high school. This is what life was like, according to the reporter: Students needed passes "to do almost anything—go to the toilet, carry your coat in the hall, use the coin telephone." Most outside doors were padlocked during the day, "and teacher aides are stationed, sentry-like, at posts near all exits." The locker room was kept locked during the day. Teachers stood guard in the cafeteria during the noon break, as instructions to eating students boomed from loudspeakers. The rest room doors were always kept open to prevent students from smoking or using narcotics. When the *Post* reporter took a photograph near the girls' rest room, some teachers saw the flash, erroneously assumed that she was photographing a custodian who happened to be passing by, marched her to the office, and threatened her with confiscation of the film. At the last moment the reporter bolted, as she put it, "to freedom."

Ironically, some three weeks later Taft High School had its first demonstration. It was a protest against the suspension of a black student. He had brought a copy of an Afro-American newspaper containing a controversial, anti-Semitic poem to a white girl who had requested it. In doing so, he had violated another rule, one forbidding students to bring "unauthorized materials" into the schools.

Obviously, schools vary in the extent to which their custodial atmosphere is controlling. Teachers differ in the manner and degree to which they exercise their authority vis-à-vis their students. A curriculum specialist who has visited classrooms all over the country said, "It's important for the teacher to gain control from the standpoint of the organization of the classroom; otherwise there's chaos. But the teacher should have self-discipline herself. In some of the elementary schools I visit, children themselves work out the procedures. They do their own planning, and the teachers stay more and more in the background. First they get the classroom under control, which may take a few weeks, and then they gradually pull out. If Johnny is disruptive, the class can discuss in Johnny's presence how to cope with him, because everyone is involved. But many teachers resist this idea; they feel threatened."

Regardless of the pattern, however, to some extent the pressures for conformity exist. They have to, considering the schools' role in socializing youngsters into the society, and no teacher can avoid his role in this.

[6]

The controlling aspects of school do not end at the point where cognitive learning begins. The model of the modern school resembles a factory, and it is no accident that both were born at about the same time. This was a time when the factory, too, bore considerable resemblance to a custodial institution. Curricula and materials are mandated from above, with no reference to the particular children in the classroom. The work to be done is identical for each student. Students are expected to learn what the teacher orders them to learn, irrespective of their own needs and desires. Lesson plans and teachers' guides (complete with the "right" questions to ask) form the day-to-day teaching structure. Teachers are expected—or expect themselves—to be omniscient: Both interviews and the professional literature reflect the fact that comparatively few teachers can admit they do not know something or are in error about something they have told their class. Teachers and students work toward the purpose of passing quality control inspections, *i.e.*, good marks on report cards, good scores on tests.

There are teachers who themselves feel closed in by the rigidities of the educational system, and rail against it. A Princeton art teacher who goes into various elementary classrooms to teach talked at length about the scholastic schedule teachers and students are locked into. "Teachers want it, they feel they must go from Point A to Point B in the second grade. They don't realize it really isn't going to upset the balance if we don't reach Point B then and pick it up the following year. I hear this from teachers; I hear the actual panic by the end of May. 'My God, I've still got this much to do, and I don't know how I'm going to get it done.' Education should be a big, flowing experience. . . ."

Several teachers talked about grades—about the frustrating decisions that have to be made in grading—about most students' singleminded attempts to get good marks. "You give an assignment, and they say, 'Are you going to grade this?' " bemoaned a Denver high school teacher. "It's the same thing as saying, 'Are you going to pay me for mowing your lawn?' It's this materialistic concept something for something. To me the worst thing is what's happening to the kids. They think education is stuffing facts into somebody's head and giving them a test and having them pass it. This is ridiculous. They forget it the next day, and what have you done? You've done a job, you've gotten paid for it, you've given them a little test, you've put a little mark in a little book. The kids who get an education in this country get it despite the system, not because of it."

A Los Angeles high school teacher working in an integrated school told of his attempts, in his American History class, to get away from the traditional topics of foreign relations, agriculture, and the like. All semester he had had his students look at the urban environment, the race problem. "If our teachers could get off this mechanical approach to what education is," he said, "that it's data . . . Hell, this is so darn well built into the system by such things as the College Board exams, you know. That's my tremendous guilt feeling. These kids aren't learning a doggone bit of American History as such. They've been on race the whole semester long. Maybe I'm hurting them, their future—hurting them in this respect while trying to build up their future for actual living. . . ."

For decades now the theoretical approaches to teaching have

been "pupil-centered"—meaning, at its simplest, that you do not teach a child how to use his mind by imposing information on him and having him spew it back. Schools of education have been solemnly lecturing their student teachers not to lecture when they get out there in those classrooms. The emphasis has been on the teacher as guide, the student as an active partner—discussing, analyzing, inquiring, conceptualizing. There are master teachers who do a marvelous job of eliciting this kind of response from the boys and girls in their classes, who also do wonders in making the subject under discussion come alive to illuminate the child's world and deepen his perceptions of it. Yet study after study shows that for the most part teachers do what they always have done: They talk and talk and talk.

That teachers talk too much in their classrooms has become especially apparent in recent years as a small but growing number of researchers have focused their attention exactly where the action is, right in the classroom itself, recording in minute detail the social transactions and interactions that occur. Observing thirty-five sixth-grade teachers as they interacted with individual youngsters, with groups, and with classes as a whole, Marie Hughes found that the most frequent and pervasive teacher mode was that of "control." In her context that meant a variety of teacher tasks: setting standards, structuring the classroom to give it focus, reprimanding or threatening students, and so on.[10] "The teachers directed the children in what they should do and how they should do it," Hughes observed, "what they should answer and how they should answer." Moreover, teachers rarely elicited responses calling for association of ideas, the development of inference, or the expression of personal opinion on the part of the students. (There were two sets of teachers; the ones rated "good" by their central offices were less controlling than the ones who were simply representative of their schools.)

A study by Hugh Perkins of the University of Maryland with seventy-two teachers as they reacted in two-minute segments with seventy-two fifth-graders showed that 84 percent of all the teaching acts were in the categories of "leader" or "supervisor." There was a high incidence of pupil desk work and recitation. Just 4 percent of the time was given to ideas and experiences stemming from the pupils themselves.[11]

When Arno Bellack and several associates studied 15 high school teachers and 345 students in the New York City area, they came up with similar findings—only more so. All the teachers and students were from classes in Problems in Democracy, grades ten and twelve. Bellack, helped by the teachers, had created a unit of instruction around problems of international economics.[12] The teachers were carefully trained in the concepts to be developed during the two-week course. Careful observation of the teachers while they were teaching the course showed that the ratio of teacher talk to pupil talk was three to one—meaning the teachers were on stage, as it were, two-thirds of the time. Classroom roles were clearly delineated: The teachers asked questions, the students answered, the teachers reacted to what the students had said. In other words, it was the teachers, not the students, who gave meaning to the material.

"Teachers don't discuss concepts with us," said a high school senior from Wheaton, Maryland, at a joint NEA-Magazine Publishers Association conference on student militancy, held in December, 1968. "We're being taught *at*. In effect, they're making you a regurgitating machine. You feed back what they give you."

[7]

Interview with a sixteen-year-old junior high school girl in Denver:

"This social science teacher I was telling you about, she's pretty unusual for a teacher because—well, sometimes she uses psychology, too, stuff like that. She's really nice. My political philosophy kind of comes from her philosophy. It kind of goes together with hers."

"Do you simply accept what she says?"

"No, I think about it. I have the same ideas, but she kind of brings them out, makes me think about them more."

"She gives you psychology, too?"

"Well, no—she'd kind of like to teach that more, because she thinks it's more important for us to have that than learn about the Presidents and stuff like that. Because right now we're at an age, she says, and that's right, where we need a lot of help in getting along with others. But learning about Presidents and stuff like that—it's pretty hard to learn about history that way, and psychology would really help us to get along with others. I think she's right. But in the school system you have to teach American History in the eighth grade, you know. You just have to."

"How are the other teachers in your classes?"

"Well, a lot of them are just teachers, you know—most of the time they aren't really exceptional."

"How's that?"

"Well, a lot of teachers, they don't understand the way you feel. Sometimes they don't have an open mind, like about teenagers' problems, you know. Like one of my teachers, we started talking about hippies, and he just blew up. I just acted like he'd won the argument, you know. I asked him about hippies, and he hated them because they were nonconformists and they hated the war. That's what he said about hippies. And I said, 'What's good about war?' I shouldn't have said that because teachers get mad when you talk back, and I didn't mean it that way. And he said, 'If this country isn't good enough to fight for, it isn't worth anything.' And I just let it go because, you know, I wasn't going to argue with a teacher."

"Don't teachers like the idea of your asking questions, stimulating discussion?"

"No, the other teachers don't like that. I have to ask questions before I understand anything. Especially in algebra. I have a lot of trouble with algebra. I keep asking questions and the teacher kind of shrugs me off."

"Does he shrug off the other students, too?"

"Most of the time he does, because the kids in there are exceptionally bright, practically geniuses, and I'm not a genius in algebra. Not in the least. Sometimes I'm absent and he gives me this book to read. But I can't get anything just from reading a book. I have to have it explained to me, and he doesn't take the trouble. After a while I have to pester him or I don't understand a single thing."

[8]

"No one will contend that every high school graduate is capable or even wants a higher education. What some of us do contend is that many of those being weeded out today are both desirous of a higher education and, in terms of their intelligence quotient, capable of absorbing academic training." This is how a high school student using the pseudonym "E. Smedgling" launched into an attack on school and teachers that, significantly, was given prominent space in the January, 1965, issue of *Clearing House*. "We charge that a very indifferent elementary and secondary school system is failing to prepare many fine students for the higher learning they are capable of," Smedgling, a senior, continued. He told of Mr. Canter, who was supposed to teach him economics "but with all the brazenness of a turbaned Oriental hawking his wares in a Turkish bazaar" peddled his wife's doughnuts in class, instead. He rarely gave reading assignments or tests, and hardly ever talked about the subject matter. When he fell off a ladder and broke his ankle, a substitute teacher who was an English major and knew nothing about economics took his place. Then there was Smedgling's math teacher, Mr. Gotham, a man who'd been an outstanding principal but was demoted to classroom instruction when he became too old and deaf to cope with administrative responsibilities. Doddering, having trouble with his hearing aid, he couldn't cope with the classroom either.

"We all feel sorry for Mr. Gotham and for a school system that finds it necessary to employ teachers who should have been retired years ago. We also feel sorry for ourselves, and we worry a good deal about how we will fare with the math questions we will face when we take our college entrance examinations," wrote Smedgling. He praised his auto mechanics teacher as being highly skilled and effective, but noted that this teacher spent most of his time gossiping with the mechanical drawing teacher next door. He also told of an inspiring history teacher who'd been promoted to vice-principal, and of another dynamic teacher who was awarded a fellowship and also left, to continue his university studies.

[9]

During the 1966-67 school year, as part of a long-term study of teacher effectiveness and its evaluation, the Bureau of Research of Colorado State College conducted interviews with 2,000 Colorado high school seniors.[13] The students were asked to describe, under cover of anonymity, what teacher characteristics they considered most effective and least effective, based on their experiences with the teachers they had had during their public school years. Over and over again, the students saw most the most positively, and judged as having been most effective for them, those teachers who looked upon them as individuals and showed genuine concern for them as persons. "This teacher was never too busy to see you or be interested in you," was one typical reply. "He treated you as an individual and an equal. He never looked down on you." Another, describing a teacher who was interested in the young people over and above their roles as students, explained, "The main thing is that he took a special interest in each and every one of us, not only as a student, but as an individual outside of class."

Next in order of importance the students chose those characteristics that describe enthusiasm for the subject and for the act of teaching. "By encouraging thinking and creativity among students, he inspired all of us to want to learn," said one of the Colorado high-schoolers. "The students really worked hard for him." A second youngster stated, "She made the whole class revolve around the students. Even if the subject material seemed dull, she made it interesting." A third wrote that her history teacher made the subject "so much more than dull, dry facts. Through her own research, she made us see the importance of events and situations that would ordinarily have been passed over."

Next the students chose for appreciation those teachers who cared whether the students worked or not. "This teacher always made his class a challenge," observed one of the high school respondents. "The homework was not overwhelming, but we had to work to make the grade. His tests were difficult but not impossible, and you always felt a sense of achievement when you did well. He worked us pretty hard, but he made the subject interesting." And sixth among the traits valued most by students was impartiality. "She was the first teacher I ever had that treated everyone the same," said one of the students in the study sample. "I have not had such a teacher since then." According to the author of the study, Dr. John A. Williamson, "The frequency of comments regarding this trait tends to indicate that the teacher who does not noticeably have favorites is rather rare."

Conversely, the teachers rated least effective—the teachers who turned students off—were those who exhibited traits contrary to those above. For instance, one teacher was described as having an interest "only in rushing through a class haphazardly. The class presentation showed no outside preparation." Another was depicted as "a wonderful person in general, but a very poor teacher. He wanted all the students to like him, but they ran over him instead. He was not firm enough." And a teacher who did not care whether her students learned was summed up: "She simply put in her time and earned her salary for being present in class."

In general, these findings replicate the results of other studies in which students have been queried about their teachers. What the kids ask for is not, from their point of view, all that remarkable. They want their teachers to be interested in them as individuals; to manage their classrooms competently; to be caught up in what they are teaching and in the act of teaching itself; to expect the students to work; to show impartiality; to respect student opinion.

One could argue, of course, that they are largely describing a more or less "ideal" teacher. The ideal is pretty unusual to come by, not only in teaching but in every other profession. But it could also be argued that they have a modest—that is, realistic—view of what the teacher must be if he really is to justify his role as teacher; that it only seems a way-out ideal image because much in the structure of education, and in the human transactions accomplished in it, conspires against its realization.

[10]

Ghetto Schools: Clash of Cultures

THE middle-class child may be a prisoner of the institution, but at the same time he and his teacher have a compact. In exchange for conforming to the rules, learning the lockstep way, and generally performing in the manner expected by the adults, he's placed on the academic track. This eventually brings him to college, earns him a degree, provides him with a very respectable job or career, and gains him the appropriate material rewards. Furthermore, there is between this teacher and this child a kinship. They understand each other. They speak the same language, share the same world, eat the same food (psychic and otherwise). The whole school milieu, in fact, is imbued with a conventional, traditional, muddy kind of middle-class morality replete with all its virtues and defects.

The middle-class culture is the only one the school is geared for and teachers, generally speaking, are capable of accepting.

This becomes very evident when middle-class students turn away from middle-class values. Many school people, probably the vast majority, find it quite difficult to tolerate boys and girls who have staked out positions antithetical to the dominant values. For many school people, anything resembling hippies is anathema. This is especially so in upper-middle-class communities, where teachers often tend to be more conservative and less permissive than the parents of the children they teach. As a high school teacher in Princeton stressed, in such situations teachers tend to be much stricter than parents with respect to long hair and skirt lengths. The reasons are fairly evident. With their lower-middle-class backgrounds and moderate salaries—often far too low to permit them to live in the affluent communities in which they teach—teachers are uncertain of their social position. They know some of their students look down their noses at them. They feel that the friendly manner of parents (who may invite them out to dinner or provide theater tickets for them) is at bottom an act of *noblesse oblige*. Turnover in some high-pay, high-prestige suburban areas is as high as in some ghetto schools. Niles Township, for instance, is an affluent Chicago suburb that in a three-year period, from 1964 to 1967, had a teacher turnover of 21 percent, and 20 percent of those leaving did so specifically to take teaching posts elsewhere.[1]

With teachers feeling insecure in moneyed environments, and being upwardly mobile besides, it's no surprise that they consider it an affront to witness students blatantly rejecting the very life-styles they themselves covet to some extent. A high school dropout from Scarsdale High School said that teachers considered him an outcast when as a freshman he grew a beard, let his hair grow long, and began circulating antiwar petitions. Once during his school years he was also busted on a drug charge. He said that teachers did engender good communication with "straight" kids but not with him and the few others like him. "I'm sure the teachers spent more time talking about me than with me," he said. "They'd complain to the guidance counselor who would speak to me—I thought it was the teachers who needed the talking to." Recalling that he never had a teacher who went out of his way to be interested in him, never had one taking him aside to talk about his problems, the young man said, "They didn't like my behavior, but they never bothered to try and find out why I acted the way I did. Every once in a while I proved to my teachers in each class that I could do very good work. Looking back on it, I'm dismayed—why didn't they try to find out what was wrong?"

Povl W. Toussieng of the University of Oklahoma School of Medicine has pointed out, referring to "subjective" students like this one, that they "have very little use for school, but teachers and schools alike have even less use for these particular students." [2]

If schools generally find it difficult to accommodate middle-class children who turn away from their culture, they find it even harder to work with children from blue-collar and (especially) low-income backgrounds. It is common these days to view the problem of educating low-income children solely through the prism of race. But children of the poor, whatever their background, have always had the highest dropout rate, the highest percentage scoring poorly on achievement tests, the highest percentage getting D's and F's. White, black, brown, or yellow—social class is a very reliable predictor of educational success. The higher the parental status, the more certain the child's chances for scholastic achievement; the lower the status, the more slender that chance. A massive study of economic inequities and the schools, *Education and Income,* bears striking witness to this fact. Undertaken in "Big City," an unnamed Midwestern metropolis believed to be Detroit, it showed that with one small exception all fourth-, sixth-, and eighth-graders whose family income was over $7,000 scored above grade level on the Iowa Achievement Test, while all those whose family income was below $7,000 without exception scored below grade level. The Iowa Test measures reading, vocabulary, language, work, and arithmetic skills. Many of the children of the poor have always fallen by the wayside educationally. The difference between the past and present is that owing to a variety of factors—drastically shrunk work opportunities for the unskilled, the tremendous population shift of low-income Negroes from rural to city areas, the civil rights movement, and the rise of black militancy—owing to factors such as these, more attention is being paid to children from economically disadvantaged families.

When social class and race are considered together, the inability of the public schools to reach and teach effectively most children outside the middle-class mainstream comes into sharpest focus of all. With few exceptions, the schools mirror more or less faithfully both the class and racial bias to be found overall in the larger society. They mirror the failure of the integration movement to catch hold, and they mirror the growing trend to separatism: Prior to the 1954 Supreme Court decision on integrated schools, 2.2 million Negro children attended all-Negro schools; in 1968, 2.5 million did so. Schools mirror the economic discrimination that has prevented the Negro from enjoying the nation's economic well-being: inner-city schools, most with overwhelmingly minority-group populations, get less moneys than schools in more favored areas. They mirror both the overt and covert types of social discrimination: So-called ability grouping separates the white and Negro children, and the most common staff deployment pattern is for whites and Negroes to teach in all-Negro and integrated schools and for white teachers alone to teach in all-white schools. They mirror the special discrimination that has been directed against the Negro male: By various stratagems Negro men in teaching were—and to a much lesser extent still are—denied access to high-level administrative jobs. (There's a sudden demand for —and resultant shortage of—highly qualified Negro administrators in some parts of the country.) Finally, the schools mirror the general public bias: White teachers are no more or less bigoted against Negroes than a comparable nonteaching group would be.

The schools very accurately mirror the frustration, the pain, the violence, the efforts at goodwill, the hope, the defeatism, the fury, the myriad impulses that characterize the American racial scene. More and more they mirror the racial confrontations that have become a marked feature of life in the late 1960's. Teachers in many metropolitan areas from New York City to Los Angeles voiced fear of black militant take-overs of their schools. (Not all such anxious teachers were white.) Some, white and black, described such takeovers as having been accomplished and the old administrations ousted. "I don't know how a teacher can survive today," muttered a white vice-principal in Los Angeles. "You don't know where you stand with the militants. There's no communication —if they want action, they'll uproot anyone. They came in and said, 'Either you do as we say, or we'll burn your school down.' And many of us think now that that's what they should have done. Burned the school down and started all over again. Now the teachers are leaving in droves."

This administrator was one of those who had been displaced from his old school as a result of black power demonstrations. He insisted that prior to the "intrusion of the outsiders," relationships between teachers and students in his old high school had been excellent. "They weren't learning," he admitted, "because by the time they came to us, it was too late. Something should have been done earlier. But we took a great deal of interest in them, and that counts for a lot, too."

A bit later in the interview, however, he sighed and said, "I think we do have to face the problem, and no question about it, we haven't. If you know you've failed in the set structure, then you have to find other ways of solving the problem. It would be nice to have a lot of money to spend, and all the fancy equipment and machinery . . . But it's irrelevant. When you're working on a one-to-one basis, and no one is looking over your shoulder to see if you're taking roll or giving tests, it can be done. . . ."

[2]

An eighth-grade English teacher who works in a Manhattan slum school, describing a typical workaday morning:

"I got to school at eight fifteen and punched in on the time clock. Picked up all my mail. There were the usual notices about attendance, late slips, clinic cards, directives for next week. Dragged up to the teacher's cafeteria and had a half a cup of coffee, then raced up to the fifth floor. There were two students leaning against the door as I got into my room. They weren't supposed to be there yet, and we had a three-minute conversation about that. I didn't want to hear any more stories, so I asked them to open a window. They did it wrong—you're not allowed to open the windows from the bottom, only from the top, and then only six inches. I told them to be quick about it because they're not allowed to open the windows. Then I threw them the keys and asked them to open the closet. I got out my roll book, took out the section sheets that they would carry around all day, looked at the schedule, and realized that today I'd have to make up four separate section sheets because the kids were going to two separate gym classes and two separate shop classes. And each little group has to have their own section sheet.

"By this time the students were straggling into the room, and I greeted a few of them and snarled at a few of them—you know, 'Don't knock over the desk,' 'Stop hitting her,' 'Throw your gum away,' 'Take your coat off and hang it in the closet,' 'Pick up the paper you threw on the floor,' 'Bring the potato chips up here.' Oh, and I have the kids trained to bring the knives to me in the morning; all the water guns, too, and all the Spaulding balls and nail polish, till three o'clock. And magic markers are not permitted to be used by the students because they have the unpleasant habit of writing 'Fuck you' on the walls.

"I lent four students pencils and got security from them, which was a system I'd learned—security meaning, 'Do you want a pencil? Give me something for the pencil. When you give me back the pencil, I give you back what you gave me.' Then I argued with three other students, yes, they must hang up their coats because that's the school rule. Then I took attendance by sight. 'Has anybody seen Tommy; he hasn't been in school for twenty days now.' Somebody yells out, 'Sick!' And somebody else yells out, 'Aw, shit, he's not sick.' 'All right, look, I don't want to know what his thing is, but if you see him, tell him that I have to send a truant slip, and he ought to get his body here for at least one day because then he can stay out another twenty days before I have to send out another truant slip. Give him the message, please.' The kid did show up the next day.

"Eight kids came in late. I had to change the attendance. But I also had to write down the names of the absentees on each of the four section sheets. Boys and girls separately. Then I had a state card to fill out. Then two kids came up with clinic cards. That means I had to fill out that they would leave fourth period for the eye clinic on Twenty-third Street. Then I had to write out a pass for each of these to go down to some special person and get a pass to leave the building. And I had to indicate that I'd done this on all of these sheets I already filled out. Then two kids came in carrying bass violins, and I asked, 'Where's your late pass?' 'Well, it took us a long time to come up the stairs.' 'Go get the pass.' We had a three-minute discussion on bass violins and passes before they went.

"Then finally the bell rang, and one kid dashed out the door. He's not supposed to do that until the second bell, and the principal would clobber me if he caught any of my kids out there. Then a parent walked in and said, 'I'm Willie Mae's mother, and I wanna talk to you.' I said, 'Won't you have a seat?' She sat down, and the children came running out of the room, and I had to call them back because I had to distribute the section sheets, and I had to appoint some monitors to take care of assorted things for the offices.

"So I had Willie Mae's mother sitting at my desk very irate because a letter was sent home to her about her daughter's cutting, and by that time the assistant principal, who was on the floor, was frothing at the mouth, standing at the door, literally screaming, 'Why are you not out on your post?' I pointed to the

parent, and the assistant principal ignored that and said, 'Mrs.
——, get out there on your post!' And then he said, 'Mrs. ——,
you left your bag on your desk! Don't ever leave your bag on
your desk!' So I mumbled a few words to the mother, got my
pocketbook, and went out on my post to direct traffic. It was
now three minutes after nine."

[3]

Compensatory education programs for ghetto children, designed to help them overcome so-called cultural deficits and
raise their educational levels, are started with great fanfare.
Some show much promise when they're in their initial stages,
being tried out in one or two schools. Invariably, once they're
expanded to cover a city system, they fail to produce the results
expected. Small groups of low-income youths make it through
school with a respectable education, especially when they're
given intensive instruction and their teachers and counselors
take a great deal of interest in them. Of 500 students in New
York City's College Discovery and Development Program, for
instance, 350 were graduated from high school and most have
gone on to college. Slum children aren't uneducable, as some
teachers are fond of rationalizing, but for the most part they're
not being educated. Statistics related to Negro children illustrate the point. In such critical skills as reading and verbal ability, low-income Negro children start slightly behind whites on
standard achievement tests, are more than one and a half years
behind by the time they reach the sixth grade, more than three
years behind when they're in the twelfth grade.

More striking even, because of the implications involved, is
another set of statistics. This one concerns low-income Negro children who are *ahead* of grade level in their early school
years. By the time they reach the upper primary or junior
high level, they, too, fall further and further behind. A
HARYOU study of central Harlem, for instance, reveals that 22
percent of third-grade students were reading above grade level,

while 30 percent were reading below grade level. But by the time they reached the sixth grade, only 12 percent were reading above grade level, while 81 percent were reading below it.[3] Such patterns are consistent not only for reading but for arithmetic, word knowledge, and general intelligence. As low-income youths grow older, they're caught in a triple bind: The pathology of ghetto life impinges more, they see more clearly that the future holds few rewards for them, and the ability of school and teacher and curriculum to grab them becomes much weaker.

In the metropolitan areas of the North and West, Negro youngsters are more than three times as likely as white youths to drop out of school by the time they are sixteen or seventeen. The barren educational experience Negroes have in schools is highlighted by comparisons of Selective Service Mental Test performances: During the period June, 1964, to December, 1965, 67 percent of Negro candidates but only 19 percent of whites failed the examination. And only 8 percent of all black students go on to college, compared with 50 percent of all high school graduates.

Against such bleak statistics, the black communities and the (mostly) white teachers face each other with increasing anger, bitterness, mistrust, and misconceptions—all the stuff that confrontations are made of. "I cried for education, but you white folks had your foot on my neck," screamed an anguished black mother at a U.S. Civil Rights Commission-sponsored conference on race and education. "We are being made the patsies and the villains for the whole country's neglect to the point where it makes it dangerous to go to work in certain areas," cried an outraged teacher at a school-community relations summer workshop in New York City, as colleagues cheered. "Business gets off the hook, government gets off the hook, and we are the fall guys!"[4] At an NEA staff meeting on urban problems David Spencer, chairman of New York City's IS 201 demonstration district, said, "When I go on a job, my boss looks for me to do the job, and if I'm not doing it, he'll call me and say,

'Look, Dave, I think you're a little slow, and if you can't pick it up, then you'll have to go.' Now I feel the same way about teachers. I'm tired of teachers who say, 'I've got two or three pupils here who are tops. Look what I have done.' What I see when I look is that there's twenty-four more who ain't done nothing." [5] And a matronly white teacher in Boulder, Colorado, exploded about being "so tired of taking the blame for all the problems of the Negro people. I don't like it any more than they do, but I didn't create the situation. Like every other teacher, I do the best—the very best—I can do under the circumstances. . . ."

In effect, the black communities accuse the teachers of being incompetent to teach black children. In effect, the teachers put the blame on a "cognitive deficit" that results from the cultural disadvantages under which the children labor. Both sides are trapped in a circle made all the more vicious and tragic for the extent of truth and amount of oversimplification both positions contain. Black children from ghetto neighborhoods generally don't get the kind of parental "preteaching" that schools heavily depend on in order to succeed. Nor have they learned to tolerate the boredom that permeates schools the way middle-class children have. At the same time most teachers haven't learned to utilize the strengths ghetto children have acquired. Both students and teachers, then, face profound difficulties.

[4]

A high school teacher in Cheyenne, Wyoming, commenting on his experiences with low-income students:

"The biggest struggle is with the low achievers and the poverty-level kids—these kids who are not going to college. They're turned off school, they're turned off the teacher, they hate books. They'll come into the class, no pencil, no paper, and say, 'I dare you to try and teach me something.' I'm learning to deal with them. I'm putting my books away, they're no good anyway—Galileo, the books don't even say he had trouble with the Church. So I say to the kids, 'What do you want to study?' They say, 'We want to study hippies.' Okay, so they'll study hippies—that means we'll also study Zen Buddhism, American Indians, romantic poets, the expatriates of Paris in the late 1920's—I try to teach them as much as I can about the world in relation to their interests.

"I could relate all year's history to the Cheyenne Police Department and to marijuana and to sex, and I'd really have them. But I teach them as much as I can, and I don't really know—I've been able to do this so far without getting into any trouble, and I think the principal knows what I'm doing. I'm not sure—presumably he reads my lesson-plan books.

"Well, what it all does to me personally is to keep me up nights wondering whether I should call the kids into the office for using vulgar language in class, embarrassing girls . . . I'm determined that at our next faculty meeting I'm going to throw the whole question of discipline on the table and hash it out. We're all in the same position, and we all know it, and we talk about it quietly in the lounge, but it has to be brought out in the open. The thing that has hindered its coming out in the open is that all teachers know that part of their ability as a teacher and part of the evaluation which they will receive as teachers is whether they're able to maintain discipline and whether they're able to handle their problems in the classroom.

"But the real problem with the kids is reaching them. I'm trying to reach them. It's a rough business. I should be doing a lot of reading. But this is the problem: If you're trying to reach turned off kids, you've got to spend so much of your time in the how of teaching that you won't have any time left for the what, and there should be a balance."

[5]

In the wake of books like Jonathan Kozol's *Death at an Early Age,* Herbert Kohl's *36 Children,* and James Herndon's *The*

Way It's Spozed to Be, all written by former inner-city teachers, the impression is left that ghetto schools are filled with racists, sadists, psychopathic, and hopelessly ineffectual teachers who could not possibly last in any other kind of school. There are plenty such around, and it's no trick at all to collect the anecdotes that prove their existence. For instance, the San Francisco teacher who told a colleague, "Hitler had the right idea, but he picked on the wrong people," and the Chicago teacher who deliberately gives bright Negro children lower grades than they deserve, and the Newark teacher who cuffs his third-graders and pulls their hair when they are in the yard, and the all-too-common expression of disgust heard in teachers' lounges everywhere with reference to Negro youngsters—"those animals."

Not to be ignored, however, is the other extreme—the teachers whose commitment to their students is absolute. Too often overlooked in the general condemnation of ghetto teachers, such men and women represent the highest level of personal and professional integrity. A typical example is Betty, a twenty-five-year-old white girl teaching in a Brooklyn slum section. She tutors some of her slower second-graders after school several times a week, makes home visits and invites parents to her home, encourages them to telephone her at home to discuss problems, has discarded the standard curriculum as wholly inappropriate to her youngsters ("The assistant principal knows but hasn't discussed it openly with me, and hasn't said anything to the principal"), devises social studies sections that make even the kids testing in the dull-normal range take off and join in the discussions, is learning the numbers racket (in which many of her children are involved) in hopes of working up a practical math curriculum around it, and is active in a neighborhood action group.

Such white teachers are unusual, but more are coming to work in ghetto schools all the time. They often find themselves in difficulty with conservative administrators and alienated from the other white teachers, who can neither understand their intense commitment to the black community nor their willingness to put such prodigious amounts of time and energy into their work. Between the extremes of vicious racism and intense dedication, what kinds of teachers are there in ghetto slum schools? Hopeful newcomers. Teachers transferred from other schools (sometimes because of transgressions, or because they have rocked the boat too hard). Teachers who no longer want the high-pressure atmosphere of a high-achievement white middle-class school. Teachers who have been in the school for decades, before it deteriorated, and have prerogatives they don't want to lose. Most of all, average people with training that's inadequate for a situation requiring heightened sensitivity and awareness, self-confidence, an ability to suspend stereotyped beliefs, and a thorough grounding in anthropology, sociology, and psychology. In many instances, ghetto school-teachers of whatever background must contend not only with difficult teaching assignments but with the minutiae, petty tyrannies, and bureaucratic boondoggling characteristic of many ghetto schools.

As the U.S. Riot Commission Report has pointed out, even with available federal funds ghetto schools are often overcrowded, understaffed, short of textbooks and other materials; in addition to which they have the lowest per-pupil expenditure, the highest turnover of teachers and students, and fewer experienced teachers than do middle-class schools. For many white teachers ghetto schools are a kind of educational Siberia. (Schools with special facilities, like New York City's More Effective Schools, are an exception: They have waiting lines of teachers.) The Coleman Report observes that teachers in predominantly Negro schools are less likely to want to remain there, and less likely to believe their schools have a good reputation with other teachers. At a Cleveland hearing on racial isolation in the public schools, a teacher told how he felt when he first learned he'd been assigned to an almost all-Negro school.[6] Candidly, he said, "Well, I think I was a little bit disappointed personally. I knew . . . that any time a school is predominantly Negro . . . that there is a stigma that goes with it, that it just can't be first class. I feel that this is true not only in the minds of Negroes, but also in the minds of most whites." A Los Angeles elementary school teacher, interviewed for this book, reported on the reception she received when she was transferred from a Negro school in the southern section of town to a middle-class school in west Los Angeles: "Some of the teachers looked down their noses at me. And some said, 'All those years in south Los Angeles—how could you stand it?' I was furious. I liked that school. And some of my children learned."

Having little familiarity with black students and their life-styles, white teachers often are at a loss how to reach them academically. A study by Patrick J. Groff of San Diego State College, for instance, suggests that teachers have strongly ambivalent feelings about some crucial aspects of their relationships with slum children: whether they should take a gentle approach or be authoritarian and make strong external demands; whether they should show "superior strength" in view of the child's "respect for physical prowess"; whether they should consider the child anti-intellectual or believe him to have respect for knowledge and education.[7]

Furthermore, the white teacher is much more apt to be harsh in his judgment of the black child than the black teacher is. In a study with white and black elementary school teachers in a low-income Midwestern district, David Gottlieb of Michigan State University found that much higher percentages of white than black teachers complained of parental disinterest and discipline problems.[8] Almost twice as many white as black teachers saw the youngsters as "athletic"; conversely, nearly twice as many black teachers saw them as "ambitious." Black teachers by considerable margins perceived the children as "cooperative" and "fun-loving." But white teachers in overwhelming numbers, as contrasted with black teachers, looked upon the kids as "high-strung," "impetuous," "lazy," "moody," and "talkative." Mulling over his findings, Gottlieb speculated that "the Negro teachers are less critical and less pessimistic in their evaluations of these students than the white, probably because many of them have themselves come from backgrounds similar to that of their students and yet have managed to overcome racial barriers to attain positions of responsibility and status."

"You take a brand-new white girl," explained a Negro teacher on the West Coast. "She's maybe twenty-one, twenty-two years old. She's led a nice protected life. She goes to the university and teaches in an environment where the kids are gifted or they're smart or they're nice in these demonstration schools. Very few are problems. Well, they come to San Diego, and they barely know what a colored person is. And then this white girl gets thrown down in the southeast section. She finds the kids fighting among themselves. She finds the language they use offensive. Most of the time the girls don't adjust to this . . . The teachers themselves are partly responsible for this, because if a teacher in a high school sees all these kids who are troublemakers in his class, he goes down to the counselor and says, 'Look, buddy, what are you doing packing my class with all these meatheads?' And the counselor will say, 'Oh well, I thought you could handle them.' And the teacher will say, 'No, thanks.' But the new teacher doesn't know enough to complain, doesn't have the power, doesn't have the experience." And many quit teaching within a few weeks after first entering the classroom.

There is now the conviction among some black power intellectuals that white teachers simply can't reach black children. All of the black teachers interviewed for this book flatly rejected the thesis. Some felt it's harder for white teachers to reach black youths—"especially now with things so polarized," said a Negro teacher in Denver, one who had been very active in the integration movement. "The new crop of kids is questioning more—questioning black as well as white teachers." Some felt that teachers—all teachers, regardless of ethnic background—would have to be more involved in the community. "They'll have to take part more in the social, religious, and economic life to reach black youths," commented a Negro teacher in Los Angeles. "Just being in school from nine to three and then running off to their 'other world' isn't going to do it." Some felt that things in the ghetto—not only in regard to schools but with respect to all aspects of ghetto life—wouldn't really change until some of the socially conscious young black men and women now being educated returned to the ghetto and themselves assumed more control over the institutions.

Whatever their viewpoints, however, they didn't go along with the rule-of-thumb that whites per se can't reach blacks. "Given the life experiences of the black student today, the teacher comes in with more liabilities if he's white than if he's black," explained the human relations head of a city board of education on the West Coast, himself a Negro. "The black has his own liabilities, but we feel they're not of such a dangerous nature to our children. I think a sensitive teacher, no matter what the color of his skin, can do a good job. But there aren't that many around."

In 1968 Pennsylvania State University involved itself in a program for school dropouts and a study of the program's results.[9] One facet of the evaluation was an attempt to distinguish between successful and unsuccessful teachers of slum youths. The successful teachers didn't begin immediately to teach. They started with an awareness of the "fear and frustration" with which the dropouts faced academic work, their deep personal sense of inadequacy, their many defense mechanisms. The teachers accurately perceived that the youths needed to sense acceptance and gain a measure of self-worth before academic learning could mean anything to them. And in their teaching approaches, these teachers deliberately capitalized on the students' strong points, stimulating their involvement. In other words, they started where the youths were. Strongly stressed was the personal element between the ghetto youth and his teacher.

For the average white teacher, somewhat ethnocentric to begin with, this is hardly the easiest assignment. He has no inclination to bring the relationship to a personal level. He's group-oriented to begin with, as a teacher; furthermore, he has never really come to grips with his own prejudices. He's faced with thirty youths in a situation that (many teachers insist) calls for close to a one-to-one relationship.

For several summers the New York City Board of Education ran summer institutes for teachers specifically working in ghetto areas. One of the purposes of the institutes was to bring the teachers to have a more sympathetic outlook toward the students. But when the Center for Urban Education evaluated the institutes, they found them badly run, poorly taught, and producing no change in the teachers.[10] Though they got paid for attending, many of the teachers slept through the presentations, read the papers, or did their nails, and no one took notes. Some expressed open hostility to minority groups. Some said they had become more hostile after being abused by community leaders. In a role-playing situation, according to one CUE observer, "the participant portraying the parent depicted her as being illiterate, with no husband but with many boyfriends, careless with her responsibilities, a liar, holding ambitions for her child not in keeping with her own *laissez faire* manner. When she indicated that her son 'wants to be a doctor,' the class laughed."

When the participant-teachers were queried by CUE about what they would do differently in the fall when they returned to their classrooms, 80 percent of their answers had to do with content and curriculum. Only 20 percent related to interaction with students. The CUE report concluded, "It would seem . . . that the benefits the participants received from the institutes were limited to those things they can do without any serious personal involvement with the children." Shortly after the report came out, the institutes were dropped.

Many teachers who do make well-meaning attempts to relate to ghetto youths and children do so under the old "melting pot" doctrine, that it is essential to eradicate differences. Thus, instead of "starting where the child is," a pedagogical imperative that supposedly was taught to them when they were in training, they insist on attempting to change the child to fit an educational system that has failed him in the first place.

"Even if the teacher understands the child's view of life," observes Deborah Meier, an early childhood teacher who has taught in ghetto schools in New York City and Chicago, "she sees her first and foremost task in presenting him with a different and superior view." [11] This subtly confirms the student's already poor self-image. Rather than giving the child a chance to choose from among a variety of approaches to life, the teacher seeks to "erase as much as possible of the memories, associations, and skills with which he comes to her." Though she may seek to improve his manners through the guise of play, she's both "imposing and censuring." It's her standards, not his life, that he's forced to explore at play, and he "does not lose sight of the fact that his own world is despised by his teacher as a wrong model, a bad model, or at the very least, an irrelevant one." But it's his own world he must go back to when his teacher leaves him, so "out of his need for protection and security and out of family loyalty," he's forced to "resist any entrapment that might immobilize him in dealing with his environment." The problem with the lower-class school's destructiveness toward its students isn't that it's too middle-class, Mrs. Meir concludes, "but because unlike good middle-class education (whether at home or at school), it does not respect children's learning drives and experiential backgrounds."

It's a situation fraught with tragic irony: To cope with her set of circumstances, the teacher must attempt to change the child in fundamental ways; to cope with his, he must forcibly resist (or pretend to acquiesce).

[6]

"Teacher expectation" isn't a panacea that will magically bring a student's reading level up. Nevertheless, it's a potent factor in the interaction between teacher and student.

That teachers expect a much higher level of accomplishment from middle-class than from lower-class students is something sociologists studying the schools have noted for many years. But teacher expectation really became newsworthy in 1967, when Robert Rosenthal of Harvard University and Lenore F. Jacobson, an elementary school principal in south San Francisco, published the results of an ingenious experiment they had conducted in an elementary school with a low-income Mexican-American population in south San Francisco.[12] The teachers in the school were tricked into believing that certain children could—on the basis of what purportedly were legitimate but newly developed intelligence tests—be expected to bloom intellectually. Actually, the researchers chose the children at random. What happened? In the first and second grades—though not in the fourth and fifth—the children arbitrarily designated as "spurters" actually did make gains far greater than were being made by children in a control group. Moreover, these children, though randomly selected, were now being seen by their teachers as "happier," "more curious," "more interesting," and having a "better chance of being successful in later life" than the other kids.

Since the largest gains were in the area of reasoning rather than verbal intelligence, Rosenthal and Jacobson figured that the teachers did not necessarily talk to the designated children more but communicated their expectations in "a subtler feature of the interaction of the teacher and her pupils. Her tone of voice, facial expression, touch and posture may be the means by which—probably quite unwittingly—she communicates her expectations to the pupils."

One of the more intriguing aspects of the Rosenthal-Jacobson findings was that when control group children—those not designated as "spurters"—made unexpected intellectual gains, their teachers failed to hold them in higher esteem. On the contrary, "the more they gained, the less favorably they were rated . . . Evidently it is likely to be difficult for a slow-track child, even if his IQ is rising, to be seen by his teacher as well-adjusted and as a potentially successful student." Even if a child changes for the better, it seems, strongly held preconceived notions on the teacher's part do not necessarily undergo revision. It follows, therefore, that some academically successful low-income children succeed in spite of their teachers, not because of them.

The Rosenthal-Jacobson teacher-expectation study has been attacked on methodological and analytical grounds, but few critics argue against the basic contention that expectation is a factor in the creation of change—or in keeping change from taking place. Study after study and informed description after informed description tells of a defeatism common to many ghetto schools—one that infects almost every member of the instructional staff from the administrators on down. Too many principals feel, as did those cited in a report on a major metropolitan school system, that "there isn't too much we can do with our children. Most of them are slow learners." [13] One study showed 43 percent of the principals in low-status schools but only 17 percent of the ones in high-status schools wanting to obtain principalships of greater responsibility and more prestige.[14] Weak or uncaring principals are especially deleterious to ghetto schools. Too many teachers pick up the cue from their principals and lower their expectations, their hope and their enthusiasm for teaching the children. Yet, as has been demonstrated in several inner-city schools in New York City, Philadelphia and elsewhere, a strong and positively oriented principal can bring up the achievement level of the students in his school.

And too many children are caught in the kind of vicious circle described by Helen H. Davidson and Gerhard Lang in

Journal of Experimental Education: The kids do badly in school. They have a negative perception of their teachers' feelings toward them. They do worse as a result of those negative perceptions. This in turn aggravates the teachers' negative attitude, etc., etc.[15] The principal finding of the Coleman Report —that Negro children achieve more in integrated schools with a predominantly middle-class clientele—may well be associated in part with the higher expectations had by everybody, from principals to pupils, in such schools.

The belief that low-income children have low potential and are going to do badly becomes institutionalized in the common practice of "tracking," grouping children according to ability. With intelligence or reading tests the most usual basis for such grouping, the ghetto poor almost always find themselves in the lowest ability group, the slowest classes, the general or vocational (nonacademic) tracks. Both intelligence and reading tests have been bitterly attacked on grounds of cultural bias and reliability. That large numbers of ghetto children need remedial or compensatory education whether they are located in integrated or segregated schools is a fact of life. If tracking meant that they would get such help and then be moved on to higher-level tracks, there would be a sound educational basis for it. In actual practice tracking most often becomes an educational excuse for segregation. Slow-tracked kids get the inexperienced or apathetic teachers, they get watered-down curriculum, they get an atmosphere that says they are dumb and cannot learn. But they hardly ever get the chance to move out of a milieu so heavily laden with a self-fulfilling, self-defeating atmosphere of failure, even when the school is integrated.

". . . I felt good when I was with my class, but when they went and separated us—that changed us," said a Midwestern high school girl, describing the effects of tracking upon herself and her classmates. "That changed our ideas, our thinking, the way we thought about each other and turned us to enemies about each other—because they said I was dumb, and they were smart." [16] A San Diego high school teacher, vehemently attacking the tracking system, said, "It's devastating. I have some students who have been tracked—they've been together so long they know every move each of them will make. Just by a look they can get a conspiracy going. Every substitute teacher that comes, says, 'This is the worst experience I've ever had in my life.' And I know he isn't exaggerating, because I have it every day with them. There are five students in there who, given the chance, would be serious about their work. But it's controlled in a different direction. So this one group has no model of what a good student could be. Either in his attitude toward learning something or in his behavior."

Almost inevitably, it seems, the physical tracking of the children dovetails with the mental track upon which many school people consciously or unconsciously operate. It's a mental track that almost literally rejects the possibility of academic success for minority-group children. No more eloquent proof exists than the harrowing stories concerned teachers everywhere tell of bright or even gifted black or Hispanic youngsters. These are youngsters who have displayed high levels of academic achievement but whom guidance counselors nevertheless shunt to noncollege tracks, or discourage from applying for college admission, on the grounds that they aim too high. And everywhere, too, one hears of instances in which concerned teachers (white or black) fight such bias on behalf of individual children for whom they have particular regard.

[7]

"The school is supposed to be a reinforcement of the home life," said the fourth-grade teacher who has taught in several ghetto schools in New York City. "But if the home life is so terrible, it's a completely different environment from home. And this presents tremendous amounts of friction because what the kids see at school isn't what they see at home, and vice versa. As a teacher you're an authority figure. Your role is parental insofar as you're there to provide certain things for the children. One is emotional warmth. Another is some kind of empathy or compassion for them. Another, that they have to feel you care about them. They need something from you. The factual knowledge can come only when they feel comfortable with you in other ways. On any level, if the kids don't feel some kind of interest or warmth on your part, you've had it. You're a caretaker, guardian, custodian, parent, prison warden, and teacher. And very often, at least in my case, the teacher [instructor] role comes last. I could spend the entire day mediating fights and breaking up arguments and maintaining discipline in the room, if I get them on the wrong day."

[8]

"The first year in the inner-city school is the testing period. That's when most of them drop out," said a veteran eighth-grade teacher who has taught in several East Coast ghetto schools. "Some teachers only last a couple of weeks; you come to find out they've walked into the office, said, 'I can't take it,' and quit cold. PhD's come in full of ideas but can't stand the gaff and leave to go into college teaching. The kids test unmercifully. The weak, effeminate male is backed up against the wall. If the teacher survives that first year, he'll make it. Even though he doesn't have the same kids next year, word passes around: This is a tough teacher, a tough class. It helps if the male teacher is physically powerful, but he has to have the brains to know how to use his power. But all don't have to be physical fighters; they can handle the kids in other ways."

Other teachers can do it, he said, by never smiling. Each teacher knows when to use his own technique, knows when to turn his back on something and pretend it had not happened. Some of the women also use physical force, the teacher said, slapping girls with 18-inch rulers to control classes; they are, he added, considered to be some of the best teachers.

"A pattern of violence expected from students and counter-force from teachers creates a brutalizing atmosphere in which any learning would be hard," notes Dr. Kenneth Clark in his study of Harlem, *Dark Ghetto*.[17] Discipline becomes the end, not the means, and education in many ghetto schools principally consists in keeping order. "I fight more as a teacher than I ever did as a kid, I'll tell you that," said an inner-city junior high school teacher, formerly a cab driver. He described a recent incident in which two former students (dropouts) had jumped a fellow teacher after class let out one day, and he'd come to his colleague's rescue.

Truly disturbed children, the ones who suddenly and periodically erupt into violence or withdraw into utter passivity, are the ones that frustrate and anguish teachers most. They set off the others, teachers say, and they can't cope with them.

An inner-city elementary school teacher talked of a disruptive boy in her bilingual class. ("You only need one to make the class a shambles.") One day he climbed atop a bank of cabinets at the back of the classroom and whooped it up during the middle of an English lesson. He refused to listen to her and would not come down. A consultant from one of the local universities happened to be in the room at the time. "That woman told me I was paying too much attention to the child and that's what the problem was," said the teacher, outraged. "Can you imagine? The boy was climbing on top of the cabinets, and she told me I was paying too much attention to him!"

Untrained to work with such children, possibly not fully adept at classroom management, probably unwittingly doing many things to bring on disruptions, many teachers would like nothing better than to see them out of the classroom.

Actually, in most areas, the situation with respect to disturbed children in ghetto schools is a shambles. (There are plenty of disturbed children in middle-class schools, too, but their parents can afford private treatment.) In a few cities teachers have won the unilateral right to remove from the classroom any child they deem to be disruptive. It's a dangerous power in view of the fact that some teachers consider any ob-

streperous child, any behavior problem, as "disruptive."
("They keep sending kids down to me to handle," said a principal in Cheyenne, Wyoming, disgustedly. "Their position is,
all they want to do is teach.") Frequently, children are suspended from school or transferred to another school entirely.
These procedures help at times, but far too often they are used
thoughtlessly, punitively, or simply to get rid of the problem.
According to the New York Civil Liberties Union and other
private organizations, a growing number of suspensions in New
York involve youngsters who are not disturbed in the ordinary
sense but who take part in demonstrations, defy dress codes, and
hold nonconformist political views. Though parents are to be
notified in long-term suspension cases, this procedure is often
disregarded by school people who are eloquent with respect to
their own due process rights but lack the same fervor when it
comes to children.

Some schools in New York and elsewhere have special guidance classes, and a number of districts throughout the country
have special schools for disturbed children. Most do not, and
the quality of such classes and such schools ranges from excellent to brutal, many of them weighed toward the latter end of
the spectrum. A teacher in a Harlem-based junior high school
told of "the huts, the cages in back, where 'career guidance' is
located. The principal is very careful not to know what's going
on out there." What goes on? Forty-five boys who are incipient
high school dropouts are placed in the "cages" at the end of
the eighth grade, ostensibly to prepare them for some kind of
vocation. "More than half are above average in intelligence,
you know. Beautiful, clever kids who know where it's at and
give everybody a hard time . . . Pushers, thieves . . . a
sprinkling of morons, too. Usually the first month out there
the kids literally get bounced off the walls—money is set aside
every year to repair the windows. The kids challenge the teachers to a fight, and the teachers have to establish that they can
beat any kid in the class. So only teachers are hired who can do
this . . . The teachers teach the bright ones separately. And

they ram it, you know, with a steel ruler in one hand—'You're gonna learn this because I said so. And if you don't learn it, I'll break your ass.' The bright ones usually learn more in that year than in all the eight before. And for that, heaven be praised."

A Los Angeles teacher told of working in "social adjustment classes" for extremely disturbed children. The only criterion for entry is an IQ over 40. She gets third- and fourth-graders who cannot spell "cat." Though she has had psychology classes at UCLA's Psychology Clinic, she gets no advice, no help, to deal with the eight or ten hostile and destructive children out of a class of twelve. She must develop her own highly individualized program and has spent hundreds of dollars of her own money buying equipment. She talked of how draining it is to be with these troubled youngsters all day, every day, and she talked of the satisfactions: "Seeing these little boys who were repeating school being won over, being upset if they have to miss school, bringing them up to grade level." But many children are totally excluded from school until there is an opening, she said. They simply wait at home, doing nothing, because there are not enough facilities for them. And in many instances the classes are run by teachers who simply make of it a "punitive situation." On the whole, she said, "social adjustment classes are a wastebasket for extremely disturbed children." If nothing else, society is consistent: It permits the pathology-inducing ghettos to exist and then takes as callous a view of the children spawned from them.

[9]

Both for the child born into ghetto life, who in time becomes a student in one of his neighborhood's schools, and for the man or woman who eventually comes to teach in that school, it's a world that neither of them made. A world which, in many respects by now, has them reacting to each other as adversaries. Yet it is one in which both must function as best they can, each with his particular complement of human characteristics, each adapting to the given circumstances in ways that sustain him psychically.

Whatever the reasons that brought them to ghetto schools, most teachers are not so cynical that initially they do not want to do a good teaching job. Within the framework of their talents, they try. Some try very hard indeed, in the face of a multitude of obstacles. Some relatively few ghetto teachers enjoy the exhilaration of success, of seeing their pupils flower as persons and grow academically. But over a period of time if a teacher's efforts bear little fruit, he tries less hard. More and more he resigns himself to the specter of failure. Yet a ghetto teacher no more than a ghetto child can accept personal failure without serious damage to his self-esteem. And so, like the child, he builds up the defenses that will protect him from the denigration of his self.

In an unconscious process, then, he de-escalates his personal and professional commitment—a process that for some teachers takes months, for others, many years. The continual parade of angry, violent, passive, or withdrawn children becomes less shocking, more blunted, to eyes and ears. That he is really not reaching many of the children becomes more bearable as he weaves about himself a network of insulating myths: The children are stupid, they are animals, the parents don't care, the failure lies with teachers earlier in the youngsters' lives. He becomes increasingly anesthetized to the spectacle of needful youngsters whose needs he cannot fulfill, cannot even fully comprehend. The hypocrisies to which he must become a part in playing the game of "education" do not seem so hypocritical, after all.

The teacher may become a law-and-order educator, running a quiet and unproductive class with a bunch of kids made docile. He may channel his energies into being a pal, inviting kids to dinner, to outings, counseling them—abandoning any hope or pretense of teaching them to read and write and add. He may concentrate his efforts on the two or three kids who are self-starters, whose highly motivated personalities will ensure them success. He may simply featherbed as best he can through the months and years. He may withdraw into his private little world, doggedly "teaching" classes out of control, oblivious to the noise and confusion around him.

However he does it, he finds the defensive ways that will protect his innermost self from failure and futility. Defensiveness is a bond he shares with the children he cannot teach, and the irony of it is that neither of them knows it.

[11]

The School as Fortress

"YOU parents yell about this and scream about that. But in the end you're going to take your children out and put them in private schools, or let them finish naturally and they'll graduate out. And you'll be gone. But I was here in the school before you came, and I'll still be here when you'll have forgotten all about the school. I'll be here until my thirty years are up."

The woman who voiced those remarks was a very bitter and disillusioned elementary school teacher on Manhattan's Upper West Side. She and the parents to whom her words were directed had just emerged from an angry meeting of a parent-teacher-principal council, a council set up in this school in the wake of the teacher strike of 1968. New York City is a special situation: The massive strike was ideologically and politically, more than educationally, centered; it brought teachers and parents close together or drove wide chasms between them in ways altogether different from the normal teacher-parent relationship, where the focus is on Johnny's reading or Mary's arithmetic problems. In the increasingly aggrieved, hostile

219

contacts between white teachers and black or Hispanic parents, there are deep emotions at play by now that transcend immediate educational concern.

Yet even in the best of circumstances the relationship between the parents of a school-going child and that child's teacher isn't an easy one. This is especially true on the elementary and junior high school levels, where parent-teacher contacts are much more frequent than they are on the high school level. By its very nature the parent-teacher relationship produces strong tensions that inhibit easy human contact. The fact of educational life that that angry Manhattan elementary school teacher was referring to—parents' involvement with the school's being so fleeting in comparison with that of the career teachers'—is one element responsible for producing this tension. There are a number of others. Willard Waller, whose observations of teachers produced a classic sociological study, *The Sociology of Teaching*, was convinced that "parents and teachers are natural enemies," each destined to put down the other.[1] Waller studied teachers in the early 1930's, before teacher strikes became habitual, before public schools became battlegrounds, so these factors played no part in his conclusions. "The chasm is frequently covered over," he wrote, "for neither parents nor teachers wish to admit to themselves the uncomfortable implications of their animosity, but on occasion it can make itself clear enough."

Strong stuff. Many parents—and teachers—will reject it outright. They'll point to all the instances of parent-teacher cooperation, to the way both groups work together on projects of one kind or another for the betterment of the schools. They'll say that in general parents and teachers want exactly the same things—learning to take hold, children to move from grade to grade knowing more, thinking more, becoming more skillful in meeting the demands of their environment. They'll say that in most schools (big-city schools excepted) there is an atmosphere of friendly cooperation. All this is true. Yet it's also true that the parent-teacher relationship is a paradoxical one:

The very things that unite these two groups also serve to create wide gulfs between them. Their goals may be the same: Both want the same good things to happen to the children in school. But the investment they make in those children is quite different. The way they view the goals—the way they view failure to reach those goals, for that matter—is quite different. They operate, one might say, from very dissimilar psychological bases.

The parent's investment is relatively simple. He wishes his child would do well in school, and often he brings to that wish impulses arising from his own ego needs (not an unmixed blessing). The teacher's investment is much more complicated since he represents not only himself individually but a profession and an institution as well, and since his place in the community has a different perspective from the parent's. Even if teachers as a group weren't as security-minded as they are, this alone would force them into a protectionist role. Yes, teachers and parents work together in some respects, but until very recently at any rate, it has been more of an accommodation they have worked out to ameliorate the effect of the tensions between them.

Learning to live together is not the same as wanting to live together. The relative paucity of teacher-parent friendships— not something superficial like having tea together once a year but real, deep, warm friendships—illustrates that. In a study of teacher prestige and how its level can be raised, educational researcher Don-Chean Chu commented that teachers "often find themselves on the fringes of the social community." [2] When it analyzed the attitudes of 199 New York State communities in 1963, the New York State Citizens Committee for the Public Schools discovered that in only 33 percent of the communities do parents generally invite their children's teachers to their homes.[3] *No* community indicated that its residents invited teachers in as often as they did other acquaintances. Seven years earlier, by contrast, 13 percent of the communities indicated that their residents did invite teachers as often.

In other words, parents and teachers don't generally form friendships; whatever close contact there was is diminishing. This is in marked contrast to such professions as medicine and law, where friendships between the professional and his client are more common. (New York City may be in the vanguard of a new trend, however, since as a result of the decentralization issue, teachers and parents are working closely together outside of school and forming relationships on a new basis.)

This is not to claim that no teacher ordinarily has a friendship with a nonteacher, of course, only to suggest that it's most common for teachers to socialize with other teachers and least common for them to socialize with parents of children in their schools. The custom seems so natural it's simply accepted, and when an interviewer brings it up, the most frequent reaction is on the order of, "Well, I never thought about it, but it's true." A man who had been teaching school in Denver for forty-two years talked about his friends, mentioned that a few among them were *not* teachers, and, quite without realizing the implication, said, "They've even forgotten that I'm a teacher." A Cheyenne teacher told of the time, not long before, when she, her husband, and her children were having dinner in a Chinese restaurant. They encountered one of the pupils in her class and his parents also eating there. This time it was the parent who unconsciously uttered the thought, "Teachers are a breed apart." What she actually said was, "That's strange, I never think of teachers as having children!"

But of course the feeling of apartness is not one-sided. In talking with teachers all over the nation, one gains the impression that teachers so rarely invite parents to *their* homes as a way of initiating a friendship as to render it statistically unmeasurable. There are walls between parents and teachers, walls symptomatic of the public school itself in its relationship to the wider community, for in some respects the school takes on the characteristics of a fortress, and at all costs the enemy must be kept outside.

[2]

"Has the public image of the teacher changed? Many would insist that it has slipped from a place next to motherhood, love, and religion down the scale to a spot close to mothers-in-law, income tax, and measles."

—from an article in the *Minnesota Journal of Education*.[4]

[3]

How teachers and parents relate is governed in part by the teacher's place in the community. Tensions would sprout in any event, but their intensity is related to the prestige of the teacher among those who, in effect, make up his constituency. Teachers who reside in districts where they are highly respected, where they are numbered among the most important people in the community, are apt to view parents quite differently from teachers who live in areas where they are taken for granted or, worse, held in fairly low esteem. Putting it another way, it seems reasonable to suppose that a strong correlation exists between the extent to which a teacher feels he's valued and the degree to which he perceives parents as a threat.

Actually, while communities do exist where teachers are highly respected, they are relatively few in number. In some parts of the country one hears from teachers that they feel *less* well regarded now than they did two or three decades ago. This doesn't necessarily mean that lower esteem is related to lower teacher standards. It may be that higher levels of education are more common among the population as a whole; hence, teachers are held less in awe than in the past. At any rate, teachers do not occupy a very lofty place in most communities, as an NEA poll taken in 1966 makes very clear. Fewer than three out of every ten teachers saw themselves blessed with high prestige. Nearly two-thirds of this nationwide sample of teachers characterized their prestige, as they saw it, as "medium." One out of ten thought that in their communities teachers were held in very low esteem. The downward trend of teacher prestige is underscored by the fact that three years earlier a similar NEA poll showed a larger percentage of teachers judging their prestige as high and a smaller percentage judging it as low. Furthermore, the earlier poll showed that close to half the teachers felt they deserved more prestige than the community actually gave them. In effect, they distinctly felt shortchanged in terms of status.

Women teachers consider educators to occupy a higher place than men teachers do—probably because teaching is considered to be a much better-paying job for women than for men. Ironically, in the South, where teacher pay is lowest, teacher prestige is very high. "By Southern thinking, teaching is a thing that's extra special," said a high school teacher from King's Mountain, a community of 10,000 in the southwestern farming country of North Carolina. "I know of instances where we have some people in industry who came into the vocational program, and left higher paying jobs to do so, because to them teaching had prestige. And then they were surprised to learn that they didn't get paid for prestige."

By far the more common attitude, especially in well-to-do areas, is the one expressed by another high school teacher, this one teaching (but not living) in affluent Cherry Creek, Colorado: "A large segment of the population expects the public education system to get students into the college of the parents' choice. If the schools will do this, the parents are satisfied with them, with the teachers. If the student doesn't learn very much, doesn't receive a great deal of controversial-type stimulating knowledge, or become excited about the process of learning—really, a lot of parents don't care. Does the community accord teachers respect? No and yes. Most of the parents haven't even thought of the question. But there is a core of informed, concerned parents who rally behind teachers, who realize the quality of the educational system is directly tied to the quality of teachers. They fight for us. But they're a minority."

On the other hand, it can be an exceedingly painful experience for some teachers not fully sure of their own competence when the informed, concerned parents constitute the vast majority of the community. A high school teacher in Princeton, New Jersey, where many parents are affiliated with Princeton University, Educational Testing Service, Radio Corporation of America, or other brain-powered institutions, said that some good teachers enjoy the stimulation and invite parents in to talk about their specialties. But some other good teachers are reluctant to take jobs there. "It's a devastating feeling for teachers to come to the first Parents' Night in October. Here she is, facing the head of the University math department, or the director of testing at ETS, or a physicist from RCA, and now she's going to talk about math. They'll be kind, and they'll say, 'Okay,' or they'll say, 'You're wrong,' and try to help her, but it's pressure. And teachers have left in the middle of the year because they couldn't take this pressure."

[4]

Even when there's internal strife, most school systems close ranks as soon as danger is perceived from the outside. It's an automatic reaction, common to all bureaucracies, to put up fortifications against interference from the outside world. Inevitably, as sociologist Howard S. Becker put it in a long essay on secrecy and solidarity in school systems, schools tend to "try to become self-contained systems of power . . . erect[ing] barriers designed to keep outsiders on the outside and preventing the surround[ing] society from directly affecting the institution's operation." When a really threatening onslaught against those barriers is made—witness the movement toward community control—the resulting battle is apt to be violent.[5]

As far as the schools are concerned, they do not, of course, see themselves as putting up defenses against parents. They are quick to point out that well, yes, public education should be public, but education today is a highly complex technical process that demands a great deal of expertise. Hence, they say, only those persons having that expertise—the professionals —can be and should be directly involved in making the decisions and carrying out the policies that lead to successful teaching and learning. "Consequently, the phrase 'parent participation' for most school personnel has come to mean only such activities as conferences between individual parents and teachers, monthly PTA meetings, and booster clubs for extracurricular activities," observed Warner Bloomberg, Jr., and John Kincaid of the University of Wisconsin's Department of Urban Affairs in a study of the issue. "Such devices give mom and pop much more of a feeling of having a 'real part' to play in the life of the school, provide a means of personal understanding of the school's educational tasks, and enable adults in the community to make useful, though relatively minor, contributions of time, money and personal interest to the life of the school. Relatively few professional educators or critics have questioned the adequacy of these means for the goals stipulated, and even fewer have urged a basic reconstruction of the character and content of school-community relations. . . ." [6]

Few have questioned it because the self-protective, self-maintaining tendency of the educational institution is so strong and manifests itself in so many ways: in the perpetuation of the myth that school is above politics, in the assumption of a professional jargon really based on commonsense notions rather than on technical assumptions, in the failure of most school systems to adequately communicate with parents on what goes on inside the institution. For the most part, parents are, as Becker pointed out, "allowed to see the schools in action only when there is plenty of warning and a 'show' of some kind has been prepared for them." In many schools "Open School Night" has become a painful fetish. An Illinois teacher who admitted she dreaded the "ordeal" said she and her colleagues gave visiting parents the "administrative handshake—we move them along." Three Cheyenne grade school teachers said parents could stop in and observe their classrooms any time, without advance notice; this is uncommon.

The protectionist ways of school systems are clearly seen by a kind of evasiveness school staffs have, until recently, shown when briefing the public on conditions inside their schools. They've always insisted there were no major problems even when the schools were falling apart at the seams. And in the very defensive way in which much of the profession reacted to criticism, a defensiveness some educators themselves decry. The NEA even runs a blacklist of sorts: The *NEA Handbook* states that one of the functions of its Professional Rights and Responsibilities Commission is "to gather information about the various individuals and groups who criticize or oppose education and to make résumés of their activities." [7]

From school superintendent to classroom teacher, members of the teaching profession too often give the impression that disapproval of anything they do or say is close to blasphemy— at the very least a reckless act with malicious overtones. This permeates the school atmosphere at every level and gives rise to the feeling, "My school, right or wrong, we do not wash our soiled linen in public." The impression one is left with, then, is that the schools are really not the public's business. It's a feeling that comes across very strongly when teachers are asked to comment on their principals. Almost invariably, one of the major aspects teachers talk about is whether the principal "sticks up for his teachers." If he supports the teacher against parents and students—even in situations where the teacher is flatly in the wrong—then he already has an abundance of points in his favor insofar as his staff is concerned. If he criticizes teachers in front of parents or students or if he fails to put on a strong show of support—this overshadows much of what he does that would otherwise merit teacher approval.

Said a Winston-Salem high school teacher, reminiscing about a principal she had revered when she was teaching in a Thomasville, North Carolina, junior high, "We loved him. He always backed us. Even if he didn't think a teacher was right, he backed her." Even teachers not as vehement about it insisted that staff members should never be made to seem in the wrong in front of a parent or pupil because—an oft-used phrase— "it undermines the teacher's authority." At worst, the teachers said, the principal should make some neutral public noises if right was not wholly on the side of the teacher and chastise her afterward in the privacy of his office. It rarely seemed to occur to the teachers being interviewed that this might be a narrow, insular attitude. It was a rare teacher who acknowledged that the practice could distort the true picture for a concerned parent and undermine any confidence pupils have in the fairness of schools, undermine, in effect, confidence in authority.

Why this vehemently protectionist pose, one potentially destructive? Admitting that something has gone wrong is to let outsiders gain insight into the inner workings of the institution, according to Becker. Therefore, no loyal staff member can ever admit any error on the part of any other staff member, "even if this necessitates open lying, for to admit such a thing would be to admit the parents into the power structure of the school." This is the mortal fear of administrators and teachers: that parents will invade the sacrosanct corridors the staff considers its very own, will tell them how to run the school, will tell them how to teach.

Becker pointed out that the wall of solidarity which schools put up against outsiders—how ironic for parents to be considered outsiders!—"works to perfection with lower-class parents who are easily intimidated by middle-class institutions," but "not at all well with the middle-class parent who knows how to make trouble for the school and will do so without compunction if not satisfied." [8] Becker wrote from the perspective of the Chicago school system and before the militant black segment of the lower-income group began to inject itself into school affairs in ways the school systems dread most. But plenty of middle-class parents, too, are kept at arm's length except in those patterns the schools have deemed socially acceptable, and feel they cannot really influence the workings of the school. An extensive Stanford University study of school-community relationships, *Voters and Their Schools,* brought into sharp relief the really impotent feeling parents have about their children's schools.[9] Large numbers feel they lack any voice in school affairs except in the voting booth and "have little sense of any efficacy in their relationship to the schools. They despair of their own ability to do anything, of the possibility that school officials might care about what they think, and they find educational policy too complicated for them."

Many parents, like members of any other group, possess a wide range of skills, specialties, and ideas that might be useful to the teacher or the administrator and ultimately be a gain for the pupils. But the purposeful distancing of parents results in either their talents not being put to the service of the school or their talents being diverted by the professionals into "safer" channels. Parents may, ironically, be the most underutilized resource a school has.

Furthermore, some significant school budget and bond issue defeats probably occur at least in part because a significant proportion of parents feel alienated from the school. Bloomberg and Kincaid point out that administrators, "who are usually more knowledgeable about politics than most of their teachers," value passivity in the community because "it helps them maintain unchallenged control over their schools and the system as a whole, securing it from 'interference' by 'outsiders' to a greater degree than almost any other public institution." But the "passive surface of many 'good' school districts often conceals a good deal of antagonism toward and mistrust of the schools," which finally coalesces the dissidents and produces a taxpayers' revolt.[10] Needless to say, such a revolt rarely springs up from those citizens who have been "co-opted into the PTA's, mothers clubs, and booster clubs." As for teachers, say Bloomberg and Kincaid, since so many "maintain, or at

least try to maintain, this same pattern of passivity and author-
ity-dominated flow of communication in their classrooms, it is
not surprising that they see nothing wrong with having it
writ large in the school district."

What about the PTA's and parents' associations of all kinds
that abound throughout the country? Don't they serve as a
bridge between school and community? In a sense they do, but
they also illustrate the way schools have built up guards
against outside interference and intrusion. In fact, as educational critic James D. Koerner has bluntly stated, "the PTA, as
presumably everybody knows, is usually a creature of the local
administration." [11] Citing studies to back up his contention,
Koerner added that studies are not needed to corroborate
the obvious, "that the American PTA is rarely anything more
than a coffee-and-cookies organization based on vague goodwill and gullibility. It is chiefly useful to the administration
for raising money for special projects and persuading parents
who are interested enough to attend meetings that the local
schools are in the front ranks of American education." Though
it has an elaborate administrative structure, operates on national, state, and district levels, disseminates much informa-
tional literature, has standing legislative committees, and car-
ries on other lobbying activities, it is, Koerner maintains, a
member of the educational establishment, "failing to be
more than an administrative rubber stamp, it simply sustains
the existing order."

In many small-town and suburban communities (as well as
in some urban centers like New York) fiscally conservative
parents band together with like-minded citizens to fight school
taxes and vote down school bond issues. PTA's and other edu-
cation-minded parents' groups often provide effective counter-
political action to hammer away at lies and provide a climate
supportive of the schools. Valuable as this is, it doesn't presuppose a really significant relationship between the school
and the community which it serves. Fighting for school
support doesn't necessarily mean being involved in meaningful

and constructive debate with the schools on educational issues of concern to all. It doesn't mean parents individually feel a real sense of kinship with the schools they are paying for, the schools that have a profound effect on their children's economic and social future. For that matter, despite all the rhetoric about PTA's, meetings are generally badly attended by both parents and teachers.

Even when a parents' group is politically powerful, relatively speaking, it does not mean parents feel they have a pipeline to the power structure behind the bureaucracy. In his examination of New York City's Board of Education, sociologist David Rogers studied the effectiveness of parents' organizations in the city.[12] One of the most powerful is the United Parents Association. Yet even UPA finds itself as isolated from the school system as the bureaucrats can manage to keep it. A white middle-class parent from the Midwood section of Brooklyn told him, "The board is still operating under its old assumptions that parents don't understand anything." Another commented, "They [the principals] don't think that parents have a right to know or say anything." Rogers concluded that "distrust of school officials by white middle-class parents is deep."

When parents and teachers around the country are asked about PTA activities, a few describe narrowly activist groups or individual officers bent on self-interest. "They become PTA presidents to get close to the principals," said a Los Angeles parent contemptuously. An organizational-minded Cheyenne high school math teacher described instances in which "a parent has gotten angry at a teacher, started rumors flying, and the PTA was quickly organized to get rid of the teacher." There was an account by a teacher in Newton, Massachusetts, of what he described as an "excellent" elementary school that fell prey to parental interference. They became dissatisfied with the way the school was being run, and the local PTA group began visiting classes, writing reports, holding conferences with the principal, and insisting on changes. The principal, according to this teacher-informant, then told teachers "they would have to knuckle under." This brought on severe morale problems, which were not ameliorated until a new principal took over.

The vast majority of informants, however, described practical but "safe" PTA activities: mothers assisting nurses with eye examinations; working in the school library; tending the azalea plants; organizing Back-to-School Nights; buying needed sports equipment (rather than, as some parents have objected, pressuring the local board to buy it); putting on fashion shows for students; giving teachers a dinner once a year. "Most of our meetings consist in reading the minutes of the last meeting and boring business reports," said a New Jersey parent who attends her PTA sporadically. And a Princeton, New Jersey, PTA president emphatically stated, "We try to be as helpful to the teachers as we possibly can, but we're very careful not to intrude on their professional affairs."

[5]

How three teachers view parental involvement in the schools:

A high school teacher in El Cajon, California, discussing the PTA: "They're a necessary evil. If you've got to pass a tax issue or a board election, they're a source of woman power, where you can get them on the phone . . . And they get a little prestige out of being the president or the committee chairman, and in many instances they work very hard. So we tolerate them with the idea that when we need them, they're there. But they have very little influence on school policy."

A Denver high school teacher, recalling how leery he used to be about parents: "I started out with this orientation, and I'd say within the past five years I've gotten over it. I decided, 'You're no threat to me at all.' Before, I resented the parents. But then I said, 'Look, if you've got any answers at all, why shouldn't I be willing to share them with you? At least, let's talk things over. And I'm not going to back down just because you say so. And I don't expect you to back down either. But let's have some dialogue."

A junior high school teacher in Cheyenne, on parent-teacher conferences: "I think there's been a big wall between teachers and parents. We have built up this wall in talking in professional terms. We have to prove everything on paper—that Johnny's up to ninety-two percent or down to forty-two percent, and it seems like such a technical thing, school and teaching. I am with the child eight hours a day—but have we really emphasized the personal aspects of teaching? We've always done all of the talking, like I'm doing now. And many times I think we approach it as if we had to prove we were teaching something rather than that we were working with people."

[6]

The hands-off climate engendered by the school institution accomplishes two things when it's successful: It keeps parents with energy and interest busy doing useful work, and it deflects any real threat to the school's power structure. But it also serves to diminish the kind of contact teachers find important in keeping their classrooms running. There are parents, not otherwise occupied, whose hobby it is to make life miserable for school people. But the biggest complaint of school superintendents, principals, and classroom teachers is parent apathy, not overinvolvement. The biggest complaint is about parents who do *not* attend PTA meetings, do *not* visit the schools, do *not* respond to teachers' notes or phone calls, do *not* react to their children's school problems. Yet this is inevitable. The school can't remove itself from the community and at the same time expect the community to respond on the limited and arbitrary terms it has set up. It cannot create a variety of constraints and then not expect to have these permeate the entire school atmosphere, right down to the teacher-parent level. Yet this contradictory relationship is what is often sought by schools. A study of parent-teacher relations brings out the four

main reasons parents hesitate to visit their children's schools
—reasons that speak volumes about the gulf between teachers and parents: (1) the teacher would make things more difficult for the child if there were parental interference; (2)
teachers won't change their minds; (3) teachers won't listen
to parents; they think there is only one side to a story—the
teachers' side; (4) teachers are too busy to listen.[13]

But many parents do visit their children's schools, especially
to take part in parent-teacher conferences that occur two to
four times a year. These conferences are the acid test. They
force a confrontation between two people who personify the
two most powerful influences on the child, at least the younger
child—home and school. Both parent and teacher see the child
from their own particular frames of reference. Both bring to
the meeting their unique conceptions, misconceptions, anxieties, and a range of feelings that lie submerged. Both are, in a
sense, on trial.

The parent is on trial first of all because the child is his, an
extension of his own ego. Whatever comments the teacher
makes about the youngster, good or bad, are a reflection on
himself. Thus, he comes to the conference charged with a certain sensitivity that can easily turn into oversensitiveness. In
effect, the parent says to himself, "It's me the teacher is really
criticizing, not my child." It's an emotion-charged situation,
further complicated at times by feelings of rivalry on the parent's part.

The teacher also comes to the conference feeling he'll be
judged, and for somewhat the same reasons. The child is his
student, and he feels—unconsciously if not consciously—that
his own teaching ability is tied to the youngster's progress. In
any event he's pretty sure the parent thinks so. Therefore, in a
way the student becomes an extension of the teacher's ego, too.
This renders him vulnerable to fears that he won't be able to
control the situation. If the parent utters words of appreciation—words that rarely come but that he yearns for—all
well and good. But there's always the danger that the parent

will berate him, and gain the upper hand during the course of the interview. "Parents know how to bitch, but they don't know how to praise," muttered an elementary school teacher in New York City.

"Very powerful feelings may be evoked by parents," observed Fritz Redl, a psychiatrist who has studied school-related mental health problems. "All people, teachers included, are inclined to react to any authority figure somewhat after the way they did toward their own parents. Echoes of childhood rebellion or deference mock the tones of confidence with which they would like to speak. . . ." [14]

What are teachers' gripes about parents? Teachers object to parents who push their children to excel in everything, who refuse to accept the fact that youngsters develop gradually and don't show the same rate of accomplishment in all areas. They object to parents who want their children to be on the college track even if they aren't college material. A San Diego high school teacher said wryly, "With few exceptions, the school gives in to the parents anyhow. The feeling is, if the parent insists upon it, every kid should be given the opportunity of failing." Teachers object to parents who, when a problem is brought up, say, "Well, he never acts that way at home," implying that the teacher is at fault. They object to parents who compare report cards and then demand to know why their children failed to do as some others. They object to parents who do not show consistency in dealing with problems. "The parent comes in to discuss Johnny's problems and seems to show a great deal of concern," explained a Denver career teacher. "She wants to know, 'Why is he doing this? What can I do to help?' It's heartening, and I work out a really solid program for improvement. In a week's time the whole thing falls through because the parent is too busy to follow through on it."

Such gripes have substance, yet it does seem as though communication—more precisely, lack of communication—might be exacerbating such kinds of parent behavior. If teachers do not speak up, if schools do not invite mothers and fathers in to explain honestly and straightforwardly their plans and programs and problems, if no effort is made to illuminate the ways in which parents can help or hinder, misconceptions are bound to occur, and the patterns of parent behavior that teachers object to will arise more often than they otherwise would.

While many teachers try to make parents as comfortable as possible during parent-teacher conferences, others attempt to hurry the conference, or deliberately seat themselves behind their desks in a show of authority. And as relations between teachers and parents grow increasingly strained, especially in ghetto areas, administrators are putting tight reins on what their teachers can and cannot say, further inhibiting communication. In a junior high school near Harlem, for instance, teachers are given a mimeographed rules sheet that tells them what to say to parents. One rule advises teachers to remain courteous at all times; this is certainly a positive approach— except that, as one reads on, one learns that "this helps steal the thunder of the parent who is ready to blame the teacher for his child's inadequacy." The message therefore is: Don't be courteous to the parent because he merits respect; do it because that is the way you can manipulate him. A teacher who works at that school pointed to another bit of advice to faculty members. It began, "Enlist the cooperation of the parent. . . ." The teacher explained that he and his fellow teachers understood that to be shorthand for, "You do all the talking; don't let the parent get a word in edgewise."

Teachers at the school are also given a set of thirty-seven comments from which they can choose one or more to utilize on report cards, but they are not allowed to write their own messages without special administrative permission. The teacher who exhibited the list also decoded the comments as teachers understand them. Examples:

Comment: "Needs to pay greater attention in class."
Interpretation: "The kid goes to sleep."
Comment: "Should take greater part in her classwork."
Interpretation: "The kid never opens her mouth."

Comment: "Makes no effort to answer questions in class."

Interpretation: "He doesn't understand what you're talking about."

Comment: "His constant talking interferes with his learning and that of others."

Interpretation: "He swings from the light fixture and is constantly in the dean's office."

Comment: "Has trouble getting along with others."

Interpretation: "He was suspended four times for getting into fights with others."

Comment: "Often disrespectful to teachers."

Interpretation: "He told the teacher to go screw herself."

Communication? Yes, but a kind that is oblique and patronizing. It is a way of warding off the parents. When a school is imbued with the philosophy that it must preserve itself as a fortress, it really has no choice: This, unfortunately, is the only kind of language it can use.

[12]

The Limits of Professionalism

[1]

PROFESSIONALISM is a word much used by teachers these days. The NEA in particular puts out a veritable cascade of materials about the subject. The AFT, having less money to spend, is more restrained; but during the 1968 teacher strikes in New York City teachers belonging to its UFT affiliate made extravagant use of the word. No community people, they vowed, would tell them—the professionals—how to run their classrooms.

Without question, a commitment to professionalism can be a strong, healthy psychological force in refining standards and otherwise upgrading a field. This has certainly happened in the teaching field. But professionalism can also be a protective shell leading to insularity and irresponsibility. This also happens. It happens too often with teachers and administrators who use it to cover up personal incompetence. As, for instance, in the case of a fifth-grade boy in Yonkers, New York, who had the temerity to correct his teacher when she made a spelling error on the blackboard. She gave the boy a harsh tongue-lashing, and when his angry father came to school the next day to protest, she said, "*I* am the professional!" A parent in a Los Angeles school reported an almost similar incident. When she complained to the principal that her daughter's teacher was habitually speaking ungrammatically, the principal eyed her balefully and demanded, "Are *you* a professional?" It turned out that the mother did have teaching credentials, an obvious irrelevancy.

If these were isolated instances, they wouldn't be worth commenting about. But such cases are far from uncommon with school people who have mistaken the uses of professionalism. Nor is another case uncommon—that of big-city schools whose accountability runs up a professional chain of command to an amorphous central office run by professionals, successfully excluding the communities they serve. Hiding behind a wall of professionalism, then, school people protect themselves from criticism—while simultaneously expecting unlimited parental cooperation. By this kind of obdurateness they create extremist attitudes in parents or at least provide the climate in which extremism flourishes—and then use the extremists as an excuse for warding off all parents.

Teachers have always had problems justifying themselves as full-fledged professionals. Whether they are depends on one's definitions and could be argued from now till doomsday. To be sure, they engaged in intellectual preparation for their work. This preparation has a theoretical basis of sorts. Refined knowledge is dealt with. There is an ethical standard behind the transaction. On the other hand, they're hired by the city just like any other public servant. Unlike risk-taking professionals, they get paid on the basis of a special salary schedule. They're protected by tenure and due process. Seniority prevails over competence within their ranks. When finally they put away their chalk for the last time, they're the recipients of lifetime retirement. Over the years, a kind of compact seems to have been worked out: low pay, high security. Unlike the accustomed image of professionals, they even walk off the job now and then, in some cities there being more "now" than then. They have devised contractual protection against trans-fers, in many cases, that prevents experienced teachers from being shifted to ghetto schools, where they're most needed—something like a neurosurgeon agreeing to treat only head-aches.

Then what are teachers? Legally, they're quasipublic officers. One teacher quaintly and with good humor defined teaching as "an occupation within a calling." Does it really matter? It doesn't matter if you're a teacher in Denmark or Russia or China, where teachers have always been highly regarded. It matters in the United States, where teachers do not have such high esteem and where professionals generally have come to be the aristocrats of the middle class.

However, if one indicator of professionalism is to be involved in one's professional organization, to take an active interest in bettering conditions for one's field and one's clientele, the professionalism of teachers is still very limited. This is clearly seen in a study, conducted in the early 1960's, of beginning teachers' attitudes toward their organizations. Many "had very little understanding of the functions of the national or-ganization," and, furthermore, they "could not seem to care less." These teachers, mostly NEA members, were "unenthu-siastic, uninformed members of their professional organiza-tions." The few union members interviewed also expressed "a degree of reluctance about their membership." [1] A later study of New York State Teachers Association members depicted association leaders as having a high degree of interest in activities and conditions that would professionalize teaching.[2] The ordinary classroom teachers displayed no such interest. They wanted to teach, period. They showed "little interest in vital educational matters other than teacher welfare." The conclusion, according to the study, is that "teachers tend not to accept responsibilities necessary for professional status."

A teachers' union organizer in the Rocky Mountain area bewailed his own inability to get teachers really involved in educational matters outside their own classrooms. "It disappoints me, and I'm often very critical of my colleagues for being willing to spend so little time on matters that are so important," he said. "In many cases they race to get to a part-time job. Or it's a feeling of, 'I've never been able to do anything in this school, and now I just don't give a damn. Nobody asks for my advice, nobody gives it due when I do give it, so why should I go out of my way?' Really, I have such great hopes that when teachers get themselves organized and exercise some power, they'll find themselves revitalized." He told of a woman teacher who taught in the school auditorium, trying to conduct class with another class going on at the same time, and children not able to see over one another's heads. "A teacher like that has it very comfortable. She ought to be sued for mal-practice. She ought to say she won't teach under those con-ditions. A doctor won't operate in filth and then, when the pa-tent dies, say, 'It wasn't my fault.' But teachers do this daily. They can say, 'So what if the kids are two years behind? It wasn't my fault.' "

A teacher in San Diego put it more succinctly. "When you call a salary meeting, eighty percent of the teachers show up. When you call a curriculum meeting, twenty percent show up."

Most teachers are women—single women with friends to see, shopping to do; married women with families to hurry home to. Men teachers run off to their second jobs. This doesn't mean they're not doing effective work in their classrooms. It does mean they have a narrower orientation to their pro-fession and a weaker commitment to it. "Let us define a career teacher as one who plans to, and actually does, make a life oc-cupation of teaching; one who is philosophically, emotionally, and spiritually committed to teaching and all that's involved; and who is growth committed, that is, never satisfied with what he's doing and how well he's doing it, and who fully intends to keep on growing for the rest of his life," commented Walter K. Beggs of the University of Nebraska at TEPS' 1963-64 con-vention. "I would guess that, if you apply this definition, about one out of four teachers presently practicing would qualify as a career teacher."

[2]

Born of the reckless way in which unscrupulous school boards once manipulated teachers' salaries, the single salary schedule burst into full life and is the way most school districts pay their teachers today. The single salary schedule, practically an NEA invention, assumes something about teachers no educator would dream of assuming about students—that all teachers are alike and equal in their capacities. That it doesn't matter what's taught or who teaches it. That the skills they bring into the classroom, the effort they expend, and the results they obtain, are identical. Pay is based on years of experience and level of education—the assumption being that the more experience a teacher garners, and the more education he has, the better teacher he'll be. Both assumptions are questionable—in fact, after five years or so on the job the teacher reaches a plateau in terms of effectiveness, and after twenty or twenty-five years goes into a decline. At any rate, teachers aren't paid in accordance with their worth or with any relation to the market value of their specialties.

Then why not increase the salaries of really excellent potential and practicing teachers—in order to draw them in and retain them? That brings on merit pay, which pays teachers according to ability, provides incentives for other teachers to improve their competence, and fashions a climate that rewards excellence. A small number of smaller districts, most of which wouldn't be able to hang on to the abler teachers without it, use merit pay plans. For the most part, however, merit pay is a dirty phrase among the teaching ranks. During the past several decades more than one hundred school districts actually did try such plans. Most quickly fell apart. Bickering, jealousies, and charges of favoritism brought the plans to ruin.

Even a few top-rated teachers interviewed for this book flatly stated they wouldn't dream of working in a district that had a merit plan. The fact that they would be getting a high level of pay didn't matter. There are intrinsic satisfactions in teaching, they insisted, that provide their own reward. Now, teaching has always drawn its share of altruistically minded people (for that matter, possibly more than its share). But the fact remains that many excellent teachers do leave the nation's classrooms because there's too much of a discrepancy between the salary they get as teachers and what they could be getting elsewhere.

While teachers object to merit pay for a number of reasons, a primary objection rests on the determination of teacher effectiveness. Though administrators supposedly evaluate teachers for tenure and other purposes, teachers say merit pay based on administrative ratings are fraught with hazards: principals or department heads would pick favorites, settling higher pay on teachers who are most conformistic. At the same time, teachers are reluctant to evaluate each other and would hardly allow students to participate (though studies show that students are fairest and most accurate). The NEA has had a long-standing resolution calling for a wholly objective evaluation for merit pay purposes. Since teaching involves some qualitative aspects that defy completely objective measurement, and since researchers have been trying unsuccessfully for fifty years to come up with effective and objective rating scales, the whole thing is akin to chasing after the Holy Grail. One is forced to conclude that the posture of teachers in this respect is not altogether credible. For that matter, if teaching is so mysterious that criteria for teacher effectiveness can't be set up, or the best and worst teachers pinpointed, then either education is in worse trouble than one suspects or the old canard—"anybody can teach"—really holds true.

In actuality, of course, the best teachers have a ready reputation around a school, even when they're not formally so designated. The school clerks know it; the more involved parents know it. As an exhaustive report on North Carolina schools has pointed out, "The top ten percent of any given faculty can be recognized as to competence. They are excellent teachers with most students under most circumstances. Most principals, fellow teachers, students, and parents can reach reasonable agreement on the ten percent of the faculty who are least competent." [3] As for the ones in between, maybe their worth can be reasonably determined without there being required the hairline accuracy needed to determine the worth of a diamond.

The whole issue of merit pay is fraught with complications—emotional as well as technical ones. It would be useless to minimize them. But if the teachers' organizations created more of a climate of goodwill toward the concept, it's likely that they'd be more acceptable and successful. On the whole, younger teachers are more receptive, but it's the older teachers who usually control the organizations.

Nevertheless, as teachers' salaries move to increasingly higher levels, there's correspondingly greater pressure on the part of school boards and the general public for some financial distinctions among teachers in terms of their competence. As the president of a Westchester County school board said, "We're not forever going to subsidize the adolescence of teachers. They can't have their economic cake and eat it, too. Not when they start going into the ten-thousand- twenty-thousand-dollar scale. The taxpayers won't stand for it."

If this mood grows, and the more pragmatic teacher-leaders come to appreciate that fact, some of the difficulties surrounding merit pay may yet prove surmountable.

[3]

Most teachers, with the possible exception of beginners, hate being evaluated. This holds true not only in connection with merit-pay plans but in general. Here again, highly rated teachers have the same attitude as do the more average ones. In fact, there are excellent teachers who sometimes move from one district to another, and take a pay cut in the bargain, just to be in a school that has less supervision. For that matter, nobody working in the schools, including principals and superintendents, likes being evaluated. (When the concept of a national assessment of schools was first proposed by USOE and the Carnegie Foundation, superintendents hit the roof even though only regions were to be compared.) Quite possibly, not wanting to be evaluated is a common human characteristic (though in circumstances other than school, people who take pride in their work usually enjoy showing it off). In any event, evaluation *is* a fact of life in most human situations. Even doctors in their isolated offices are evaluated—if only by patients who either remain with them or leave for someone they think can do a better job of doctoring them. Schoolchildren are not, of course, afforded a similar choice of practitioner. Even if they get a poor one they're stuck—they can't choose someone else. (Perhaps older students and the parents of younger ones should have the right to select their own teachers each year, in place of arbitrary assignment. Since most would throng to the best teachers on each grade level, there would be tremendous pressure on the school administration to force an upgrading all around.)

Evaluation of teachers means: (1) classroom observations; (2) other indicators of competence—for instance, how well the kids learn or how often discipline problems are sent down to the office. The purposes of evaluation are: (1) to offer help and advice to teachers; (2) to provide programs of remediation for those who need it; (3) to have evaluation reports in file as per board of education regulations; (4) to gauge, generally, the competence of individual teachers. Teachers resist and resent evaluation—especially classroom observation—because: (1) they're insecure; (2) an isolated classroom observation is discontinuous and artificial; (3) the observer (usually an administrator or supervisor) might catch them on an off day; (4) they tend to see the visit as an intrusion; (5) it's often done so badly. An NEA study shows that only 36 percent of the teachers surveyed expressed confidence in the evaluations they received and—incredibly—21 percent didn't even know whether or not they had received a written evaluation.[4]

Generally, teachers prize classroom autonomy above all, and consider intrusion unprofessional. But viewed in another light, meaningful evaluation tied to consultation is very directly a concomitant of professional growth. Good teachers do sit down after a hard day with the kids and mull over in their own minds what went right and what went wrong. But such postmortems are of necessity limited because teachers can't get outside their skins. As Ira J. Gordon put it in *Studying the Child in School,* the teacher "not only manipulates the flow of materials and transactions among children, but is also a crucial variable in the learning situation itself." [5]

It's tempting to say, leave the professional alone in his classroom to do his job. But even the good teacher builds up habits or, as a result of his day-to-day classroom exposure, insensitivities that inhibit his teaching effectiveness. Naturally, somebody coming in to observe once in a while enters an artificial situation in which the teacher tries to be at his best. It's disappointing that team teaching, which could result in frank exchanges among teachers, generally hasn't seemed to do so. Of course, critical exchange isn't the easiest of human transactions.

The best administrators and supervisors act as guides, as counselors, as "teachers of teachers" with consummate tact and perception. But classroom observation, on the whole, is extremely haphazard. Many teachers interviewed for this book hadn't been observed in years. A North Carolina teacher was outraged; he was to be observed because he was transferring from one school to another, and it had been ten years since anybody had observed him teach. A high school teacher in Great Neck, New York, a wealthy bedroom community near Manhattan, said teachers in his school were evaluated on the basis of how well students did on the Regents tests. A Denver

248]   WHAT'S HAPPENED TO TEACHER?

teacher said his principal "walked in and out" once yearly to fulfill the central board requirements.

The impression a naïve outsider might have, that teacher and supervisor sit down in a professional manner to discuss the teacher's classroom work, must be rudely shattered. It happens sometimes. It doesn't happen often. The NEA poll showed that only 30 percent of the teachers reported desirable outcomes following evaluation. (Many left the question about outcome blank.) A study of 242 schoolteachers in thirty-six districts, as reported in the *American School Board Journal*, shows that 25 percent never taught in schools with any kind of supervision. Another 25 percent said the help they were getting was ineffective. Some made notations about supervisors who were obnoxious and opinionated, or had the habit of criticizing teachers in front of their classes. Much classroom observation everywhere is very superficial—a brief look inside, a hurried few minutes spent going over a checklist. Margaret Stevenson, executive secretary of NEA's Association of Classroom Teachers, points out that many principals are former shop or gym teachers and aren't really qualified to appraise teachers. In truth, nitpickers can find the silliest things to gripe about. ("He criticizes if there's so much as a piece of paper on the floor," said a Raleigh teacher, "and I'm scared to do projects; he might walk in when things are messy.") Evaluation can be used to harass. A guidance counselor in San Diego was one of several nonadministrative persons who suggested, "Take evaluation out of the administrators' hands—let the master teachers do it."

Since the trend is to more teacher participation in all school affairs, it could be more than an idle suggestion. If master teachers take over, it's presumably because they feel they can do a better job. But that implies accepting professional responsibility for competence and incompetence among the staff. It's difficult, thus far, to be optimistic about anything like that.

[4]

If merit pay is a dirty word to most teachers, tenure is almost a sacred one. As it has worked out, tenure is the closest thing to an ironclad promise of job security with no strings attached. It goes a long way toward making teaching the most secure occupation of any, where professional aspirations are involved. What tenure provides is a guarantee that teachers can't be dismissed from their jobs except for certain specified causes— usually immorality, dishonesty, willful neglect of duty, or mal-feasance. Dismissal is preceded by elaborate due process procedures. These include a hearing, right of counsel, chance to subpoena witnesses, opportunity to appeal, etc. More than thirty states and a number of cities in nontenure states have established tenure laws.

Like so many other conventions in the teaching field, tenure goes back to the history of teachers—specifically, to wholesale and arbitrary dismissals which took place periodically up to and including the 1930's. Underlying many such dismissals is a cruel fact of life for teachers—they're vulnerable to community pressure, to false accusations from vengeful children, to charges of incompetence from parents disappointed in their youngsters' progress, to arbitrary and capricious dismissal by their superiors.

What's happened to Negro teachers in the South, where tenure laws are weak or nonexistent, illustrates the point. Since the 1954 Supreme Court decision on desegregation, hundreds of Negro teachers have been dismissed from school systems that were desegregated. Both black and white teachers have been let go for becoming politically active or taking up unpopular causes. Neither the ACLU nor the teachers' organizations are in short supply of cases involving teachers dismissed or not rehired for having taken part in civil rights or antiwar demonstrations—or, as in the case of a high school

English teacher, for having criticized local educational practices. Following New York City's 1968 teachers' strikes, some
principals harassed teachers who had taught during the strike,
and attempted to dismiss probationary (nontenure) teachers.

Ostensibly, then, tenure exists to protect the teacher from
capricious acts, to let him teach in peace, to allow him freedom
of speech in class. Unfortunately, relatively few teachers take
advantage of this freedom to discuss controversial subjects—
and, because they do not, those who do are rendered more vulnerable to harassment, intimidation, and dismissal proceedings, tenure or no tenure.

If tenure hasn't done all it was meant to do, it has done something it wasn't supposed to—it has further sapped the incen-
tive of many teachers to improve their competence or to bring
to their jobs a strong professional motivation. It's not a question
of tenure alone. It's a question of too many individuals with
low job motivation—sheltered by a single salary schedule,
shielded by tenure—doing work that, despite its apparent
challenges, can easily become routinized—coasting along.
"This is ready-made for mediocrity," admitted a Princeton
high school teacher. "Schoolteaching works on the honor system,
and I'm afraid a number of my colleagues around the country
country don't have too much honor."

In almost every district one finds model teachers, master
teachers, teachers who exemplify the highest standards of
dedication and performance. In almost every district one also
finds teachers who can't control their classrooms, can't control their students, can't teach. Yet they remain as teachers.
In almost every district one finds pure and simple timeserv-
ers and, worse, teachers who can't control themselves and who
make school a cruel, unbearable experience for some or all
of the children whose minds they're supposed to be enriching.
Yet they, too, remain as teachers.

Sometimes the teacher shortage is cited as a reason why the
profession hasn't faced up to this problem. But the teacher

shortage has been lessening considerably in many areas. Moreover, it's a dubious assumption that thirty children with an unfit teacher are better off than if they were spread out through
other classes, with better teachers, even if that meant a
greater teacher-pupil ratio. Especially when there's nothing
definitive to say that smaller class size leads to better learning,
and a good deal to say that better teaching leads to better learning. Teachers know very well which of their colleagues do
such a poor teaching job that it turns out to be a lost year for
the students in that class. Teachers know—because they talk
about it among themselves—which of their colleagues are
sadists, or voyeurs, or too hysterical to contain themselves or
their classes. But though they abhor such things, they close
their eyes to them because, as one put it, "Listen, we have to
live with each other."

Individual teachers in such instances are, of course, caught
between professional responsibility and group loyalty. It's
obvious which has to win. But the ramifications go deeper.
Three factors surrounding the incompetent or unstable
teacher tend to protect him: (1) dismissal procedures are
onerous; (2) administrators don't want to stick their necks
out, either, though it's their job to provide the best possible
environment for the children; (3) the teachers' organizations
haven't assumed their share of responsibility.

Numerous administrators complained about the difficulty
of getting rid of incompetents. One in Los Angeles, echoing
many others, explained, "It's so difficult to prove incompetence.
How do you prove, in what amounts to a court of law, that no
matter how hard you've tried to work with a teacher, he won't
spark the kids, can't plan a lesson, doesn't manage his class
properly, or is a cruelly sarcastic kind of person, destructive to
the kids? You have to think like a lawyer. During the hearing
you have to justify everything you say. There are people there
who watch everything you do or say. People from the personnel division, from the teachers' organization. The whole thing

is very difficult to get through. Almost impossible. Practically the only way to remove a teacher is when he has tb, is a Communist, or molests a child."

Dr. Edward Pino, superintendent of schools in Cherry Creek, Colorado, summed it up: "It's far easier to fire an incompetent janitor than an incompetent teacher. Short of rape or murder, once a teacher is hired, you're stuck with him."

Often, however, administrators don't try too hard. They don't want the bad publicity that might result, or they don't want to risk strained relations with the staff.

The pervading atmosphere, that only the most extreme criminal act will pry an incompetent teacher from the classroom, keeps schoolchildren, who have no recourse, locked in with teachers who exhibit the grossest kind of behavior. Interviewing members of New York City's United Parents Association, education writer Bernard Bard was told of one teacher who picked up youngsters by the ears and threw them into a corner. When the parent complained, the principal said, "The teacher has emotional problems at home, so we have to expect that from time to time." Another parent reported the case of a teacher who tried to tell her young impressionable students that *they* were mentally disturbed. In this instance the principal said he could take no action because "before you know it, I'll have the superintendent on my back." [6] It goes without saying that, given the teacher population as a whole, such teachers are well in the minority. But to the child who has one, the teacher constitutes a terrifying majority of one. Note that with more than 55,000 teachers on the payroll, New York City's Board of Education has formally discharged only twelve teachers in a five-year period.

When a principal really wants to get rid of an undesirable teacher, he's much more apt to "play the game," as they say in administrative circles, than to attempt dismissal. The game is that first the principal tries to persuade the teacher to resign, and then perhaps tries to harass him to do so. Failing that, he uses his persuasion to get the teacher to seek a transfer to another school. Sometimes, when personality clashes are at the bottom of the problem, this works out well for the teacher. But what happens all too often is that the teacher is really unfit, gets shunted from school to school, district to district, in his pocket glowing letters of recommendation from administrators only too glad to be rid of him. Sometimes involuntary transfers are arranged with the connivance of the school superintendent, especially if the teachers' organization looks the other way. It was the collapse of this game in New York City that was the immediate cause in bringing on the Ocean Hill-Brownsville-UFT due process fracas. In a book recounting the New York City teachers' strike, Martin Mayer observed that "one of the survival skills of a New York school administrator is the ability to slough off bad staff onto other districts, and there are literally hundreds of incompetent (some of them mentally ill) teachers drifting about the school system." [7]

But the game can rebound. A Boulder teacher who had a penchant for slapping children's faces was persuaded to transfer five times in six years—and finally wound up full circle back at his original school.

Teachers' groups say they're helpless to do anything about the situation because they don't control entry into the profession. It's true that screening is almost nonexistent at the teacher training institutes ("These people paid for their education, how can we counsel them out," said a professor of education in Colorado). Screening is slipshod at the point of hiring, and that apparently holds true for some of the best districts. "We want to accept the principal's decision," said a Princeton teacher, "but we can't do so any longer." He explained that he and a group of his colleagues are demanding a voice in tenure decisions. "There are too many incompetent administrative decisions, too many incompetent people coming in. We've reached the point where we won't work with such teachers." At the same time, he said, many of his coworkers don't feel teachers should intrude in this area.

Yet the fact that teachers don't control entry is only half the story. While stressing the need for professionalism, the professionals don't utilize the resources they do have. A Los Angeles vice-principal, a former classroom teacher who insisted that teachers are "the most unappreciated occupational group in the nation," nevertheless recounted the difficulties he had when trying to dismiss a teacher whose classes were chaotic, who couldn't be helped, and who refused to budge from the school. "At the hearing, the teacher's people will want to discount and disqualify everything you produce against him," he said. "It's hard to get teachers to testify against one of their own, too." In fact, according to Donald L. Conrad, associate secretary of NEA's Professional Rights and Responsibilities Commission, about one teacher a year is asked to relinquish membership in the million-member organization. Two are suspended, five censured. Most, if not all, such cases involve contract violations. A survey by the *Harvard Law Review*, which in 1968 polled forty-seven state and local NEA affiliates, brought only fourteen replies. All fourteen claimed to have the power to adjudicate ethics cases but—with the exception of Minnesota, which processed ten or twelve a year—very few had such cases referred to them.[8]

Lacking certification and hiring powers certainly wouldn't prevent the teachers' organizations from working with state or local bodies to provide for revision of tenure regulations— say, to provide for renewable tenure on a five- or seven-year basis, as some educators suggest, with performance as one of the criteria. Nothing prevents the NEA from setting up its own criteria for teacher training institutions. Nothing prevents the NEA—or AFT, for that matter—from setting up its own standards and examinations for membership admission to its national, state, and local associations. Too often, as the New York State Teachers Association study showed, "the local association's advancement committee is no more than a salary committee," its other functions more social than professional.[9] Parents and other parties should be able to file complaints about alleged incompetence or other questionable teacher behavior with the local association, for investigation, just as anyone can file a complaint against a doctor or lawyer with their respective associations. This would not require state sanction, as do Professional Practices Commissions or other legally constituted bodies. An NEA official, however, predicted a different trend for the future: (1) strong due process procedures for probationary teachers—who are, of course, the most vulnerable to harassment; (2) national tenure.

Ideally, a balance exists between the practitioner's right to be safeguarded against unfair practices and the client's right to be protected against untoward acts on the part of the practitioner. The ideal is always difficult to achieve. Every professional group closes ranks to protect its own; teachers are hardly an exception. But teachers are the exception in that they seem to want—at this juncture, at least—the best of both worlds: the security of the civil servant and the prestige and rewards of the professional. More than that, they want a major say in matters of educational policy while getting tenure protection. In other words, they want power without accountability, which is basically an antidemocratic stance.

[5]

Among some of the educators most concerned with the professionalization of teaching—NEA's TEPS and the anti-establishment people in the forefront—the answer to some of these problems is clear. The answer they propose is the establishment of a career line within the teaching ranks, with certification at each level renewable after several years. The idea jelled when the input of federal funds created new roles for teachers in specialized work. It was fashioned by the TEPS group into a full-fledged differentiated staffing concept. Already being experimentally implemented in a few schools in Kansas City, Missouri; Temple City, California; and elsewhere, and being seriously considered by state legislatures in Massachusetts, Florida, and elsewhere, differentiated staffing with differentiated pay is based on the kind of functional specialization common to science and industry. In other words, teachers' personal talents and inclinations would guide their job choices, make their roles more manageable, and provide more challenging positions for those teachers for whom teaching is a full-fledged career. Thus, some teachers would specialize in large-group instruction, others in small-group work, in remedial work, and so forth. While a number of differentiated staffing models are on the drawing board, their basic component is the same—a hierarchical pattern that begins with the master teacher, works its way down through several layers of associate-type teachers, and winds up at the bottom with interns and paraprofessionals.

Master teachers would be in the classroom part of the time, working in the area of curriculum development and with other teachers for the balance of the week. "Take a fifth-grade class," explained Mary C. Nesbitt, state president of the North Carolina Classroom Teachers Association. "Any fifth-grade class. You won't have five expert teachers. You might have one. You might have two, if you're real lucky. You probably have a first-year teacher here who needs help. You probably have one over here who's been there too long. If you have someone with real ability to coordinate and get cooperation from these teachers, she'd be weaving a total program, getting the best out of all these teachers. The saddest thing I know is where children are exposed to a poor situation this year, maybe two years in a row, and then they're problems. . . ."

By no means are all teachers and teacher groups overjoyed by this drastic reorganization, especially since it would eventually do away with the single salary schedule, current slipshod evaluation practices, and tenure (as it presently exists). Some see it as "back-door merit pay." AFT's sociologist Robert D. Bhaerman objects to the differentiated pay feature.[10] Opinion is sharply divided within the NEA itself, and among teacher groups in the various states where it's being promoted.

The image of master teachers electrifying the whole staff with their skill and their enthusiasm, thus raising the overall level of teaching and learning, is, of course, an appealing one. So is the prospect of luring and keeping more high-caliber teachers. Differentiated staffing adapts itself ideally to flexible scheduling and other innovative approaches that show promise of improving the educational climate. Whether it will work out as conceived will depend to a considerable extent on how well the whole "team" of teachers is able to integrate its efforts. Whatever happens, one thing is fairly evident: Those teachers who are more ambitious and aggressive and are at a stage where they find full-time classroom work too confining but don't want to stop being teachers, need another teaching level for their energies. Hopefully it will also lead to good things for the educational process. What would be useful for all teachers, however, not just those striking out for the top reaches of a new hierarchy, is a climate of receptivity and creativity that would encourage them to think and explore and feel their way to a deeper concept of what it means to be a teacher.

[6]

Reading the critical literature about teachers these days, one is struck by a number of expectations. The contemporary teacher is supposed to respond equally well to each student regardless of the student's background. He's supposed to start "where the child is" and, from that point, lead him to utilize his fullest capacities. He's supposed to relate the curriculum to the child, finding ways to transform the subject into a sound value system consonant with the needs of today's (and tomorrow's) world. He's supposed to act as a "change agent," providing the student not only with the promise of a better life but with the social, emotional, and subject-matter strengths to bring this about. He's supposed to equip the child with the skills he needs in a society in which the only constancy is inconstancy. Finally, he's supposed to be committed to his own professional growth—reading, researching, running around the world for culture during his summer hiatus.

There are within the teaching ranks highly perceptive, intelligent, strongly motivated people, and more of those coming into the schools now. But there are—let's face it—also has-beens and losers who couldn't make the money they're making now in any other profession. Most teachers are at neither extreme. Most are well-meaning, rather ordinary people, who want to do well at their craft—a difficult and demanding craft —who have somewhat plebeian tastes and a more parochial outlook than the times perhaps call for.

Given the expectations, given even a portion of them, their training is hopelessly inadequate. It will take a revolution in technique and considerable sums of money to transform teacher training. And as Felix C. Robb, director of the Southern Association of Colleges and Schools, has pointed out, it will take what's in very short supply now: "turned-on" professors to turn on student teachers.[11] Robb also suggested that "one million well-qualified, genuinely professional teachers" supplemented by teacher aides might be a more worthy goal for a teachers' association than playing the numbers game and trying for two million members.

Collectively, teachers are emerging from a state of semiservitude, which to some extent explains both the extremes of militancy and passivity which they at times display. Still at the bottom of a rather rigid hierarchy, their professional freedom of choice is restricted. Though this is slowly changing, they've had little or nothing to say about the curriculum, textbooks, or school policies. Kept somewhat infantilized, they've nevertheless been asked to perform some of the most brilliant pedagogical pyrotechnics this side of Mark Hopkins. And in a sense, to provide the answers to some of the nation's most troubling social problems. For the teachers to do so, with skill and clarity and sureness, would require a transformation in teacher education. But even now, given all the handicaps, the best of them rise up to the challenge with the kind of talent and devotion we have in mind when we speak of the "dedicated teacher."

In emerging from the lowly status into which they had been placed, teachers—through their organizations—have an overriding concern with their welfare these days. Yes, they want conditions bettered for the children—but it's fundamentally a fight for teacher betterment that's being waged at present. This is, of course, inevitable and understandable—especially given a public that has been known more for its shabby than for its generous treatment of teachers.

All the same, it's disheartening that the revolution for teacher well-being could not count the child's heartbeat, as well as the teacher's pennies. When, for instance, a group of teachers in one of New York City's most prestigious high schools protests a principal's request for an emergency faculty meeting after school to discuss slashing cuts in the educational budget —when it protests this meeting on the grounds that it is being held "on their own time"—one must wonder what is being lost as well as gained.[12]

For teachers, their emergence comes at an ironic time. They're not alone in becoming more outspoken, insisting upon being heard, and making a new place for themselves in the sun. Minority groups and students, too, are demanding the same things at the same time, and it is going to be a learning process for everyone concerned. Parents and students will have to learn the difficult art of distinguishing between involvement and intrusion; teachers can't do their work under threat of constant interference.

As for teachers, they'll have to learn to give way, in a sense, at the same time they're getting their way. Parents of all colors and socioeconomic groups are questioning more. In wealthy suburbs, as well as in ghetto areas, they're asking questions about quality education—partly because they themselves are better educated and know more what to ask, partly because education is becoming much more expensive. As teachers' pay reaches higher levels, parental concern about competence will inevitably increase. As an increasing number of innovative programs are being launched, they'll want to know that these are worth the price. This new demand for accountability is bound to go past school boards and superintendents of schools right to where the action is—the schools themselves and the people who run them. As teachers gain more autonomy, more control over the instructional process, parents will want to be sure that major policy decisions are in everyone's interest. Pressures will heighten to hold teachers accountable for the progress of students.

Furthermore, as teachers grow organizationally and politically stronger, and their strikes possibly take on a different character, more centered on issues relating to politics and social change, the result may be quite a different relationship between teacher and community. Indeed, the very fact of current strikes is causing changes in the way teachers look at the community and in the way the community looks at them.

His growing militancy, the racial crisis, educational innovation and technology—all such complex events have been impinging on the contemporary teacher with great force, and he has neither had the time, the psychic room, nor the scope to absorb them all. In other words, he's like most other people—somewhat confused, bewildered, hoping for the best, groping to make things come out all right.

As teacher talks to his class about the Napoleonic Wars, trying to get beneath the surface of dates and events—as he bends over Mary's desk to help her with her fractions, trying to make her *see* the system—he faces a different kind of complexity, at once simpler and more complicated than the worldly one. In the interchange between teacher and student, that most primitive of relationships, is where, ultimately, he may find the higher level of professionalism he seeks.

Notes

Chapter 1

1. "And Teachers Want More, Too," *U.S. News & World Report* (March 3, 1969).
2. John H. Fischer, "The Teacher's Role Is Growing," New York *Times* (January 12, 1968).
3. B. Othanel Smith, *Teachers for the Real World* (Washington, D.C., The American Association of Colleges for Teacher Education, 1969), p. 106.
4. Anthony Oettinger and Sandra Marks, "Educational Technology: New Myths and Old Realities," *Harvard Educational Review* (Fall, 1968).
5. "Teacher Opinion Poll," *NEA Journal* (May, 1960).
6. David Asubel, *Educational Psychology* (New York, Holt, Rinehart & Winston, 1968), p. 412.
7. S. E. Frost, Jr., *Introduction to American Education* (New York, Doubleday & Company, 1962), pp. 319–20.
8. W. Wolf and W. C. Wolf, Jr., "Teacher Dropouts Still a Dilemma," *School and Society* (April 18, 1964).

Chapter 2

1. G. C. Lee, "The Changing Role of the Teacher," in J. I. Goodlad, ed., *The Changing American School* (Chicago, National Society for the Study of Education, 1966), p. 16.
2. Research Division, National Education Association, *The American Public School Teacher,* 1965–66 (Washington, D.C., National Education Association, 1967).

3. Harmon Zeigler, *The Political Life of American Teachers* (Englewood Cliffs, N.J., Prentice-Hall, 1967), Ch. 2.

4. Research Division, National Education Association, *Reading and Recreational Interests of Classroom Teachers* (Washington, D.C., National Education Association, 1967), pp. 7–13.

5. *Ibid.* See also, Perry London, *et al.*, "Teachers' Use of Leisure," *Teachers College Record* (March, 1964).

6. *Ibid.*

7. *Ibid.*

8. William S. Learned and Ben D. Wood, *The Student and His Knowledge* (New York, The Carnegie Foundation for the Advancement of Teaching, 1938), pp. 340–44.

9. Dael Wolfle, *America's Resource of Specialized Talent* (New York, Harper & Brothers, 1954), Ch. 7.

10. Chester W. Harris, ed., *Encyclopedia of Educational Research* (New York, The Macmillan Company, 1960), p. 1359.

11. J. Scott Hunter, *The Academic and Financial Status of Graduate Students—Spring 1965* (Washington, D.C., U.S. Government Printing Office, 1967), p. 15.

12. Philip R. Harvey, *et al.*, *Graduate Record Examination Special Report* (Princeton, N.J., Educational Testing Service, 1965), pp. 1–29. Also, personal communication with William H. Angoff of ETS.

13. R. B. Fox, "Factors Influencing the Career Choices of Prospective Teachers," *The Journal of Teacher Education* (December, 1961).

14. G. Lang, "Motives in Selecting Elementary and Secondary School Teaching," *Journal of Experimental Education* (September, 1960).

15. William V. Hicks and F. H. Blackington, *Introduction to Education* (Columbus, Ohio, Charles E. Merrill Books, 1965), pp. 25–26.

16. J. Gillis, "Personality Needs of Future Teachers," *Educational and Psychological Measurement,* Vol. XXIV, No. 3 (Fall, 1964).

17. E. Eisner, "Situation Potentials and Personality Needs in Teaching," *The Journal of Teacher Education* (September, 1961).

18. J. M. Stephens, "Traits of Successful Teachers: Men or Angels?" *Theory into Practice* (April, 1963).

19. Lindley J. Stiles, *Introduction to College: Education* (New York, G. P. Putnam's Sons, 1969), p. 153.
20. D. G. Ryans, *Characteristics of Teachers* (Washington, D.C., American Council on Education, 1960).
21. Asubel, *op. cit.*
22. Louis Kaplan, *Mental Health and Human Relations in Education* (New York, Harper & Brothers, 1959), pp. 66–67.
23. Ronald M. Pavalko, "Aspirants to Teaching: Some Differences Between High School Senior Boys and Girls Planning on a Career in Teaching," *Sociology and Social Research* (October, 1965).
24. *Ibid.*
25. U.S. Office of Education, "Beginning Teachers. Status and Career Orientations. Final Report on the Survey of New Teachers in the Public Schools, 1956–57." (Washington, D.C., U.S. Government Printing Office, 1961). Circulars.
26. R. O. Carlson, "Variation and Myth in the Social Status of Teachers," *The Journal of Educational Sociology* (November, 1961).

Chapter 3

1. Department of Health, Education, and Welfare, *Digest of Educational Statistics, 1967* (Washington, D.C., U.S. Government Printing Office, 1967).
2. "U.S. Report Finds Gains in Schools," New York *Times* (January 19, 1969).
3. E. H. Harper, "Elementary Teachers' Knowledge of Basic Arithmetic Concepts and Symbols," *Arithmetic Teacher* (December, 1964).
4. A. Huettig and J. M. Newell, "Attitudes Toward Introduction of Modern Mathematics Program by Teachers with Large and Small Number of Years' Experience," *Arithmetic Teacher* (February, 1966).
5. R. E. Reys, "Mathematical Competencies of Elementary Education Majors," *The Journal of Educational Research* (February, 1968).
6. W. M. Perel and P. D. Vairo, "Are Teachers Devoted to Their Disciplines?" *Journal of Secondary Education* (December, 1966).

7. National School Public Relations Association, *Education U.S.A.* (December 12, 1968). Weekly report.

8. John C. Flanagan, *Project Talent* (Pittsburgh, Project Talent Office, University of Pittsburgh, 1964), Ch. 3, p. 86.

9. National School Public Relations Association, *Education U.S.A.* (March 13, 1967). Weekly report.

10. G. S. Kleinman, "Needed: Elemenary School Science Consultants," *School Science and Mathematics* (November, 1965).

11. F. R. Wittacre and P. D. Vairo, "Archimedes, Have We Failed You?" *Peabody Journal of Education* (March, 1968).

12. Elementary Science Study, *Newsletter*, No. 16 (October, 1968).

13. R. F. Byrnes, "Our First Need: Improved Teaching," *Bulletin of the National Association of Secondary School Principals* (May, 1967).

14. J. W. McKenney, "Teaching the Bill of Rights in California," *Saturday Review* (March 19, 1966). *See also,* H. H. Remmers and D. H. Radler, *The American Teenager* (New York, Charter Books, 1957), Ch. 8.

15. B. Bard, "The Blackboard," New York *Post* (August 10, 1968).

16. E. F. Stamm, "Knowledge of World Affairs," *Journal of Teacher Education* (March, 1962).

17. H. Taylor, *The World and the American Teacher* (Washington, D.C., The American Association of Colleges for Teacher Education, 1968), Ch. 1.

18. National Council of Teachers of English, *The National Interest and the Continuing Education of Teachers of English* (Champaign, Ill., National Council of Teachers of English, 1964), pp. 1–71.

19. National School Public Relations Association, *Education U.S.A.* (October 21, 1968). Weekly report.

20. M. Karl Openshaw, "Chicago," in *Development of the Career Teacher* (Washington, D.C., National Education Association, 1964), p. 42.

21. National School Public Relations Association, *Education U.S.A.* (September 23, 1968). Weekly report.

22. *Ibid.*

23. *Ibid.*

24. J. M. Stephens, *The Process of Schooling* (New York, Holt, Rinehart & Winston, 1967), p. 81.

25. National School Public Relations Association, *Education U.S.A.* (April 17, 1967). Weekly report.
26. John I. Goodlad, "Editorial," *National Elementary Principal* (November, 1967).
27. D. Lewin, "Go Slow on Non-Grading," *Elementary School Journal* (December, 1966).

Chapter 4

1. Willard S. Elsbree, *The American Teacher* (New York, American Book Company, 1939), p. 63.
2. *Ibid.*, pp. 26-27.
3. *Ibid.*, p. 81.
4. *Ibid.*, p. 38.
5. P. Odegard, *The American Public Mind* (New York, Columbia University Press, 1930), Ch. 6.
6. Elsbree, *op. cit.*, p. 169.
7. H. G. Good, *A History of American Education* (New York, The Macmillan Company, 1956).
8. Elsbree, *op. cit.*
9. Odegard, *op. cit.*
10. *Ibid.*
11. Carroll Atkinson and Eugene T. Maleska, *The Story of Education* (New York, Bantam Books, 1962), p. 104.
12. M. Belok and F. Dowling, "The Teacher Image and the Teacher Shortage," *Phi Delta Kappan* (March, 1961).
13. E. L. Furness, "The Image of the High School Teacher in American Literature," *Educational Forum* (May, 1960).
14. Louis Harris, *et al.,* "Crisis in the High Schools," *Life* (May 16, 1969).
15. National School Public Relations Association, *Education U.S.A.* (April 1, 1968). Weekly report.
16. Hillel Black, *The American Schoolbook* (New York, William Morrow & Company, 1967), Ch. 7.

Chapter 5

1. Committee on Educational Finance, *Financial Status of the Public Schools, 1968* (Washington, D.C., National Education Association, 1968), p. 73.

2. *Ibid.*, p. 43.
3. National Education Association, *What Everyone Should Know About Financing Our Schools* (Washington, D.C., National Education Association, 1968), p. 29.
4. C. P. Kindleberger, *Economic Development* (New York, McGraw-Hill Book Company, 1965). Also, *International Yearbook of Education, 1965.*
5. Committee on Educational Finance, *op. cit.*, p. 51.
6. R. J. Shockley, *Your Future in Elementary School Teaching* New York, Richard Rosen Press, 1961), pp. 46–47.
7. "And Teachers Want More, Too," *op. cit.*
8. Research Division, National Education Association, "City Worker's Family Budget," *NEA Research Bulletin* (May, 1968).
9. Research Division, National Education Association, *Extra Pay for Extra Duties, 1967–1968* (Washington, D.C., National Education Association, 1968), pp. 1–69.

Chapter 6

1. John Chaffee, Jr., "First Manpower Assessment," *American Education* (February, 1969).
2. Smith, *op. cit.*
3. John Macdonald, "Teacher Education: Analysis and Recommendations," in *The Teacher and His Staff* (Washington, D.C., National Education Association, 1969), pp. 1–2.
4. Institute for Development of Educational Activities, *A Symposium on the Training of Teachers for Elementary Schools* (Melbourne, Fla., Institute for Development of Educational Activities, 1969).
5. William R. Fielder, "Albuquerque," in *Remaking the World of the Career Teacher* (Washington, D.C., National Education Association, 1966), p. 106.
6. National Commission on Teacher Education and Professional Standards, *The Assignment and Misassignment of Teachers* (Washington, D.C., National Education Association, 1965), pp. 1–68.

Chapter 7

1. National Education Association, *Teacher Strikes and Work Stoppages, January 1940 to July 1968* (Washington, D.C., National Education Association, November, 1968). Research memo.
2. "Teacher Opinion Poll." *Today's Education* (September, 1968).
3. Edgar B. Wesley, *NEA: The First Hundred Years* (New York, Harper & Brothers, 1957), p. 339.
4. Francis Keppel, *The Necessary Revolution in American Education* (New York, Harper & Row, 1966), p. 91.
5. Research Division, National Education Association, *Estimates of School Statistics, 1968–69* (Washington, D.C., National Education Association, 1968), pp. 12–15.
6. Myron Lieberman, *Education as a Profession* (Englewood Cliffs, N.J., Prentice-Hall, 1956), pp. 1–540.
7. Joseph Azzarelli, "Four Viewpoints," in F. W. Lutz and J. J. Azzarelli, eds., *Struggle for Power in Education* (New York, The Center for Applied Research in Education, 1966), Ch. 1.
8. Laurence Iannaccone, *Politics in Education* (New York, The Center for Applied Research in Education, 1967), Ch. 2.
9. For an excellent brief account of NEA's history, *see* Peter Janssen, "NEA: The Reluctant Dragon," *Saturday Review* (June 17, 1967).
10. David Rogers, *110 Livingston Street* (New York, Random House, 1968), p. 199.
11. Zeigler, *op. cit.,* p. 61.

Chapter 8

1. "NEA Finds Principals Spend Less Time with the Community," *Education News* (September 9, 1968). Weekly report.
2. K. Goldhammer, *et al., Issues and Problems in Contemporary Education Administration* (Eugene, Ore., The Center for the Advanced Study of Education Administration, 1967), p. 31.
3. Carl O. Olson, "Should Principals Teach," *NEA Journal* (March, 1968).
4. Ralph B. Kimbrough, *Political Power and Educational Decision-Making* (Chicago, Rand McNally and Company, 1964).
5. Hicks, *op. cit.,* p. 316.

6. Bernard Bard, "The Blackboard," New York *Post* (March 15, 1969).
7. Max Ehrlich, "The Anatomy of Conflict: Claims of the Parties at Interest," in *The Struggle for Power in the Public Schools* (Washington, D.C., National Committee for Support of the Public Schools, 1968), pp. 34–35.

Chapter 9

1. P. W. Jackson, *Life in Classrooms* (New York, Holt, Rinehart & Winston, 1968), p. 149.
2. *Ibid.*, Ch. 2.
3. *Ibid.*, p. 48.
4. Remmers and Radler, *op. cit.*, Ch. 5.
5. D. Mallery, *High School Students Speak Out* (New York, Harper & Brothers, 1962), p. 146.
6. G. W. Allport, "Crisis in Normal Personality Development," *Teachers College Record,* Vol. 66, No. 3 (December, 1964).
7. Oswald Hall, "The Social Structure of the Teaching Profession," in *The Struggle for Power in Education* (New York, The Center for Applied Research in Education, 1966), Ch. 3.
8. "Discipline, Not the Worst Problem But Bad," *Grade Teacher* (September, 1968).
9. L. Van Gelder, "A Reporter Goes to School," New York *Post* (February 17–21, 1969).
10. W. B. Waetjen, "Recent Analyses of Teaching," *Bulletin of the National Association of Secondary School Principals* (December, 1966).
11. *Ibid.*
12. *Ibid.*
13. John A. Williamson, "Seniors Comment on Their Best and Poorest Teachers," *Colorado Journal of Educational Research* (Spring, 1968).

Chapter 10

1. Jack Kleinert, "Teacher Turnover in an Affluent School District," *Clearing House* (January, 1968).
2. P. W. Toussieng, "The American School's Intolerance of In-

difference." Speech delivered at the Convention of the American Orthopsychiatric Association, April 1, 1969.

3. W. E. Schafer and K. Polk, "Delinquency and the Schools," in *Task Force Report: Juvenile Delinquency and Youth* (Washington, D.C., U.S. Government Printing Office, 1967), p. 235.

4. Bernard Bard and Nancy Hicks, "The Negro and the Schools," New York *Post* (September 11, 1968).

5. D. Spencer, "A Harlem Parent Speaks," *NEA Journal* (March, 1968).

6. U.S. Commission on Civil Rights, *Racial Isolation in the Public Schools* (Washington, D.C., U.S. Government Printing Office, 1967), pp. 103–5.

7. P. J. Groff, "Culturally Deprived Children: Opinions of Teachers on the Views of Riessman," *Exceptional Children,* Vol. 31, No. 2 (October, 1964).

8. D. Gottlieb, "Teaching and Students: The View of Negro and White Teachers," *Sociology of Education,* Vol. 37, No. 4 (Summer, 1964).

9. J. J. Kaufman, *et al., The School Environment and Programs for Dropouts* (University Park, Pa., Institute for Human Resources, The Pennsylvania State University, 1968).

10. M. S. King, *Summer Teacher Training Institute in Poverty Areas in New York City* (New York, Center for Urban Education, 1968).

11. D. Meier, "Learning Not to Learn," *Dissent* (November–December, 1968).

12. R. Rosenthal and L. F. Jacobson, "Teacher Expectations for the Disadvantaged," *Scientific American* (April, 1968).

13. Schafer and Polk, *op. cit.,* p. 236.

14. R. E. Herriot, *et al., Social Class and the Urban School* (New York, John Wiley & Sons, 1966), p. 130.

15. H. H. Davidson and G. Lang, "Children's Perceptions of Their Teachers' Feelings Toward Them Related to Self-Perception, School Achievement and Behavior," *Journal of Experimental Education* (December, 1960).

16. Schafer and Polk, *op. cit.,* p. 241.

17. K. B. Clark, *Dark Ghetto* (New York, Harper & Row, 1965), p. 134.

Chapter 11

1. W. Waller, *The Sociology of Teaching* (New York, John Wiley & Sons, 1965), p. 68.
2. Don-Chean Chu, "How Can Teachers' Prestige Be Raised?" *Journal of Experimental Education* (Summer, 1964).
3. New York State Citizens Committee for the Public Schools, *Teachers in Our Community* (January–June, 1964).
4. N. Huffman, "Images of Teachers," *Minnesota Journal of Education* (March, 1964).
5. H. S. Becker, "Schools and Systems of Stratification," in A. H. Halsey, *et al.*, eds., *Education, Economy and Society* (New York, The Free Press of Glencoe, 1964), pp. 101–2.
6. Warner Bloomberg, Jr., and John Kincaid, "Parent Participation: Practical Policy or Another Panacea?" *The Urban Review* (June, 1968).
7. National Education Association, *NEA Handbook, 1968–69* (Washington, D.C., National Education Association, 1968), p. 126.
8. Becker, *op. cit.*, p. 102.
9. R. Carter, *Voters and Their Schools* (Stanford, Calif., School of Education, Institute for Communication Research, 1960).
10. Bloomberg and Kincaid, *op. cit.*
11. J. D. Koerner, *Who Controls American Education?* (Boston, Beacon Press, 1968), p. 147.
12. Rogers, *op. cit.*, p. 181.
13. F. Redl and W. Wattenberg, *Mental Hygiene in Teaching* (New York, Harcourt, Brace & Company, 1951), p. 456.
14. *Ibid.*, p. 454.

Chapter 12

1. H. J. Hermanowicz, "The Pluralistic World of Beginning Teachers," in *The Real World of the Beginning Teacher* (Washington, D.C., National Education Association, 1966), pp. 23–24.
2. V. G. Jeffers, "Teaching as a Profession," *National Elementary Principal*, Vol. XLVII, No. 5 (April, 1968).
3. The Governor's Study Commission, *The Report of the Governor's Study Commission on the Public Schools of North Carolina*

(Raleigh, N.C., The Governor's Study Commission on the Public School System of North Carolina, 1968).

4. H. Davis, "What Teachers Say About Evaluation of Teachers," *NEA Journal* (February, 1965).
5. I. J. Gordon, *Studying the Child in School* (New York, John Wiley & Sons, 1966), p. 89.
6. B. Bard, "Mentally Unfit Teachers," *Ladies Home Journal* (February, 1969).
7. M. Mayer, *The Teachers Strike* (New York, Harper & Row, 1968), p. 39.
8. "Developments in the Law; Academic Freedom," *Harvard Law Review* (1968).
9. Jeffers, *op. cit.*
10. R. D. Bhaerman, "Quality Teaching," *American Teacher* (March, 1969).
11. F. C. Robb, "Teachers: The Need and the Task." Speech delivered at the Ninth Charles W. Hunt Lecture, 1968.
12. P. Harnett, "Calling the Cops on the 14-Year-Olds," *The Village Voice* (June 12, 1969).

Index

273